Constructing International Security
Alliances, Deterrence, and Moral Hazard

Constructing International Security helps policy makers and students recognize effective third-party strategies for balancing deterrence and restraint in security relationships. Brett V. Benson shows that there are systematic differences among types of security commitments. Understanding these commitments is key, because commitments – such as formal military alliances and extended deterrence threats – form the basis of international security order. Benson argues that sometimes the optimal commitment conditions military assistance on specific hostile actions the adversary might take. At other times, he finds, it is best to be ambiguous by leaving an ally and adversary uncertain about whether the third party will intervene. Such uncertainty transfers risk to the ally, thereby reducing the ally's motivation to behave too aggressively. The choice of security commitment depends on how well defenders can observe hostilities leading to war and on their evaluations of dispute settlements, their ally's security, and the relative strength of the defender.

Brett V. Benson is Assistant Professor of Political Science and Asian Studies at Vanderbilt University. His research concentrates on alliances, deterrence, nuclear disarmament, and international arms sales. He also studies Chinese politics and East Asia relations.

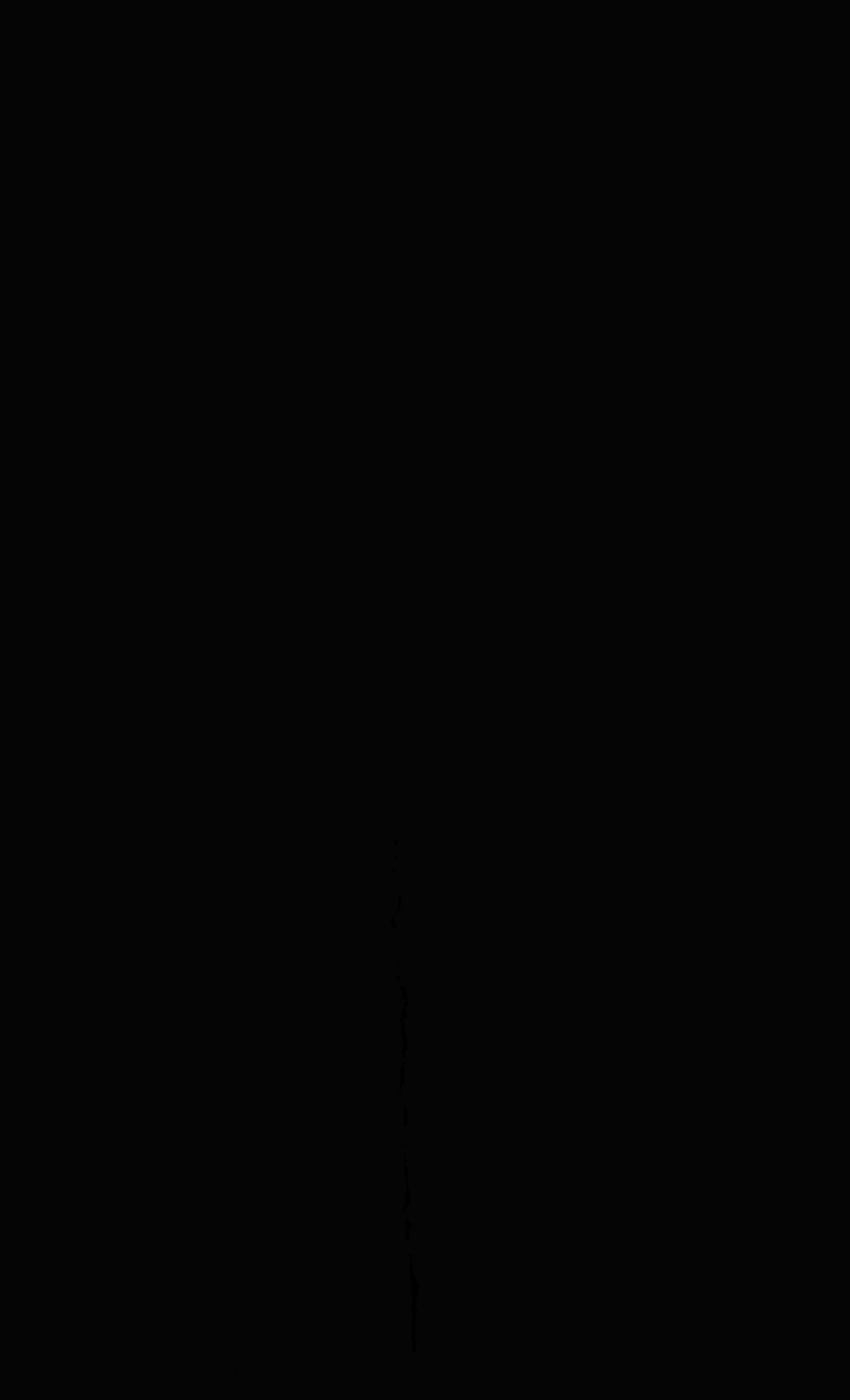

Constructing International Security
Alliances, Deterrence, and Moral Hazard

BRETT V. BENSON
Vanderbilt University

CAMBRIDGE UNIVERSITY PRESS
Cambridge, New York, Melbourne, Madrid, Cape Town,
Singapore, São Paulo, Delhi, Mexico City

Cambridge University Press
32 Avenue of the Americas, New York, NY 10013-2473, USA

www.cambridge.org
Information on this title: www.cambridge.org/9781107658196

© Brett V. Benson 2012

This publication is in copyright. Subject to statutory exception
and to the provisions of relevant collective licensing agreements,
no reproduction of any part may take place without the written
permission of Cambridge University Press.

First published 2012

A catalog record for this publication is available from the British Library.

Library of Congress Cataloging in Publication Data
Benson, Brett V., 1973–
Constructing international security : alliances, deterrence, and moral hazard / Brett V. Benson.
pages cm
Includes bibliographical references and index.
ISBN 978-1-107-02724-4 (hardback) – ISBN 978-1-107-65819-6 (paperback)
1. Security, International.   I. Title.
JZ5588.B46   2013
355'.031–dc23   2012016722

ISBN 978-1-107-02724-4 Hardback
ISBN 978-1-107-65819-6 Paperback

Cambridge University Press has no responsibility for the persistence or accuracy of URLs for
external or third-party Internet Web sites referred to in this publication and does not guarantee
that any content on such Web sites is, or will remain, accurate or appropriate.

For Lacy

Contents

Preface		*page* ix
Acknowledgments		xi
1	Understanding the Design of Security Commitments	1
2	A Typology of Third-Party Commitments	17
3	Time Consistency and Entrapment	43
4	Evidence of Moral Hazard in Military Alliances	71
5	A Theory of Commitment Design	90
6	Testing the Implications for Alliance Design	128
7	Deterrent Commitments in East Asia	142
8	Constructing Security in Today's World	169
References		191
Index		201

Preface

The inspiration for this book is the policy of "strategic ambiguity," which is the United States' strategy for addressing the dispute between China and Taiwan. I first became aware of the politics of the Taiwan Strait when I lived in Taiwan 20 years ago. I have a vivid memory of visiting Taiwan's west coast and looking out over the Taiwan Strait from the vantage point of an empty pillbox, which was constructed decades before in anticipation of an attack by Chinese Communist soldiers. Taiwan has many such reminders of its tense relationship with mainland China, a relationship I did not fully appreciate or understand when I was only 19 years old.

A friend from Taiwan, who did his military service on the island of Quemoy, left an indelible impression on me. He was a proud descendant of the Sun family – of Sun Yatsen – and spoke longingly about Taiwan being reunited with China; yet, he served as a soldier charged with the responsibility of defending a tiny island from mainland China. I was struck by the strength of his convictions and the peculiarity of the dispute separating him from his ancestral home. Equally remarkable to me was the symbolic value of the tiny and militarily useless island of Quemoy. For a period of time in the 1950s, the world, including millions of Americans who had no idea what or where Quemoy was, feared there might be a war, perhaps involving nuclear weapons, over a piece of land smaller than Staten Island that lay just a few kilometers off of China's coast. In researching this book, I have had the opportunity to revisit and explore in greater depth these early impressions. More important, I have learned that embedded in the narrow politics of the Taiwan Strait are valuable general lessons for the study of international politics.

Acknowledgments

This book is the culmination of years of input, guidance, and support from many valued influences. I owe my deepest debt of gratitude to Emerson Niou, who was my primary advisor in graduate school. As an undergraduate student studying political philosophy, I wondered how I might wed my disparate interests in philosophy and Chinese politics. Emerson guided me to the study of rigorous political theory and international politics, exposing me to a new world of formal methods and positive political theory. The road was long and often bumpy, but Emerson was consistently supportive and masterfully matched my comparative advantages to my interests. He taught me how to think big but with discipline. I owe Emerson more than words can express.

I am also indebted to my other advisors in graduate school. Mike Munger helped walk me through my move from Nietzsche to John Nash. He patiently sat through hours of white board sessions watching me struggle with Greek (not the kind I might have used to study the words of the ancients!). Chris Gelpi, Bob Keohane, David Soskice, and John Aldrich taught me how to do scientific research. This book began as a dissertation on a narrow topic, and even though the final product does not resemble my dissertation, these mentors set the trajectory for the project.

My research was also shaped by many conversations with fellow graduate students at Duke. I would be remiss if I did not extend special thanks to Jorge Bravo and Giacomo Chiozza, who both continued to influence my thinking long after graduate school. Both have spent many hours engaging with me about my ideas. I have benefited immensely from their keen insight and candid advice. As my office neighbor at Duke and again as a colleague at Vanderbilt, Giacomo was in the unfortunate position of being the first in the line of fire when I struggled with a tough question or thought I had a big idea. Fortunately for me, he has a gift for quickly connecting to the main issues. I thank him for clarifying my thinking on many occasions.

I am grateful to several participants in a conference held at Vanderbilt. Bob Powell, Jim Morrow, Erik Gartzke, Karen Mingst, Peter Rosendorff, and Michael Tomz generously gave their time to travel to Nashville and comment on drafts of my book chapters. They provided valuable advice and criticism, and I have worked hard to implement their suggestions. I offer additional thanks to Bob, Jim, and Erik for providing especially detailed comments and offering follow-up guidance. Their additional feedback gave my research an important clarity of focus and boost of momentum.

I spent a year as a Fellow in the Quantitative and Analytical Political Science Program (QAPS) at Princeton, which provided me with the time and the ideal environment to think and write. Special thanks goes to Adam Meirowitz, who read and reread several drafts. Few people I have met think as clearly as he does. I bothered him incessantly with many of the thorny puzzles. He was patient beyond expected protocol and made an enormous impact on my thinking and the final product. A friend pointed out that the acronym of the book's subtitle, "Alliances, Deterrence, and Moral Hazard" (ADM), is named after him. It is a coincidence but not an inappropriate one. Kris Ramsay encouraged me to sharpen my arguments and took extra effort to offer ideas about how they could be improved. Kris has high standards, and his ideas, thoughtful advice, and steady commitment to quality scholarship have not only improved my work but also inspired me as a scholar.

I am also grateful to others at Princeton. Among those are Alex Hirsch, Matias Iaryczower, Kosuke Imai, Nolan McCarty, and John Londregan, who constitute the core of the QAPS program that supported my stay at Princeton; Joanne Gowa, who shaped my thinking more than she knows through numerous conversations; and my officemate, Marc Ratkovic, whom I tormented with chats about parts of my project and various aspects of the book process.

My research benefited from the support of the East-West Center (EWC) in Honolulu, HI, where I resided as a Fellow. My stay at the EWC provided a welcome uninterrupted stretch of writing. I also had access to two valuable resources in fellow resident scholars Victor Cha and Michael Green. Victor and Michael generously donated their time to listen to me present parts of my research and provide detailed comments about the East Asian military alliances that I discuss in the book. I have taken special effort to implement their suggestions. I would also like to thank Denny Roy, who has thousands of great ideas about Asia. My book is significantly improved as a result of the support of the EWC and input from Victor, Michael, and Denny.

I cannot say enough about the supportive environment I have enjoyed at Vanderbilt. My department sponsored a conference for my research and the college kindly granted me a yearlong sabbatical to work on my project. My research has benefited from the input of colleagues Jim Ray, Michaela Mattes, Carol Atkinson, Dave Lewis, and Bruce Oppenheimer. I am appreciative of John Geer's advice and generous support, which have guided me through the many challenges of developing and publishing a book. Josh Clinton, who read

Acknowledgments

multiple drafts and contributed valuable feedback, deserves a special note of thanks for going above and beyond what colleagues and friends typically do for each other.

There are numerous other people who have provided input as discussants, panelists, and friends. While there are too many to list, a few were particularly influential at critical points in the process. Among these are Andy Kydd, Jack Levy, Doug Gibler, and Paul Poast. I am also indebted to John Vasquez, who has advised me on a number of occasions throughout the book process and has provided insightful comments on my work. I thank Ashley Leeds for her data, research, and valuable input.

My research assistants deserve a great deal of credit. Patrick Bentley, Laura Cantley, and Frank Wilson were tasked with a range of responsibilities, including coding data, digging through historical texts, and editing drafts. I want to thank Lisa Camner for reading and editing the manuscript as well. I am deeply grateful to the anonymous reviewers of the book manuscript. They generously provided pages and pages (and pages!) of constructive comments and criticism. I took great care to follow their recommendations. The final product bears the distinct mark of these reviewers' contributions.

I am especially grateful to my wife, Lacy, and our two children, Max and Joey. I had many moments of insight through the process of writing the book, but for every such high point there were many more dark hours of frustration and struggle. As many know, those that live with us take the brunt of the hardship while those that live away from us get to enjoy the flashes of brilliance. This project was conceived, developed, and completed on the strong shoulders of my family. Lacy is unlike any other person I have met – she is patient, consistent, and always alight when it is darkest. It is for this reason that I have dedicated the book to her.

Finally, I would like to say a few words in honor of my parents. They have sacrificed a lot for the benefit of their children. I owe them more than I will ever be able to say for taking the effort to provide life experiences for us. It would be an enormous oversight not to thank them for investing in 600 acres of hay fields when I was six, a tractor when I was seven, and a hundred head of cattle when I was eight.

1

Understanding the Design of Security Commitments

The claim that ambiguity can maintain peace in a crisis challenges our intuition. Ambiguous, weak, and fumbling commitments have been blamed for many wars. Most famous, perhaps, is England's vague commitment to France and Russia during the July 1914 crisis. Sir Edward Grey, British foreign minister, refused both to promise neutrality to Germany and to extend security guarantees to Russia and France beyond the loose alliance framework established by the 1904 Entente Cordiale between Britain and France and the 1907 Anglo-Russian Entente. Many claim that, at a minimum, Grey's strategy failed to prevent an avoidable escalation of conflict and may even have caused Germany and Austria, as well as France and Russia, to act on misperceptions about Britain's intentions (Albertini 1957; Snyder 1984; Trachtenberg 1991). Similarly, scholars have argued that weak third-party military commitments to European powers, especially Czechoslovakia and Poland, failed to deter Germany in 1938 and 1939 (Taylor 1961; Morrow 1993). More recently, critics have charged that mixed signals from the United States in 1990 about how it would respond to Iraqi aggression on its southern border opened the door for Saddam Hussein's invasion of Kuwait. Had the United States declared its intention to respond militarily, the argument goes, war may very well have been avoided (Jervis 1994).

Prevailing wisdom maintains that third-party defenders have the best shot at reducing misperception and war if they extend strong, well-defined public pledges of military support to their allies (Fearon 1997; Huth 1999; Schelling 1960; Zagare and Kilgour 2000). However, governments often do not fully flesh out the details of many commitments, including formal military alliances. Of 259 alliances formed between 1816 and 2000 and designed to deter threats to allies, 74 promised to defend the ally no matter what, 139 conditioned third-party intervention on the initiation of conflict by a non-alliance member, and

46 were "ambiguous" in that signatories did not have automatic contractual obligations to intervene on behalf of fellow alliance members in war.[1]

International security commitments are often incomplete because it is simply not possible to anticipate every potential incident covered by the scope of the promise. However, many are deliberately designed to be ambiguous. Consider, for example, the U.S. commitment to defend several small island groupings just off the coast of China during the Quemoy crisis. In 1954, the Chinese Communist Party Leader and Chairman of the People's Republic of China (PRC), Mao Zedong, declared that Taiwan should be "liberated" and began shelling the island of Quemoy, which was held by Chiang Kaishek and the Chinese Nationalists and was a stepping-stone to a PRC invasion of Taiwan. The Eisenhower administration sought to deter further Communist advances on the offshore islands, and especially Taiwan. The textbook strategy for deterrence maintains that the United States should have committed transparently and irrevocably to defend all Nationalist-held territories. Instead, Eisenhower deliberately created uncertainty about whether the United States would intervene to defend the offshore islands. In a formal treaty signed in 1954 between the United States and the Republic of China (the government led by Chiang), the United States agreed to defend Taiwan, the Pescadores, and "such other territories as may be determined by mutual agreement." Secretary of State John Foster Dulles described the strategy as "deterrence by uncertainty" (Chang and Di 1993, 1511). He commented that the treaty "stakes out unqualifiedly our interests in Formosa [Taiwan] and the Pescadores and does so on a basis which will not enable the Chinese Nationalists to involve us in a war with Communist China" (Garver 1997, 114).

Clearly, there was a belief in Washington that firm commitment to the offshore islands posed unwelcome risks, which did not exist for the Pescadores and Taiwan. Members of the Eisenhower administration worried that an overly firm commitment to the offshore islands might enable Chiang to entrap the United States in a war with the Chinese Communists on mainland China, whereas his ability to take advantage of a firm commitment to the Pescadores and Taiwan in a similar fashion was limited. The hesitation to commit to the offshore islands stemmed from the fact the islands were small, located just a few miles off the coast of China's mainland, and scattered along China's long coastline. Additionally, they served as staging points for ongoing skirmishes. Many hostilities targeting and originating from these territories would, therefore, be especially difficult to monitor, making it difficult to assess blame and punish instigators of conflict. Consequently, not only were they difficult to defend from a PRC invasion, but they also presented an opportunity for Chiang to provoke the Chinese Communists.

This example brings into sharp relief the impact of moral hazard in alliances. Moral hazard results when an actor is enticed to behave aggressively because

[1] The typology of alliances developed in Chapter 2 discusses the details of these alliances.

it is insulated from the risks of its actions. It occurs, in this context, when the protégé country, which is the beneficiary of a third party's security guarantee, is emboldened to belligerent action because the third party has promised to provide military support if the protégé is involved in conflict.[2] Consequently, third-party defenders who are motivated to design extended security commitments with the objective of protecting the protégé while preserving the status quo will also worry about the effect of the security commitment on the protégé's behavior. Thus, the third party will design alliances with the protégé's incentives in mind.

The phenomenon of moral hazard lies at the heart of a central tension in forming extended deterrence commitments. A third-party defender wishing to protect a protégé can best deter an adversary's challenges to the protégé by forming a maximally credible and firm commitment, but such commitments risk emboldening protégés not only to resist the adversary's challenges but also to provoke the adversary in an attempt to gain concessions (e.g., more territory). How can leaders deter enemies while restraining allies? This dilemma is a long-standing fascination of international politics scholarship. Glenn Snyder and Paul Diesing (1977, 432) identify the problem as the "deterrence-versus-restraint" dilemma. Robert Jervis calls it "dual deterrence" (1994, 122–124). James Fearon, who states that this is a common historical problem, refers to it as "the problem of moral hazard in alliances and extended deterrence" (1997, 84).

However ubiquitous this conundrum is, the puzzle of how leaders design commitment mechanisms to resolve it remains largely unanswered. This mechanism design problem in extended deterrence and alliance formation can be examined through three fundamental questions. First, how do third-party defenders balance the demands of deterrence with the risks of moral hazard? Second, what does an ambiguous commitment mechanism look like in theory and practice? Third, why do defenders ever opt for ambiguity when transparent alternatives exist? This book offers answers to these questions. The primary thesis is that leaders form many different kinds of security commitments in practice, with much of this variation explained by the moral hazard they face. Furthermore, under certain conditions, a probabilistic commitment is often deliberately incorporated into alliance contracts to deter threats while simultaneously restraining allies.

The Content of Commitments

In addressing the first question regarding how to balance the demands of deterrence with the risk of moral hazard, one of the book's central claims is that the

---

[2] More generally, moral hazard is a concern in a large and diverse set of contracting environments ranging from decisions about medical care and insurance (Arrow 1963; Shavell 1979), corporate investment, driving behavior (Holmstrom 1979), electoral politics (Banks and Sundaram 1993), and the behavior of athletes (Goff 1997).

content of the commitments in alliance contracts matters a great deal for structuring leaders' incentives. The argument begins with the empirical observation that leaders use a broader menu of contracts to form interstate alliances than is traditionally recognized. Throughout recorded history, leaders have promised other states military assistance, usually expressed in policy pronouncements or formal alliance treaties. Scholars have conventionally categorized these commitments as either "offensive" or "defensive," according to whether the objective is to gain concessions for alliance members from nonmembers or to protect alliance members against nonmembers. However, these categories are not exhaustive, nor do they fully capture the dimensions of variation among interstate alliances.

To illustrate this variation, consider the traditional category of "defensive" alliances, which are formed with the objective of deterring a threat to a protégé. To achieve this goal, an ally may choose to make an unequivocal and unconditional commitment to come automatically to the aid of alliance members, even in the face of moral hazard. Such commitments may involve a pledge of unlimited support or may specify clearly the amount of support to be transferred to the ally. The Soviet Union's alliance with Romania in 1948 is an example of an unconditional commitment to deter German aggression, because the objective of the agreement was to defend alliance members and it did not restrict military intervention to a specific action or condition. At other times, allies write ambiguous alliance contracts, such as Eisenhower's 1954 alliance with the Chinese Nationalists. These contracts leave open the question as to whether the defender will actually intervene if there is war. Another option is a conditional commitment. Leaders often promise military assistance on the condition that the adversary initiates the hostilities. In other words, the third party will often try to limit its commitment to conflicts that do not result from aggression by the protégé. For example, in 1912 the United Kingdom formed a conditional deterrent commitment to protect Belgian neutrality. In the treaty, the United Kingdom stipulated that it would wait until either France or Germany attacked the other before it would intervene to protect Belgium, which sits between the two powers. Conditional commitments occur frequently in alliances and might, under some conditions, help reduce the risk-taking behavior that can result from moral hazard.

To make sense of this rich variation in commitments, the book presents a novel typology of military alliances that facilitates the development of a theory about the distinctions observed in practice. The promises and threats contained in military commitments typically conform to a basic structure with an antecedent condition that, if realized, invokes a consequent obligation. The historical record shows that the terms of both antecedents and consequents exhibit systematic variation, which makes it possible to classify commitments into coherent categories based on these differences. As might be expected, some of the categories of military alliance generated by the typology overlap existing conceptions of commitment, but the typology also uncovers types of commitments that are not present in theory and yet are routinely adopted in practice.

Many of the alliances considered here, including most of the examples cited previously, have traditionally been thought of as simply "defensive" pacts. However, these alliances, which share the objective of deterring threats to allies, have important categorical differences. Given these differences, a valid question is why previous research has not studied in depth the variation in the content of interstate military alliances, including the variation among extended deterrence commitments. In the existing literature, extended deterrence commitments are usually viewed as having a binary quality – one is committed or one is not – rather than as a mechanism that can take different forms and serve different purposes depending on the conditions and obligations built into the pledge.

The binary viewpoint results from the emphasis on credibility. As in Fearon's (1997) hands-tying and sunk-costs model, commitment is thought to occur once an actor has expended sufficiently high costs to convince others of the credibility of its intentions. This intuition has dominated our thinking about commitment since Schelling (2006) emphasized the importance of irrevocably binding oneself to a future action to attain credibility. Furthermore, scholars have often assumed that states have a strong *preference* to be fully committed to an act. As the examples that open this chapter demonstrate, many scholars hold the view that the lack of a credible commitment has contributed to war. As a result, scholars, pundits, and policy makers alike have theorized how states might make their commitments credible.

The problem is particularly acute in the case of third-party commitments, since it is not immediately credible that a third party will actually provide assistance to another actor when so doing imposes costs on itself. Few people doubt a leader's resolve to defend his or her own country against attack. It is considerably harder to believe that a country's leader and people will deliver on a promise to fight for another country when remaining uninvolved does not put their own safety at risk. Consequently, the dominant research question has been: How can third-party actors bind themselves to the security of another state and foreswear abandoning that state when harm befalls it? With the focus on becoming committed and establishing credibility, it is unsurprising that the dominant concept of commitment is binary, yes or no. This viewpoint makes it difficult to imagine an option other than automatic intervention or nonintervention, such as a deliberately ambiguous commitment.

In practice, however, ambiguous commitments are common. A classic example is the long-standing U.S. policy of strategic ambiguity toward the Taiwan Strait. The U.S. government is unwilling to "become committed" in the conventional sense of establishing a credible threat to defend Taiwan if China attacks. However, U.S. policy is definitely not equivalent to noncommitment. Rather, there is a commitment, which is acknowledged by the United States, Taiwan, and China, but it is not clear whether that commitment obligates the

United States to defend Taiwan automatically if there is war between China and Taiwan.

One possible explanation for this situation is that the Taiwan Strait environment consists of unique circumstances that led to the emergence and persistence of an ambiguous policy in the early 1950s, and the resilient peace between China and Taiwan is unrelated to the U.S. commitment. However, there is another possibility, which is that third-party states routinely and purposely form ambiguous commitments because in many contexts, an irrevocable stand will cause the protected state to react too much. In these instances, ambiguity is a virtue and it is a mistake to view wishy-washiness as a missed opportunity. This is the argument pursued in this book. In the subsequent chapters, I develop general explanations for ambiguous commitments, and I illustrate that under certain conditions, the uncertainty generated by ambiguity has a positive, though counter-intuitive, effect on interstate peace.

Although credibility does play a role in shaping actors' behavior when forming military commitments, this book takes a broader look at the determinants of treaty design. A central contention is that leaders' goals of credibility are tempered, and occasionally overshadowed, by worries about the dangers of overcommitment, which may tempt the protégé state to engage in risky, aggressive behavior. Fortunately for third-party leaders, ambiguous commitment to defend an ally can discourage aggression (or at least too much aggression) because the protégé state now faces doubt about whether its alliance partner will, figuratively, have its back. If ambiguity is sufficient to deter aggression by both the protégé and the opponent, then guaranteed commitment may be inefficient and may even cause behavior inconsistent with the third party's deterrence goals. To explore these matters further, this book deals with the *content* of commitments to support another actor militarily, with a particular focus on understanding why leaders often deviate from the "standard" of full commitment and opt instead for ambiguous or probabilistic commitments that build in discretion for the third party to assist or to abandon according to its preference.

Characterizing Ambiguity as Probabilistic Commitment

The second objective of the book is to flesh out our understanding of what an "ambiguous commitment" looks like in both theory and practice. How and why do states create uncertainty about their commitments to their protégés? The previous section established that states use a variety of types of commitments, including ones that involve ambiguity, in their alliances. Now the goal is to develop a concept of ambiguous commitment that can be modeled theoretically and tested empirically. A number of scholars, including Fearon (1997), Zagare and Kilgour (2006), and Snyder (1984, 1997), have identified specific mechanisms through which a third-party state might form an ambiguous commitment. In the paragraphs that follow, I summarize their contributions and consider their suitability as a general framework for ambiguous commitments. Ultimately, however, I conclude that although these models are an important point of departure, they are incomplete, as they either lack theoretical coherence or fail to encompass the full spectrum of commitments in the historical record.

Fearon (1997) reflects on the "puzzle" of "partial commitments," which are frequently observed in practice but do not obtain in equilibrium in his theory. He seems to have two types of mechanisms in mind. In one, a defender takes a costly action to signal commitment, but then reneges. Weak defenders might use this mechanism to bluff others into believing their commitment, but ultimately choose to back down in the face of a challenge they do not think they can win. The second mechanism Fearon mentions is a "half-hearted" signal in which a defender incurs a small cost that is less than the value needed to communicate a credible commitment. This mechanism is used by defenders that intend to assist the protégé even without the signal but that use the small cost to bluff an ambiguous commitment in order to restrain the protégé.

The first kind of bluffing is problematic not only because it is not equilibrium behavior in Fearon's model but also because, empirically, alliance members tend to keep their commitments (Leeds 2003a; Leeds, Long, and Mitchell 2000). The second mechanism – feigning weakness – does not obtain in equilibrium in Fearon's model because the challenger will infer that anything less than full commitment conveys unwillingness to intervene. This logic echoes Schelling's problem with the United States' use of ambiguity in the Quemoy crisis: "Any loopholes the threatening party leaves himself, if they are visible to the threatened party, weaken the visible commitment and hence reduce the credibility of the threat. (An example may be the ambiguous treatment of Quemoy in the Formosa Resolution and Treaty)" (1960, 40).

Fearon's and Schelling's observations that leaders, in fact, select ambiguous commitments despite the seeming irrationality of such choices result because they do not incorporate moral hazard into their theories. Weak signals based on partial or incomplete payments of costs are indeed irrational when the model does not take into account the protégé's response to the third party's signal. However, it is possible to imagine how a weak signal might be sustained in equilibrium if a protégé can be influenced by the signal and the adversary knows this.

Although the theory developed in this book fully considers moral hazard, the notion of ambiguity offered here steers clear of weak commitments or feints of weakness. The primary reason is that it is a challenge to identify such weak commitments in practice. Few, if any, alliances specify a level of military support that is obviously too low to be credible. Furthermore, although it may be that forming a firm and credible commitment does not entail high sunk costs or hands-tying, it is difficult to know this without also being able to identify empirically what the "critical value" of credibility is – in other words, the value of the cost that must be paid to make the commitment credible in the eyes of both the protégé and the adversary.

Moreover, observed diplomatic signals of weakness might result from other factors unrelated to moral hazard, such as the defender feeling torn between conflicting domestic and international pressures. For example, Grey's weakness in 1914 could be attributed to his desire to respond to the growing international emergency in the Balkans while simultaneously fearing backlash from a domestic audience dead set on neutrality (Levy 1990; Zagare and Kilgour 2006). Weak signals naturally result from these kinds of conflicting pressures. Thomas Christensen (1996) explains that weak, limping financial support from the United States to the Chinese Nationalists in the waning months of the Chinese Civil War in the late 1940s stemmed from the Truman administration's desire to abandon the Nationalists because of the on-the-ground reality that the Nationalists would soon lose the war, while simultaneously appeasing the strong domestic China lobby back in Washington. We would, therefore, be mistaken if we attributed the weak U.S. support of the Nationalists at that time as a shrewd strategy to deter the Chinese Communists from attacking the Nationalists while restraining the Nationalists from attacking the Communists.

If the theory offered in this book does not identify an ambiguous commitment mechanism as bluffing, then a potentially promising alternative is a mixed strategy. This is the approach taken by Frank Zagare and Marc Kilgour (2006), who develop a theoretical model of conflict with moral hazard and show that an equilibrium exists in which the defender randomizes between defending and abandoning its protégé to maximize the deterrent effect on the adversary while also restraining the protégé. However, to induce a mixed strategy equilibrium, the theory hinges critically on an assumption that protégés possess options for punishing defenders for not defending. In particular, Zagare and Kilgour's theory gives protégés the option of realigning with another state, and defenders do not know whether the protégé is the type to punish them by realigning.

In framing the problem this way, Zagare and Kilgour criticize Crawford's (2003) claim that simultaneously achieving deterrence and restraint is possible only when the protégé does not have outside alignment options. Zagare and Kilgour show that if the protégé has outside alignment options, the defender's deterrence threat against the adversary is most effective when the protégé can, in fact, also threaten to realign if the defender does not protect it. However, building a theory on the availability of outside alignment options, while making it attractive in examining the tractability of one explanation for ambiguous commitments, also makes it overly restrictive as a general framework for analyzing the problem of deterrence versus restraint; mixed strategies in the theory depend critically on the assumption that the defender cares about the threat of realignment, and it is uncertain about whether the protégé is of the type that would actually carry out the threat. This does not appear to be a natural way of thinking about many historical examples. In the Quemoy crisis, for instance, the United States did not worry that Chiang might realign with another state. Furthermore, in today's Taiwan Strait crisis, the United States is the only prospective defender for Taiwan and, should the United States abandon it, Taiwan does not have other means by which it can punish the United States. The goal of the present study is to develop a concept of ambiguity that captures the idea that the defender's commitment generates probabilistic uncertainty, without also being dependent on the restrictive conditions necessary to induce mixed strategies in equilibrium.

Another way to characterize an ambiguous commitment is to think about the defender's strategy as an attempt to send simultaneous yet conflicting signals to the adversary and protégé. In Snyder's account (1984), deterrence and restraint can best be achieved by a strategy that instills and maintains opposite and pessimistic beliefs about the third-party defender's response in the event of war – the adversary should believe the defender will respond, and the protégé should believe that the defender is unlikely to. Instilling conflicting beliefs is a complicated diplomatic feat requiring at least two separate – and, preferably, private – messages. This was, in fact, Eisenhower's move in the Quemoy crisis. Not only was the public language of the formal treaty ambiguous, but the United States also insisted on the exchange of secret treaty notes with the Chinese Nationalists. Those notes clearly stipulated that the United States would use its discretion to determine whether to assist the Nationalists. Meanwhile, in an effort to send a conflicting message to Mao Zedong, both Dulles and Eisenhower boasted cavalierly about how the United States would not hesitate to use nuclear weapons against Communist China.

Identifying conflicting signals presents both theoretical and empirical challenges. Empirically, most signals of this kind are likely to be made in secret; others, made in public, would need to be distinguished from the noise of diplomatic exchanges. Given this research hurdle, it is worthwhile to take another approach. On the theoretical front, it is not clear whether a strategy of fooling both sides could be sustained in equilibrium. A commitment to issue conflicting signals might well unravel because the protégé and the adversary both recognize the third party's problem of simultaneously delivering on its conflicting obligations when the commitment is challenged.

Nevertheless, we might reasonably assume that if a single, observable ambiguous signal can be shown in theory to satisfy a defender's dual demands of deterrence and restraint, then multiple directional signals tailored both to deter and to restrain would also achieve the same objective, if such a strategy can be sustained in equilibrium. Indeed, it may often be the case that a defender will issue an ambiguous public commitment, which by itself is sufficient to satisfy the deterrence-versus-restraint dilemma, and then reinforce the message with secret but conflicting statements to the disputants. Therefore, for theoretical purposes, it is sufficient to demonstrate the conditions under which a single ambiguous instrument will be preferred to transparent and unambiguous alternatives in order to balance deterrence and moral hazard. Following this approach facilitates the empirical analysis because the comparative statics on the observable signal are testable, whereas directional private signals are not (unless the researcher happens to be privy to the secret communications, as in the case of the Quemoy crisis). This approach can also be used in a qualitative analysis of a specific case.

As a result, the characterization of ambiguity developed in this book is a single public *ex ante* probabilistic commitment to perhaps intervene. This mechanism is conceptually distinct from feints of weakness, mixed strategies, and conflicting signals described earlier. In making a probabilistic commitment, the defender makes a promise, as credible as any transparent and unconditional signal, that with some probability it will intervene. In other words, leaders can design contracts to specifically stipulate that third parties might or might not intervene when there is war. In so doing, a defender may condition its response on or delegate the decision to intervene to some factor or decision-making mechanism external to the tripartite game. In practice, this might look like a promise that explicitly conditions the transfer of military assistance on the realization of some random process beyond the control of the third party and protégé. For example, the third party might benefit if it can commit to intervene with a 25 percent chance. It could, therefore, promise to intervene if two randomly selected world leaders are taller than a third randomly selected leader. In practice, many alliance commitments delegate the ultimate decision to intervene to some external decision-making body, and it is not known at the time the agreement is formed what the decision will be.

Why Ambiguity?

The theory in the book demonstrates that the third-party defender's choice of commitment mechanism to best satisfy the competing demands of deterrence and restraint depends on four main factors: the defender's power relative to the protégé and the adversary; the defender's preference for the protégé's security; the defender's preferences for how disputes involving its protégé are settled; and the observability of the hostile actions leading to war between the protégé and the adversary. Moral hazard is less of an issue if the defender values the protégé's security and shares the protégé's preferences for the settlement of the dispute. Divergent preferences, on the other hand, lead the defender to be vigilant about incorporating into the commitment mechanism specific conditions or ambiguity to reduce the moral hazard that occurs from an unconditional commitment. Powerful defenders are especially cautious because the size of the moral hazard distortion is correlated with how much the protégé expects to benefit from the third-party defender's assistance. One might think that a powerful third party could simply write a contract that specifies a promise to transfer only a limited amount of military assistance to the protégé when the *casus foederis* of the alliance contract has been triggered. Such a commitment, however, may not be credible if the defender has strong incentives to prevail in the war once it chooses to intervene. The inability to limit transfers in war complicates the contracting problem, not only because the defender cannot credibly commit to a certain level of support, but also because it exacerbates moral hazard. Also problematic is the observability of disputants' hostile actions. If the protégé recognizes that it cannot be blamed for its behavior in the lead-up to war because the defender cannot observe the interactions between the adversary and protégé, including hostile actions, then it will have an incentive to behave aggressively toward the adversary.

The most effective mechanisms for managing moral hazard are conditionality and ambiguity. Under certain conditions, the optimal alliance involves conditioning military assistance on specific actions the adversary might take to initiate hostilities. In other circumstances, the most effective commitment mechanism explicitly gives the defender discretion to create uncertainty about its decision to intervene. Such uncertainty transfers risk to the protégé, thereby reducing the extent to which moral hazard influences the protégé.

The obvious next question is this: What circumstances make an ambiguous commitment optimal and what circumstances make conditional commitment optimal? Given that a conditional commitment can solve the deter-and-restrain dilemma, scholars and policy makers have suggested that this mechanism is strictly preferable to an ambiguous commitment precisely because it avoids ambiguity. For example, several scholars and policy makers have recommended that the current U.S. policy of strategic ambiguity toward Taiwan and China be replaced with an unambiguous conditional commitment to defend Taiwan if and only if China attacks it without provocation.[3] If Taiwan provokes a war by moving toward independence, then it has no promise of protection. In spite of the seeming appeal of this approach, the United States continues to use strategic ambiguity. As noted earlier, this is not the only instance of ambiguous commitment in history; many other leaders have also chosen ambiguous commitments over unambiguous, conditional ones. The persistence use of ambiguity in deterrence situations suggests that there may be advantages to ambiguity that cannot be achieved with conditionality, or that other factors might constrain leaders' ability to make unambiguous, conditional commitments. Identifying these factors and explaining their relationship with the content of the commitment have eluded scholars for decades.

The theory in this book posits two explanations for the selection of ambiguous commitments. First, compared with unambiguous alternatives, including conditional commitments, uncertainty lowers the protégé's expected payoff to conflict, thereby reducing its willingness to take stances that are overly aggressive. Inducing moderate behavior in the protégé is a priority for the third-party defender when its preferences diverge from those of the protégé for the ideal policy settlement that results if war is avoided. In 1954, the United States valued the preservation of the Chinese Nationalists and would have fought for their survival on Taiwan, but the Eisenhower administration preferred a

---

[3] See Joseph S. Nye, Jr., "A Taiwan Deal," *Washington Post* (March 8, 1998), sec. C.; and Christensen (2002).

moderate solution to the Quemoy crisis, including the possibility of conceding some island groupings to the Chinese Communists. On the other hand, the Nationalists wanted to fight to keep all the offshore islands and, if possible, expand the conflict onto China's mainland. Because the United States was sufficiently powerful to swing the balance of power between the Nationalists and the Communists dramatically in favor of the Nationalists, an ambiguous commitment avoided extreme claims over the mainland (by the Nationalists) and Taiwan (by the Communists) that might have resulted from a firm U.S. policy of either unambiguous support or neutrality.

Ambiguous treaties can also be optimal when it is simply not possible for the third party to determine whether a conflict occurred because the protégé was aggressive or because the adversary was aggressive. If the defender cannot observe hostilities, it cannot condition a response on disputants' actions. To continue with the Quemoy example, the United States favored ambiguity in its commitment to the offshore islands but not for the Pescadores or Taiwan because the very close proximity of the Chinese Nationalists on the offshore islands to the Communists on the mainland, combined with the ongoing hostilities between the two belligerents, made it nearly impossible for the United States to observe and therefore to punish actions leading to war over the offshore islands.

Overview of the Argument

In sum, this book develops a theory that derives conditions under which a defender will select a single, ambiguous commitment instrument from a menu of commitment mechanisms that appear in practice. This menu includes a defender's guarantee of unconditional intervention, a promise of intervention conditional on a disputant's action in the conflict process, or a pledge to intervene probabilistically. The theory improves on existing models by incorporating moral hazard and considering variation in the defender's power and preferences so as not to restrict inferences to limiting cases. The defender may be so powerful as to be decisive in a war with the protégé against the adversary, or it may be just slightly more powerful than the protégé itself, and is thus not decisive in war. Additionally, the defender may have a range of preferences regarding both its appetite for fighting a war on the protégé's behalf as well as its ideal policy settlement if war can be avoided. Extensions of the model also consider variations in the level of observability of hostile actions as well as the credibility of the defender's commitment to limit intervention in war.

The theory demonstrates, and empirical evidence confirms, that pledges of military assistance can induce moral hazard on the part of the protégé. This problem is not easily resolved, however, because third-party defenders often cannot simply limit the amount of their assistance in war. There is often coarseness to intervention decisions that inhibits a leader's ability to fine-tune the amount of military assistance to transfer during war. Once war has broken

Understanding the Design of Security Commitments

out, powerful incentives may drive leaders either to provide overly large transfers of support or to stay out of the conflict altogether. This is both good news and bad news for the protégé, for in many circumstances it can exploit the third party's overcommitment for its own advantage during crisis bargaining. However, it also means that the third party will abandon the protégé under some conditions when both would have benefited from being able to agree on just the right amount of military assistance.

The design of interstate military alliances affects these expected inefficiencies in war. Commitments that explicitly condition military assistance on the adversary's initiation of hostilities can deter the adversary while still inducing restraint on the part of the protégé. However, in many crises, it is impossible to observe which disputant initiated a conflict. In these cases, the optimal solution may be to design a probabilistic commitment, which deliberately creates uncertainty about whether the defender's ultimate decision will be to intervene. Deterrence by uncertainty discourages adversaries from challenging while shifting risk back onto the shoulders of the protégé. In addition to preventing conflict, probabilistic commitments also have advantages if the third party has preferences over the structure of the settlement between the protégé and adversary that is reached when war is avoided. Knowing that, with some probability, the third party will intervene if bargaining fails causes the adversary and protégé to reach a bargaining settlement that balances their expected benefits of quitting the bargaining process and fighting given that probability. Consequently, probabilistic commitments are effective mechanisms for smoothing the inefficiencies that result from the coarseness of the third party's decision to intervene in war. The finer the set of possible probabilistic pledges available to the third party, the better able the third party is to design a commitment that accords with its preferences.

The theory presented in this book results in several empirical implications, which are tested using case studies and alliance data generated from the new typology of commitments. The first implication, which derives from the discussion in Chapter 3, is that unambiguous alliance commitments, especially those that contain no conditions triggering *casus foederis*, lead revisionist alliance members to behave aggressively in crises with states targeted by the alliance. This aggression increases as the power of the third-party defender increases. An implication derived from the theoretical analysis in Chapter 5 is that concerns about moral hazard increase the likelihood that leaders will form either probabilistic or conditional alliances when their prospective alliance member is revisionist. This effect is particularly pronounced for powerful third parties, who are especially vulnerable to exploitation due to moral hazard. The theory in Chapter 5 further demonstrates that the third party's ideal foreign policy outcome also dictates the type of alliance it forms. The more congruent the third party's and the protégé's interests over war and foreign policy preferences, the more likely the alliance will be unconditional. On the other hand, the alliance is more likely to be probabilistic as their preferences diverge.

Additionally, expectations of large transfers of assistance exacerbate moral hazard, leading powerful third-party defenders relative to their protégés to be more likely to form probabilistic commitments. Finally, the more difficult it is to observe which actor is responsible for the hostilities, the less likely it is that the alliance will contain treaty terms specifying the conditions under which military assistance will be triggered.

These observable implications of the theory are tested using observational data of alliances disaggregated by type according to the theory. I compile and analyze new data of alliances and conflict spanning the years 1816 to 2000. In addition to the novel substantive contributions from the statistical analysis, my research contributes new data and measures of alliance variables derived from the typology. I also present a thorough comparison of the commitment decisions during the Quemoy crisis to other cases in which transparent mechanisms were chosen, providing further evidence for the theoretical findings. Finally, I discuss policy implications for the policy of the United States toward China and Taiwan as well as China's existing defense treaty with North Korea.

Outline of the Book

The book is organized into three main parts. The first part introduces a new typology of commitments. In the typology, which is presented in Chapter 2, I sort commitments along two dimensions: the *objective* of the promise and the *action* that triggers military obligation. A leader's promise to provide military support can have a compellent objective or be limited to deterrence. Commitments can be further partitioned into unconditional and conditional categories depending on whether the promise identifies a specific trigger that activates the commitment. A fifth category includes probabilistic commitments, which create uncertainty about whether the defender will intervene. This typology offers a new way to organize military commitments and alliance agreements and provides an important step for developing theory of different commitment types and measuring commitments for empirical analysis.

In the second part of the book, I develop a theory of moral hazard and examine the empirical data of alliances based on measures of alliance commitments derived from the typology in Chapter 2 to establish a moral hazard effect stemming from alliance commitments. Chapter 3 presents the argument that understanding the design of commitments requires that we first have a theory about the effects of moral hazard on crisis bargaining. This is not a trivial step in the argument. Leaders have a great deal of latitude in dealing with agency problems in international politics, but despite this latitude, it is not always possible for them to overcome incentive problems stemming from private information, divergent motivations, and unobservable actions. The likelihood that military alliances will overcome or become ensnared in these problems should be explained, not assumed.

Building on existing research on conflict bargaining and alliances, I combine bargaining under incomplete information with a study of incentives in the formation of *ex ante* alliance commitments. An important friction here is the fact that incentives stemming from the nature of war sometimes make it hard for an ally to commit to limited participation; once the third party's troops are on the ground, its interests may dictate against limited participation. This fact makes promises of limited assistance not credible. Accordingly, because of this time-consistency problem, the set of plausible commitments may be very coarse, and this coarseness may exacerbate moral hazard. In Chapter 4, I examine empirically the effects of alliances on the behavior of the recipients to determine whether the theoretical intuition about moral hazard offered in Chapter 3 exists in practice. The data support the claim that alliances from powerful states that are not designed to manage moral hazard are likely to lead revisionist recipients to initiate militarized disputes.

In the third part of the book, I seek to explain and test when and why leaders choose different types of commitments. In Chapter 5, I present the final piece in the theory, which draws on the approaches known as *mechanism design* and *contract theory*. I study the decision problem of trying to design commitments given what leaders expect to occur downstream when issues related to transfers of assistance and moral hazard arise. In other words, the approach is to ask what type of commitments the third-party leader would choose when it knows that the reactions by other nations (as well as by itself in the future) are governed by rationality and subject to important information constraints. I find that leaders' *ex ante* commitments can sometimes anticipate and smooth out coarse intervention decisions and thereby shift risk onto the shoulders of the protégé. Moreover, the optimal decision depends on several factors. In Chapter 5, I discuss conditions under which leaders will choose different commitment mechanisms. The theory developed here, which helps to explain why ambiguous and flexible commitments are observed in practice, produces a wide range of testable implications about the nature of formal alliances.

In Chapters 6 and 7, I test the results derived from the theoretical arguments in Chapter 5. In Chapter 6, I use observational alliance data generated from the typology in Chapter 2, and in Chapter 7, I develop a qualitative case study analysis from U.S. alliances in East Asia. Chapters 6 and 7 test implications deriving from the theory presented in Chapter 5. The data confirm that incongruence of policy preferences and war payoffs between the third party and protégé increase the likelihood that probabilistic and conditional alliances will be formed. Additionally, a leader's relative capabilities and the observability of initiations of conflict are also associated with the optimal design of the alliance commitment. Leaders of strong countries are less likely to make firm, unconditional commitments because the risk of exploitation is higher for a state that has sufficient power to sway war outcomes. Additionally, practical limitations in international politics inhibit actors from perfectly observing the behavior of states in sufficient detail to determine who initiated the conflict. These constraints also contribute to the likelihood that leaders will design commitments to be deliberately probabilistic.

Finally, in Chapter 8, I discuss policy implications of the theory presented in this book for current global disputes. Notably, the theory contributes to our understanding of the current U.S. commitment to Taiwan and China's commitment to North Korea.

2

A Typology of Third-Party Commitments

This chapter presents a typology of third-party security commitments.[1] These commitments are often formalized in the terms of interstate military alliances. The security commitment observed in most alliance agreements consists of a promise by one country to provide military support to another country subject to some condition. It is a statement taking the form "if x then y," where y is the promise of some kind of military support and x is the condition activating the military response. In principle, both x and y can vary a great deal. A country may promise complete support to its ally, or it may specify a given level of military support or even only the possibility of military support. It can also promise to remain neutral. Leaders can also specify numerous possible conditions or combinations of conditions to trigger their promise to deliver y. These conditions comprise the content of x and can range from highly specific (e.g., an adversary's attack and a protégé's nonintervention) to nonspecific (e.g., any conflict). Additionally, the conditions might stipulate the objective of the conflict, such as those contests limited to the water's edge (e.g., only if an adversary tries to gain concessions from the protégé) or to more aggressive pursuits (e.g., an adversary's refusal to concede some territory).

To build a theory of commitment design, it is essential to know what kinds of commitments countries form in practice and the circumstances leading to each type of commitment. In particular, we might ask whether there is any systematic variation in x and y in the empirical record. Scholars have long studied interstate military alliances and have created models, categories of types of military alliances, and datasets based on these categories to gain traction on the issue. A typology is a useful way to begin theorizing about alliance commitments, because it helps us identify and analyze the different mechanisms decision makers design to address threats. However, existing theories

---

[1] Parts of this chapter are taken from Benson (2011).

and typologies are limited because they do not fully capture the commitments in the historical record.

It is therefore useful to review these theories and to examine the historical record to develop a typology of alliance commitments that is both theoretically meaningful and historically comprehensive.

In the next section, I introduce existing theories of commitment. Then I provide four historical examples and explain why they do not fit neatly into existing theories. Using these building blocks, I propose a new typology. The new classifications encompass old categories while also uncovering previously undefined and unexplained commitment mechanisms. The typology contains five new categories of alliance commitments: unconditional compellent, conditional compellent, unconditional deterrent, conditional deterrent, and probabilistic deterrent.

Third-Party Security Commitments in International Relations

Many theories in the international relations literature examine why states make military commitments to each other. One prominent line of research is deterrence theory, which, in international relations, is the study of threats designed to convince targets that they will suffer unacceptable punishments if they undertake certain actions. In the literature on deterrence, a number of studies focus on how leaders can make credible commitments to defend themselves or an ally.[2] As in the present study, *extended* deterrence theory concentrates on third-party security commitments to an ally. However, research on extended deterrence stops short of addressing the central question asked here, which is why the contents of third-party security commitments vary. The reason for this lacuna is that the primary emphasis in these studies is on the question of how a leader can form a credible commitment when it is hard to believe that a third party would commit its resources, including the lives of its citizens, for another state. This focus leads to a conception of commitment as a state of being that obtains once a country becomes irrevocably and credibly bound to a future action.

Consider the formal setup of the basic extended deterrence problem. Figure 2.1 describes a simple extensive-form game used as a basic model in rational deterrence theory (Nalebuff 1991; Zagare and Kilgour 2000). The figure represents a two-player interaction between an *Adversary* and a third-party *Defender*. The defender's protégé does not receive a move. *Adversary* opens the interaction by deciding whether to challenge the protégé. If it does not challenge, the *Status Quo* (*SQ*) remains. If it challenges, then *Defender* either defends or does not defend the protégé. If it defends, then the outcome is a multilateral war, *War(m)*, in which *Defender* and the protégé fight together

---

[2] See, for example, Schelling (1966), Nalebuff (1986), Powell (1990), Slantchev (2005), Lebow and Stein (1989), Huth and Russett (1984), Zagare and Kilgour (2000), and Fearon (1997).

A Typology of Third-Party Commitments

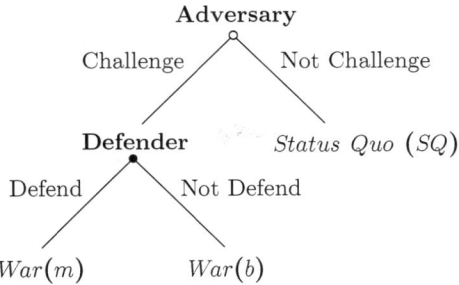

FIGURE 2.1. Extended deterrence game.

against *Adversary*. Alternatively, if it does not defend, then the game ends in bilateral war, *War(b)*, which means that the protégé is left to fight *Adversary* alone.

Adversary will not challenge unless it has some reasonable belief that its expected benefit from fighting against the protégé exceeds its value of the status quo. Thus, for the adversary to pose a threat to the protégé, there must be a significant risk that the protégé will lose a bilateral war. Suppose that *Adversary*'s preferences over outcomes are as follows: *War(b)* > *SQ* > *War(m)*. With this preference ordering, *Adversary*'s most preferred outcome is a bilateral war. Hence, for deterrence to be successful, *Defender* must defend when it gets a chance to move, because multilateral war is *Adversary*'s least preferred outcome. But why would *Adversary* believe that *Defender* prefers *SQ* > *War(m)* > *War(b)*? *Adversary* will not hesitate to challenge unless it trusts that *Defender* actually *prefers* joining a war for another state's security rather than staying out of the war and saving the costs associated with fighting.

Defender's preference for multilateral war over bilateral war might be credible if it suffers significant costs when the protégé loses. Such costs might result if a protégé's loss means that *Defender* would lose a valuable trade partner or face a new security threat from a strengthened *Adversary*. If *Defender*'s preference for multilateral war is commonly known, then defending the protégé does not require commitment, for it is already recognized to be in *Defender*'s interest. However, such a preference often lacks face validity either because it is well known that *Defender*'s interests in the preservation of the protégé do not outweigh its costs for fighting, or because *Adversary* does not know *Defender*'s war costs, capabilities, or interests in the protégé's survival. In this latter case, *Adversary* may mistake *Defender* for a weak or uninterested type even if it is strong and interested in the protégé's defense.

Both sets of circumstances – defending a protégé when doing so goes against one's immediate interests and clarifying misperceptions that one will not defend the protégé – require commitment. In the first instance, *Defender* must take some *ex ante* action that installs automatic *ex post* costs if it does not defend. Fearon (1997, 69) summarizes this point: "To be credible, a threat must have some cost or risk attached to it that might discourage an unresolved state from making it." In the second case, *Defender* must incur *ex ante* costs that a state unwilling to defend would not take. Huth (1999, 31) asserts that costly signals have the effect of "revealing information about the actual commitment of a state to defend against an attack," and, furthermore, "in the context of extended deterrence, uncertainty is likely to undermine the credibility of a defender's threat" (Huth 1988, 3). Costly military moves such as arms mobilizations, arms buildups, and deployments can separate truly committed types from uncommitted types who are trying to bluff true commitment (Slantchev 2005).

These two mechanisms, tying one's hands and incurring sunk costs, are methods for *becoming committed* (Fearon 1997). The standard for achieving commitment is that *Defender*'s costs for reneging on its promise are sufficiently high that it prefers carrying it out, and, equally important, that *Adversary* knows this. Consequently, much extended deterrence research has focused on identifying and understanding mechanisms that raise reneging costs sufficiently high to satisfy the commitment condition.[3]

Formal models, such as the standard extended deterrence game, have the advantage that they clearly denote the analytical structure of commitments made among players. The history of play at the third party's decision node indicates the antecedent conditions that must obtain before the third party decides whether to deliver its promise. The set of actions at the third party's decision node informs the content of the consequent y of the promise, if x then y. Those actions reveal what the third party promises to do and not to do if that decision node is reached. The third party's preferences reveal the objective and the limits of its commitment. If, for example, the third party clearly prefers the status quo to any other outcome, including winning a costless war, then it would prefer to fight a defensive war for the purpose of preserving the status quo than to fight an offensive war to expand the protégé's share of the pie beyond the status quo. That is, the third party would be more willing to provide full military support to fight a defensive war that protects the protégé's borders than it would be willing to fight to expand the protégé's territory. This limits the content of the commitment because the third party's delivery of y is subject to the condition that a war be defensive. On the other hand, the third party's commitment could be significantly less restrictive if it prefers expanding the protégé's share of the pie beyond the status quo in an expansionist or offensive war.

The pathway to credible commitment assumed in the basic extended deterrence game limits commitment to one simple type. This type of commitment is

---

[3] Such mechanisms include staking one's reputation on the protection of the status quo, alliance formation (Morrow 1994), trigger mechanisms or hand-tying (Schelling 1960, 1966; Fearon, 1995), commitments to gradual escalation (Schelling 1960, 1966; Nalebuff 1986), audience costs (Fearon 1994), and even contrived irrationality (Schelling 1966).

A Typology of Third-Party Commitments

TABLE 2.1. *Conditions for Third Party to Provide Military Assistance in Extended Deterrence*

		Objective	
		Preserve Status Quo	Change Status Quo
Trigger	Adversary Challenges	Extended Deterrence Threat	
	Other		
	None*		

* None applies when the treaty obligations are unconditional or the treaty terms do not specify any particular trigger condition.

located in Table 2.1, which depicts two dimensions – Objective and Trigger – that represent the possible x conditions of the commitment implied by the form of the basic extended deterrence model in Figure 2.1. The first dimension is the objective of the commitment, which depends on the third party's preferences. The second dimension, implied by the history of play, denotes the actions that trigger the third party's obligation. As can be seen from Table 2.1, these dimensions are partitioned according to the conditions in *Defender*'s commitment as implied by the basic extended deterrence game. The dimension reflecting *Defender*'s objective is divided into two partitions according to its possible preferences of non-status quo outcomes relative to the status quo. If *Defender* prefers the status quo, then it is committed to preserving it and deterrence is a priority. If it prefers something else, then deterrence is not its top priority but achieving something beyond the status quo is.

The second dimension, which captures the various histories or pathways leading to *Defender*'s decision node, identifies what actions trigger *Defender*'s commitment. The history leading to *Defender*'s decision node in the basic extended deterrence game depicted in Figure 2.1 only includes *Adversary*'s decision to initiate a challenge. The second dimension, therefore, is divided to account for only one condition in the extended deterrence game that might trigger *Defender*'s obligation to provide military assistance to defend a *Protégé*. The second dimension is partitioned into three categories: "Adversary Challenges" and "Other" and "None." The "Other" category represents the set of possible trigger conditions not included in the basic extended deterrence game, and the "None" category represents unconditional commitments that do not specify any triggers in the treaty terminology.

It is now possible to place the extended deterrence commitment in Table 2.1 according to its corresponding conditions. *Defender*'s preference for the status quo and the stipulation that the commitment depends on *Adversary* initiating a challenge put the commitment in the top left cell of Table 2.1. *Defender*'s set of actions consists of defending the protégé and fighting a war or not defending and letting the protégé fight the war by itself. The antecedent and consequent together result in the following conditional threat: if *Adversary* challenges and the objective is to preserve the status quo, then *Defender* will provide complete military support to fight a war against *Adversary*.

This is the basic form of the conditional statement studied in extended deterrence theory. As can be seen in Table 2.1, there is room below and to the right of the extended deterrence threat. It is easy to see that they could be fleshed out, which suggests that security commitments other than the extended deterrence threat are at least logically possible. As will be shown later, additional types of commitment occur when *Defenders* stipulate other conditions, x, and consequents, y. However, third-party security commitments with variation on x or y are not analyzed systematically in studies of extended deterrence. The state of *being committed*, as defined by Fearon, obtains only when *Defender* will incur unacceptably high costs for choosing not-y when x, as we have defined it, obtains, and the lack of commitment occurs when *Defender* will choose not-y regardless of x. George and Smoke (1974, 551) correctly identified this oversimplification of commitment types in extended deterrence theory: "Abstract deductivist approaches to deterrence have tended to assume that commitments have a simple 'either-or' character. One is committed or one is not."

However, world leaders form many commitments that depart from the extended deterrence standard. Such commitments include those that condition intervention on actions of the *Protégé* as well as the *Adversary*. Yet, the *Protégé* does not move in the basic extended deterrence model. Other types of commitment also include those that give defenders discretion and increase uncertainty about their willingness to defend.[4] From the perspective of rational deterrence theory, flexibility and uncertainty in commitment weaken the perception that *Defender* will actually suffer costs if it reneges, which hurts the credibility and reduces the clarity of the signal, even if the intended commitment is strong. As a result, *Defender*'s commitment is not credible and deterrence is undermined. If both flexibility and uncertainty have the effect of eroding the credibility of the deterrence threat, then states will prefer to make firm and fully transparent commitments to communicate resolve. However, as Fearon (1997) notes, "partial threats" exist in practice, and such empirical anomalies are not explained by the logic of the two-player extended deterrence model. Consequently, even if rational deterrence theory has contributed a great deal to our understanding of the mechanisms for making commitments credible, it has left open the question of why leaders choose different types of commitments.

Alliances and Third-Party Commitments

An area of international politics in which third-party security commitments are fully in play is interstate military alliances. It is impossible to say what a

---

[4] See, for example, George and Smoke (1974); Jervis (1976); Lebow (1981); and Snyder and Diesing (1977).

formal alliance is and what it does without saying something about the obligations contained therein. Leaders make promises to provide military aid, and then formalize those commitments in written contracts. Many alliances have the advantage of being formally ratified treaties, which improves their credibility. Additionally, as formal written agreements, they can be inspected and compared, which makes data collection and pattern identification possible. On examining a handful of alliances, it is immediately obvious that the commitments embedded in the terms of the agreements do not all look alike.

Few theories offer explanations for why different alliance commitments are formed, leaving the subject of alliance content understudied. Some exceptions: Morrow (1991) analyzes asymmetric alliances. Niou and Ordeshook (1994) and Smith (1995) study the choice of offensive versus defensive alliances, whereas Morrow (1994) considers leaders' decisions to form alliances with provisions for tight versus loose military coordination. Zagare and Kilgour (2003, 2006) analyze flexible commitments as mixed strategies. Snyder (1984, 1997) offers a general theory about why alliances might be flexible and ambiguous.

Much of the scholarly work on alliances has concentrated on their effects on war and conflict rather than on why their terms differ,[5] but this approach "puts the cart before the horse." Ward (1982, 26) claimed that "little work has probed the black boxes of decision making within either nations or alliances.... Nor has there been very much work which has sought to examine, understand, or predict which alliance groupings were likely to form." The problem of black-boxing alliances creates a blind spot obscuring a clear view of differences in the content (e.g., which promises are designed) and the configuration (e.g., which states ally with each other) of alliance agreements, both of which likely have implications for interstate conflict.

These are important areas of inquiry, however, because we know empirically that content affects both alliance reliability and the likelihood of conflict (Benson 2011; Leeds 2003a; Leeds 2003b; Leeds, Long, and Mitchell 2000). Assuming that alliances employ only one or two types of commitment mechanisms makes it impossible to identify competing effects caused by different commitment mechanisms. Suppose, for example, that two different types of alliance commitments lead to the same outcome, such as the likelihood that conflict occurs or the reliability of the commitment. If these two alliances are treated as the same type of commitment, then the different effects of each type will remain unidentified. Consequently, we cannot begin to analyze the effects of alliances before we know what the meaningful qualitative distinctions between different types of alliances are. That is, how can we theorize about

---

[5] See, for example, Morgenthau (1960); Waltz (1979); Singer, Bremer, and Stuckey (1972); Bremer (1992); Maoz and Russett (1993); Gartner and Siverson (1996); Smith (1996); Siverson and Tennefoss (1984); Vasquez (1993); Gibler and Vasquez (1998); Levy (1981); Colaresi and Thompson (2005); Leeds (2003b); Senese and Vasquez (2008); Benson (2011); and Johnson and Leeds (2011).

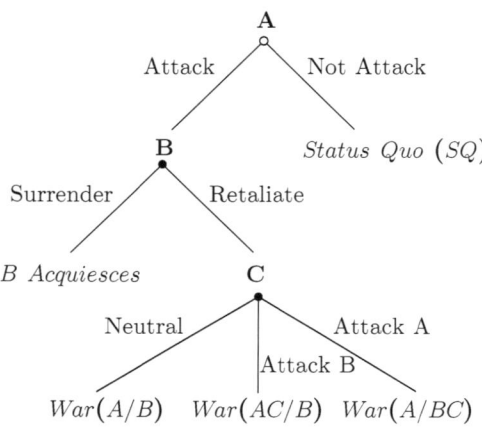

FIGURE 2.2. Alliance game.

the effects of alliance commitments if we do not know what we are theorizing about?

As a consequence of this lacuna, scholars have pointed out the need for better accounting for variation in the types of interstate alliances (Senese and Vasquez 2008; Levy 1981; Ward 1982). A useful place to start to identify and classify the range of variation is by looking at the existing classification and then adding new classes of alliance to fill the holes. An accepted way of differentiating alliance commitments is to distinguish among offensive, defensive, and nonaggression agreements. Of those three types, only offensive and defensive alliances commit third-party military assistance. What is the difference between these two types of commitments? The answer can be illustrated with the extensive form alliance game presented by Smith (1995), as this model explicitly frames alliances in terms of offense and defense (Figure 2.2).

The interaction begins with country A choosing between attacking and not attacking B. If A does not attack, then the status quo prevails. If A attacks, then B chooses whether to retaliate or surrender. Surrendering ends the game with B acquiescing and A winning its objective. War breaks out if B retaliates, at which point C must decide whether to remain neutral, join A and attack B, or join B and attack A. Remaining neutral results in a bilateral war between A and B, War(A/B). Attacking B results in a multilateral war in which A and C fight against B, War(AC/B). If C attacks A, then the outcome is a multilateral war involving B and C against A, War(A/BC).

An offensive alliance is a commitment by C to join A against B in war. A defensive alliance is a commitment by C to join B in a war against A. To assess the empirical reach of these commitments, we must examine precisely what type of promise is actually assumed by the game form.

Using the commitments analyzed by the structure of this alliance game, it is possible to refine the partitions of the dimensions begun in Table 2.1. The

A Typology of Third-Party Commitments

TABLE 2.2. *Conditions for Third Party to Provide Military Assistance in Existing Alliances Theory*

		Objective	
		Preserve Status Quo	Expand beyond Status Quo
Trigger	Adversary Attacks/ Challenges	*BC Defensive Alliance, Extended Deterrence Threat*	
	Protégé Attacks/ Challenges Other None*		*AC Offensive Alliance*

* None applies when the treaty obligations are unconditional or the treaty terms do not specify any particular trigger condition.

new categories can be seen in Table 2.2. The consequent promise, y, in both the extended deterrence model and the alliance model is the same: the third party pledges full military support in both cases. The differences pertain to the antecedent conditions, x. Consider an offensive (AC) alliance. An AC alliance in the model is analytically distinct because A and C both incur costs if C does not attack B when it gets a move. This cost is included in the model to represent the honor or reputational penalties accrued by alliance members if they renege on their alliance agreements. If those costs are sufficiently high, then C will always join A against B. The history of the game at C's decision node includes A's decision to attack B. Therefore, a war started by A is a sufficient condition for C to intervene to assist A in fighting B. The trigger dimension can be revised accordingly. As can be seen in Table 2.2, new categories of actions triggering the third party's obligations are Adversary Attacks/Challenges, Protégé Attacks/Challenges, Other, and None.

In the alliance game, it is assumed that when there is an AC alliance, the third party, C, does not prefer the status quo to war. In fact, both A and C prefer every outcome to the status quo. Their shared goal is to change the status quo at B's expense. Presumably no power wants to fight to change the status quo in a way that makes it worse off. Thus, the third party prefers to change the status quo, and the objective dimension can be adjusted to accommodate this refinement.

As can be seen in Table 2.2, an AC offensive alliance falls into the center cell in the right-hand column in the table. With this commitment, C promises to support A in waging war against B if A attacks B and B does not concede. An AC alliance is a particular kind of coercive threat in which A initiates harm against B to try to get B to make concessions to A. The threat is given force by the knowledge that C will join the fight against B if B does not capitulate.

In a defensive (BC) alliance, it is assumed that both B and C incur reputational costs if C does not attack A when it is called on to move. If those penalties are sufficiently high, then C's commitment to support B is credible. The structure of a BC commitment contains three elements. First, C promises to join B completely in a war against A. Second, C is obligated only if A first attacks B. This is clear from the game form. For C to receive a move in the game, A must first attack B and then B must retaliate. Therefore, a BC commitment excludes any obligation on the part of C to assist B if A did not initiate the conflict by attacking first. Third, the objective of the commitment is limited to deterrence. It is assumed in the model that both B and C prefer the status quo to any other outcome, which means that the status quo allocation is better for both B and C than any war outcome even if they win and do not pay war costs. This restriction on preferences limits C's obligation to defensive wars fought to preserve B's status quo allocation.[6] In other words, the third party promises to provide complete military support to its protégé in defensive wars started by A attacking B. In the table, a BC defensive alliance is classified in the top left cell alongside the conventional extended deterrence threat.

From the foregoing discussion, we can now write down the following definitions: An offensive alliance, as implied by a standard alliance game, is a formal commitment to provide full military support in the event of an offensive war that results from efforts to compel changes in the status quo. A defensive alliance is a formal commitment to provide full defensive military support if an alliance member is attacked and war ensues.

Problems Categorizing Alliances

It is noteworthy that offensive and defensive alliances occupy limited space in the two-dimensional space in Table 2.2. Alternatives to these two types of commitments are at least logically possible in formal analysis, though leaders may not actually form different types of commitments in practice. The next step, then, is to determine how well these theoretical categories of offensive and defense alliances map onto the historical record. The Alliance Treaty Obligations and Provisions (ATOP) data collection project was undertaken specifically to classify alliances into categories closely resembling obligations contained in Smith (1995).[7] Accordingly, the ATOP project categorizes military alliances as either offensive or defensive pacts.

To determine the empirical reach of the theoretically defined offensive and defensive alliances, the first step is to verify whether alliances are properly sorted and classified in the ATOP dataset according to their actual commitment

---

[6] Given B and C's shared preference for the status quo, it is not possible to say whether the equilibrium conditions for a BC alliance hold for offensive wars that expand B's gains beyond the status quo allocation. The game form restricts C's obligations to a BC alliance for deterrence.

[7] Leeds et al., 2002; Leeds 2003b.

A Typology of Third-Party Commitments

mechanism. Once ATOP's empirical categories have been examined against the theoretical counterparts, it is possible to evaluate the breadth of the existing theory's application. We may then ask: Are the two accepted categories of offensive and defensive alliance both empirically meaningful and complete? That is, do they account for the variation in actual types of alliance commitments?

There are, in fact, limitations with both the existing theoretical and empirical categories. Not surprisingly, a careful look at the content of alliances shows that the existing theoretical categories accurately match many actual alliances, but numerous others remain unaccounted for by the theory. Furthermore, although the ATOP project provides a valuable platform for examining the content of many alliance commitments, the empirical categories it employs are broader than the theory they were designed to test. Such a disconnect between the theory and the empirical data designed to test that theory suggests that the existing theoretical classification of types of alliance commitment is incomplete.

To highlight the nature of the problem with the existing alliance categories employed in ATOP, consider four alliances that are classified in the dataset as "offensive": the Pact of Steel signed between Italy and Germany in 1939; the 1832 commitment between the United Kingdom and France; the 1856 agreement among Austria, France, and the United Kingdom at the conclusion of the Crimean War; and the 1948 USSR–Romania alliance. The first three agreements are particularly important because they comprise a significant percentage of alliance agreements in ATOP data (Leeds 2003b). However, the actual terms of these agreements, as with many other alliance agreements, resist tidy classification into one broad category.

The 1939 Pact of Steel is an open-ended commitment between Germany and Italy to provide unlimited support in war. Article III states:

> If contrary to the wishes and the hopes of the contracting parties it should occur that one of them becomes involved in warlike complications with another power or powers, the other contracting party will at once assist it as an ally and will support it with all its military forces on land, sea and in the air.

This commitment declares mutual willingness to cooperate in any war, offensive or defensive. It is the broadest conceivable commitment, unconditionally binding alliance members to one another. Thus, its terms do not limit its application to a history of play in which the protégé initiates a conflict with an adversary, as in the alliance game above and Table 2.2. Since there are no trigger conditions specified in the treaty terminology, the commitment unconditionally applies to all wars involving an alliance member. I, therefore, categorize it as an unconditional commitment applicable for wars fought both for preserving and changing the status quo. It falls into both the two bottommost cells in Table 2.3.

TABLE 2.3. *Conditions for Third Party to Provide Military Assistance, Historical Alliances*

		Objective	
		Preserve Status Quo	Expand beyond Status Quo
Trigger	Adversary Attacks/ Challenges	*Extended Deterrence Threat, BC Defensive Alliance*, 1856 Austria–France–Britain	
	Adversary Attacks/ Challenges and Protégé Does Not Provoke	1882 Triple Alliance	
	Adversary Does *Not* Accede to Demands Formalized in the Alliance		1832 UK–France
	Protégé Attacks/ Challenges		*AC Offensive Alliance*
	None	1939 Pact of Steel, Post-WWII anti-German, 1939 Britain–Poland	1939 Pact of Steel

* None applies when the treaty obligations are unconditional or the treaty terms do not specify any particular trigger condition.

The 1832 agreement between the United Kingdom and France also permits offensive action. It was an alliance designed to support each other in gaining concessions from the Netherlands. It differs from the Pact of Steel because it explicitly identifies the alliance members' demands. Knowing what is demanded allows targeted countries to know how they can avoid war. Articles II and III of the treaty clearly set forth a set of compellent demands backed by a threat to use force should the target choose not to meet the conditions of the agreement:

Article II: If the Netherlands shall refuse to accept the agreement, France and the UK will embargo all Dutch vessels, and will order the respective cruisers to detain and send in all Dutch vessels which they may meet at sea; a combined British and French squadron shall be stationed off the coast of Holland, for the more effectual execution of this measure.

Article III: If on the 15th of November next ensuing, the Netherland troops should still continue within the Belgian territory, a French force shall advance into Belgium for the

A Typology of Third-Party Commitments

purpose of compelling the Netherland troops to evacuate the said territories, provided that the King of the Belgians shall have previously signified his wish for the entrance of such French force into his Dominions for the aforesaid purpose.

This alliance and the Pact of Steel are both offensive in the sense that they commit the signatories to use military force to change the status quo in a way that advantages at least one of the alliance members. Unlike the Pact of Steel, however, the 1832 agreement between the United Kingdom and France obligated alliance members to support each other militarily only if the target of the agreement refused to accede to the specific demands specified in the treaty. The treaty demanded that the Netherlands evacuate troops from Belgian territory or else France and the United Kingdom would embargo Dutch vessels and use French forces to expel the troops. If the Netherlands conceded to the demands, then the alliance members would not be committed to supporting each other in offensive military action against it. This type of commitment is different from the theoretical offensive alliance described previously, in which one country (C) makes a promise to provide military support whenever its partner (A) initiates a conflict. The 1832 UK–France agreement, which is not formally modeled by extant theories of alliances, specifies the alliance members' demands in the treaty and waits to see how the adversary will respond. It therefore occupies a new category of alliances, situated in the middle of the right-hand column of Table 2.3.

Another alliance classified as ATOP offensive that does not fit the theoretical category of offensive alliance is the 1948 USSR–Romania alliance. This agreement stipulates that the parties will actively defend one another against Germany should it "renew its policy of aggression" toward others. The agreements in ATOP are defined as offensive if alliance members commit to use military force against a non-alliance member even if that non-alliance member did not first attack an alliance member. The USSR–Romanian anti-German aggression agreement is thus classified as offensive because the provisions permit the USSR and Romania to use force against Germany when they determine that Germany is initiating aggressive conflict – but that conflict may not necessarily be directed at either the USSR or Romania. Germany might attack Poland, say, and the agreement would come into effect. However, the agreement is clearly deterrent, as it does not obligate signatories to support one another in an expansionist campaign against Germany. Furthermore, the agreement does not fit the theoretical defensive alliance category either, because mutual defense obligations do not activate upon any specific trigger. Indeed, signatories may engage in preemptive defense if they perceive Germany is renewing "a policy of aggression." This alliance is similar in form to many other alliances targeting Germany following World War II. They belong in the left-hand column in Table 2.3 in the bottom category for unconditional, because there is no specific trigger limiting a defender's obligation to histories in which an adversary first attacks. Alliance members' military obligations activate both when an adversary attacks and a protégé initiates a challenge against the adversary, as long as the purpose of fighting a war is to protect the status quo from an adversary.

Next, consider the 1856 alliance among Austria, France, and the United Kingdom at the conclusion of the Crimean War. The agreement was written to enforce provisions of the 1856 Treaty of Paris providing for the repatriation of certain territories from Russia to Turkey and the disposition of several Balkan states. Although the parties committed to use preemptive force if necessary, the intent of the treaty was to deter Russia from taking any action that would challenge the status quo as prescribed in the Treaty of Paris of 1856. It is clear that the post-Crimean War alliance is deterrent because alliance members are obligated to provide military assistance to one another only if targeted non-alliance members (i.e., Russia) seek to change the status quo. Alliance members' obligations do not extend to providing assistance to allies that take actions to move beyond the settlement established by the terms of the Treaty of Paris. Because the 1856 commitment among the United Kingdom, Austria, and France becomes active only if a nonsignatory violates the terms of the Treaty of Paris, it fits the category of commitments that condition military assistance on the adversary initiating a specific challenge, in which the alliance's objective is the preservation of the status quo. The alliance fits in the top left cell of Table 2.3.

Similar inconsistencies exist in the alliances categorized by ATOP as defensive alliances. ATOP alliances are classified as defensive if members promise "to assist a partner actively in the event of attack on the partner's sovereignty or territorial integrity" (Leeds et al., 2002). This definition, which is consistent with the defensive agreement of the alliance model, clearly excludes some deterrent alliances, such as the post-Crimean War agreement and the post-World War II Soviet alliances mentioned earlier. Additionally, it logically excludes many actual agreements that are nevertheless classified as ATOP defensive. The language of several ATOP defensive alliance agreements permits preemptive military action by alliance members or a probabilistic rather than automatic commitment to defend. Consequently, many alliances designed to deter challenges to alliance members go beyond the scope of the theoretical and empirical category of defensive alliance. To illustrate the variety of commitments included in the ATOP defensive category that do not automatically commit support if an adversary attacks an alliance member, consider the following three defensive alliances: the agreement signed by Britain and Poland a week prior to the German invasion of Poland in 1939; the Triple Alliance among Austria, Germany, and Italy signed in 1882; and the alliance signed by the United States and the Republic of China (Taiwan) in 1954.

The 1939 alliance between Britain and Poland is classified as ATOP defensive even though the type of commitment contained in the agreement does not fit the definition. It contains a threat to use preemptive force to deter a non-alliance member from attacking an alliance member. The defensive provisions of the agreement of August 25, 1939 between Britain and Poland clearly state:

A Typology of Third-Party Commitments

Article I: Should one of the parties become engaged in hostilities with a European power in consequence of aggression by the latter against that party, the other party will at once give the other party engaged in hostilities all the support and assistance in its power.

Article II: The provisions of Article I will also apply in the event of any action by a European Power which clearly threatened, directly or indirectly, the independence of one of the parties, and was of such a nature that the party in question considered it vital to resist it with armed forces. Should one of the parties become engaged in hostilities with a European power in consequence of action by that power which threatened the independence or neutrality of another European state in such a way as to constitute a clear menace to the security of that party, the provisions of Article I will apply, without prejudice, however, to the rights of the other European state concerned.

The agreement allowed signatories to use preemptive action in the event an alliance member perceived Germany to be sufficiently threatening. Although classified in ATOP as defensive, it is very similar in design to the post-World War II Soviet anti-German aggression agreements, which are categorized in ATOP as offensive. These alliances, which should be classified and studied as a separate category of deterrent agreements, belong to the cell in the bottom left-hand column in Table 2.3 defined by the objective to preserve the status quo and the no specific trigger condition.

Another anomaly is the Triple Alliance. In this alliance, Germany, Austria-Hungary, and Italy committed to assist one another if one of the contracting parties was attacked and the attack was unprovoked:

Article II: In case Italy, without direct provocation on her part, should be attacked by France for any reason whatsoever, the two other Contracting parties shall be bound to lend help and assistance with all their forces to the Party attacked. This same obligation shall devolve upon Italy in case of any aggression without direct provocation by France against Germany.

Article III: If one, or two, of the High Contracting Parties, without direct provocation on their part, should chance to be attacked and to be engaged in a war with two or more Great powers nonsignatory to the present treaty, the casus foederis will arise simultaneously for all the High Contracting Parties.

This bears some resemblance to the theoretical category of defensive alliance, with the exception of the non-provocation clause. Theoretical models of defensive alliances include costs for reneging so that alliance members do not violate the terms of their contract when the conditions for intervention have been met. However, in the case of the Triple Alliance, the signatories are not in breach of contract if they opt out of providing assistance when they interpret the conflict as having been provoked by an alliance member. This mechanism adds yet another condition to the deterrence threat in the alliance. As can be seen in Table 2.3, the alliance members are obligated to fight for one another *if* an adversary attacks *and* an alliance member does not provoke *and* the objective of the military contest is to preserve the status quo.

Other agreements signal that alliance members *might* intervene if there is conflict. The agreement between the United States and the Republic of China in 1954, for example, states that each alliance member will "act to meet the common danger *in accordance with its constitutional processes*" (emphasis added). The highlighted clause, common to many U.S. alliances, does not make military assistance automatic. It delegates ultimate decision-making power by subjecting the decision to intervene to a domestic veto player, such as the U.S. Congress. The key difference between this and other alliances is that the subsequent y is not a strict obligation. The conditional statement underlying this commitment is: if x then maybe y. Existing models of alliances do not formally analyze such probabilistic commitments, and they fall outside the theoretical category of defensive alliance. Therefore, it is not clear from theory why leaders would choose them or what their effects are.

In sum, creating a useful theory of commitments in alliances requires a clear conception of the differences that exist in alliance objectives and commitment mechanisms. Most existing theories of alliances black-box these differences. Yet, as can be seen in Table 2.3, the alliance categories established in theory do not exhaust all possibilities. Numerous well-known interstate alliances fall outside the analytic definition of offensive and defensive alliance, leaving many alliances unexplained by theory. Additionally, existing empirical categories are overly broad and do not correspond to theory. To develop a systematic theory of third-party security commitments, which can be tested with observational data of historical formal military alliances, there is need for a typology of alliances both guided by theory and grounded in empirics.

New Typology of Alliances

Given the unaccounted for heterogeneity of alliance types noted previously, I propose a novel classification of commitments based on the two main dimensions of antecedent conditions that emerged in the preceding analysis of extant deterrence and alliance theory: *objective* and *trigger*. For reasons described in the following sections, I partition the dimension that indicates the *objective* of the alliance commitment into categories of *deterrence* and *compellence*. I then sort the dimension of *trigger* conditions into groups that have *specific* triggers and those that have *no trigger*. Table 2.4 presents the dimensions of the typology and the four commitment types that result: *unconditional compellent, conditional compellent, unconditional deterrent*, and *conditional deterrent*. One additional category, *probabilistic deterrent commitments*, is not included in Table 2.4. A probabilistic deterrent commitment is distinct because the consequent of the promise is different from other commitments of military assistance. These commitments stipulate that alliance members *might* intervene if there is war. Finally, I identify a sixth category called *pure conditional*

A Typology of Third-Party Commitments

TABLE 2.4. *Typology of Third-Party Security Commitments*

		Objective	
		Deterrence	Compellence
Trigger	Specific	*Conditional Deterrent*[8] (Obligation conditional upon an alliance partner *not* forcing an offensive change in the status quo *and* a target of the alliance initiating some specified challenge against an alliance partner) 1856 UK–Austria–France 1855 UK–France–Sweden *Pure Conditional Deterrent* (Obligation conditional upon an alliance partner *not* forcing an offensive change in the status quo *and* a target of the alliance initiating some specified challenge against an alliance partner *and* an alliance partner not initiating some specified challenge against a target) 1882 Triple Alliance 1905 Britain–Japan	*Conditional Compellent* (Obligation conditional upon target not acceding to the offensive demands specified in the alliance agreement) 1832 UK–France 1854 UK–France
	None*	*Unconditional Deterrent* (Obligation conditional upon alliance partner *not* forcing an offensive change in the status quo) 1939 Britain–Poland 1939 Pact of Steel Post-WWII anti-German agreements	*Unconditional Compellent*[9] (No conditions) 1939 Pact of Steel 1942 United Nations Declaration

* None applies when the treaty obligations are unconditional or the treaty terms do not specify any particular trigger condition.

deterrence commitments, a subclass of conditional commitments in which signatories promise to intervene if and only if some condition, usually an

---

[8] This category includes the extended deterrence commitments and theoretically established alliances analyzed earlier.
[9] This category includes theoretically accepted offensive alliances.

adversary's attack or challenge, occurs. These agreements are distinct from what I eventually label as *conditional commitments*, because signatories in *conditional commitments* promise to intervene only if the condition – say, an adversary's attack – occurs and leaves unspecified what the response will be if there is war for any other reason, such as the protégé provoking the adversary. In the typology developed in Table 2.4 and the subsequent tables, *pure conditional commitments* occupy a space given by the dimensions that define the categories. As such, they become classified as a subcategory of *conditional commitments*.[10]

The first dimension – the alliance's objective – identifies what alliance members are committed to achieving. In the extended deterrence and alliance models analyzed earlier, it was possible to infer the objective from players' preferences for outcomes relative to the status quo. Commitments derived from these theories are distinguished based on whether players want to preserve or to challenge the status quo. Compellent threats seek to change the status quo at the adversary's expense and to the benefit of the party making the threat. Deterrent threats are intended to dissuade the adversary from undertaking actions to change the status quo in a way that disadvantages the party making the threat. The distinction between compellence and deterrence echoes the category of commitments in bargaining theory as established by Schelling (1960). Following bargaining theory since Schelling (1960, 1966), commitments can have compellent or deterrent objectives. As Schelling (1966, 71–72) explains:

> Deterrence and compellence differ in a number of respects, most of them corresponding to something like the difference between passives and dynamics. Deterrence involves setting the stage – by announcement, by rigging the trip-wire, by incurring the obligation, and *waiting*. The overt act is up to the opponent.... Compellence, in contrast, usually involves *initiating* an action (or an irrevocable commitment to action) that can cease, or become harmless, only if the opponent responds (emphasis in original).

The distinction between compellence and deterrence may be illustrated in a tripartite alliance model, such as the one depicted in Figure 2.2. In such models, three players – states A, B, and C – interact in a conflict sequence. State A wishes to compel a change in the status quo and has a move to harm state B, which prefers that the status quo remain unchanged. The harm ceases only if B acquiesces. If B resists, then general war settles the dispute. In forming an alliance with either A or B, C commits to intervene on that party's behalf if war breaks out. As seen earlier, in an AC alliance, C shares A's preference for challenging the status quo. Consequently, A and C promise even greater harm to B if it does not concede. The agreement commits alliance partners to initiate coercive action against B. This is a compellent commitment, as A and

---

[10] The categories in this typology need not be mutually exclusive. That is, an alliance agreement can include both deterrent and compellent provisions.

A Typology of Third-Party Commitments

C are compelling *B* to submit to a change to the status quo through the threat of military aggression. In this situation, *B* is given the last chance to stop the conflict, for the harm inflicted on *B* can cease only if *B* grants a concession to *A*, if *B* is forcibly driven into submission through defeat in war, or if *B* resists and *A* loses the ensuing war.

By contrast, in a *BC* alliance, *B* and *C* both seek to preserve the status quo by threatening *A* with negative consequences if it attacks. In forming an alliance, *B* and *C* set the stage by establishing a threat to defend the status quo – their alliance is intended to deter *A* from pursuing aggression. They then wait, and the trip wire is triggered if *A* takes action to change the status quo. The deterrence succeeds if *A* does not act.

The second dimension divides alliances depending on the conditions that trigger *casus foederis*. In Tables 2.1 through 2.3, the categories representing these conditions became ever finer as individual alliances were examined. Is it possible to create generalized nominal classifications for these distinctions that rest on less specific criteria, exhaustively include all historical commitments, and retain theoretical meaning? In bargaining theory, promises and threats can be conditional or unconditional. This is a useful guide for thinking about commitment triggers. Conditional commitments activate depending on the particular history of play, whereas unconditional commitments entail obligations for every history of play. For example, the Pact of Steel conferred wartime military obligations on alliance partners regardless of how war occurred. Likewise, the 1939 Britain–Poland deterrent alliance activated for any war involving a targeted adversary and one of the alliance partners, as long as the war was defensive in nature. However, the restriction to defensive wars is already accounted for by the deterrent objective in the other dimension. Hence, this alliance does not have any specific triggers; it does not limit mutual defense to any particular history of play. Accordingly, the trigger dimension can be partitioned according to whether the commitment includes any specific actions that activate the alliance obligations. Looking back at Table 2.3, it is clear that the first three rows (Adversary Challenges, Adversary Challenges and Protégé Does Not Provoke, and Adversary Does Not Accede to Demands) all specify a particular history that triggers the third party's obligation to deliver military assistance. Consequently, these can be collapsed into the single category of *specific* triggers in Table 2.4.

There may be one exception to the division of the trigger dimension into "specific" and "none" categories. This is the second row in Table 2.3, which captures commitments requiring the adversary to attack and the protégé not to provoke. These commitments contain specific triggers, but the non-provocation stipulation makes the third-party defender's guarantee a biconditional promise: the third party will support the protégé *if and only if* the protégé is attacked first. If the third party perceives that the adversary's attack was a response to a provocation initiated by the protégé, then the commitment explicitly threatens the protégé that the third party will not provide it support. When a war occurs, non-provocation commitments give the third party some discretion to determine whether its protégé provoked conflict. These commitments are located in the second row in Table 2.3.

The second to last row in Table 2.3 represents commitments in which third parties assist when the protégé attacks. Few historical commitments explicitly stipulate willingness to intervene if a protégé takes a hostile action against an adversary. However, many unconditional commitments imply willingness to intervene even when a protégé initiates with a hostile action. Thus, I combine the last two rows in Table 2.4: the combined category captures the third party's unconditional commitment to assist the protégé regardless of the history of play. This category includes alliances wherein the third party promises assistance whether the protégé attacks first or is itself attacked.[11]

Compellent Commitments

Let us now examine each of the four categories that result from Table 2.4 for the purpose of establishing rules for assigning individual alliances to each category. *Unconditional compellent commitments* commit members to assist each other for any type of war, regardless of who initiates. Alliances in this category either place no restrictions on *casus foederis* or they declare, in the terms of the alliance, the signatories' intention to attack an adversary immediately. The Pact of Steel is a clear example of the former, as it does not place any limitations on *casus foederis* and applies both to compellent and deterrent situations. Therefore, it is classified as both an unconditional compellent and deterrent commitment. An illustration of an alliance with a declaration to take up arms immediately against an adversary is the Declaration by the United Nations of January 1, 1942. This agreement committed all signatories to wage war immediately against Japan, Germany, and Italy. Each signatory was obligated to fight against the three opponents. Because the alliance was active immediately upon signing, no specific conditions triggered signatories' obligations to provide military assistance.

If an alliance contains a compellent threat along with specific demands the target can meet to avoid attack, the alliance is classified as *conditional compellent*. In such alliances, members are permitted to initiate force only if the adversary targeted by the threat does not acquiesce to the demands. Because the agreement spells out alliance partners' demands, the adversary targeted by the compellent threat can choose to concede before harmful action is ever initiated. In addition to the 1832 United Kingdom–France agreement described

---

[11] Although it is possible to imagine a scenario in which a third party would promise to assist only when the protégé attacks first (perhaps because it is willing to fight only if it can gain a first-strike advantage against the adversary), the wording of actual military alliances reveals that this is rarely, if ever, the case.

A Typology of Third-Party Commitments

earlier, the 1854 alliance between the United Kingdom and France is an example of a conditional compellent alliance. Article II of this alliance specifies a demand issued to Sardinia, along with a punishment for noncompliance:

The Integrity of the Ottoman Empire being violated by the Occupation of the Provinces of Moldavia and of Wallachia, and by other movements of the Russian troops, [the UK and France] have concerted, and will concert together, as to the most proper means for liberating the Territory of the Sultan from Foreign Invasion, and for accomplishing the object specified in Article I [establishing peace between Russia and Turkey]. For this purpose they engage to maintain, according to the requirements of the War, to be judged of by common agreement, sufficient Naval and Military Forces to meet those requirements, the description, number, and destination whereof shall, if occasion should arise, be determined by subsequent Arrangements.

The objective of the commitment was to change the status quo by expelling Russian troops from the Ottoman Empire. To achieve this objective, the signatories threatened to use "sufficient Naval and Military Forces to meet those requirements." Implicit in the threat is the willingness not to attack Russia if it withdraws from Ottoman territory.

Deterrent Commitments

As with compellent commitments, deterrent alliances can be distinguished by the conditions that require members to provide assistance. Deterrent commitments can be classified as *conditional* or *unconditional*, depending on the specificity of the trigger activating the alliance. *Conditional deterrent commitments* become active if a target of the alliance takes a specified hostile action. Specific triggers include "an attack on one is an attack on all," "in the case... of being menaced in its nationality and independence," "in case of a threat or aggression," "if one of the parties is the victim of aggression," and "stand as one country in defense against any aggression." A third-party defender is bound by the commitment to defend a protégé if a targeted adversary takes a prohibited action. If the adversary does not initiate the specified action, then third parties are under no obligation to assist. Because they are designed to deter a specified action considered hostile by the signatories, conditional deterrent alliances are similar to extended deterrence threats and defensive alliances in alliance models.

As discussed previously, the 1856 commitment among the United Kingdom, Austria, and France becomes active if a targeted adversary violates the terms of the 1856 Treaty of Paris. Another example of a conditional deterrent alliance is the 1855 agreement among the United Kingdom, France, and Sweden. The alliance treaty states that signatories' obligations are triggered if Russia makes a demand of Sweden for territorial concessions.

Unconditional deterrent commitments permit protégés to use preemptive force against a threatening adversary. This commitment stands in stark contrast with conditional deterrent alliances, which obligate alliance partners to wait until an adversary takes an overt hostile action. The label "unconditional" reflects the fact that the alliance does not stipulate any specific actions that would trigger the alliance. Alliances are classified as unconditional deterrent if they simply declare that "A will defend B" without specifying any particular action the adversary must take to trigger the alliance obligations. This broadens alliance obligations to include engaging in preemptive or active defense. Deterrent alliances are distinct from compellent commitments, however, in that they are clearly designed to preserve the status quo. Some alliances, such as the post-World War II Soviet anti-German aggression agreements, activate if the targeted adversary merely indicates that it might have aggressive or expansionist aims. They are deterrent because they are designed to preserve the status quo from any possible act of revisionism on the part of an adversary. Alliance members are under no obligation to provide military assistance if a fellow signatory engages in a war to expand into German territory.

Another type of alliance agreement is a *probabilistic deterrent commitment*. These alliance agreements explicitly state that signatories may or may not provide assistance. An alliance is probabilistic if the wording of the commitment clearly allows signatories to escape from the agreement once the alliance is active. For example, some agreements explicitly state that alliance members "may" assist one another in the event of attack. A common method for establishing a probabilistic mechanism in an alliance agreement is to delegate intervention decisions to a random process beyond the direct control of the signatories. For example, the Collective Security Organization of the Commonwealth of Independent States, signed in 1993, established a Council of Heads of States, and then promised that signatories would assist fellow alliance members if both the Council and the countries' domestic legislatures agreed. Another example, mentioned earlier, is the 1954 United States–Republic of China agreement. Similar to the U.S.–China alliance, many of the commitments signed by the United States after World War II do not make military assistance automatic. Instead, they require that the U.S. decision be made "in accordance with its constitutional processes." This removes the ultimate decision from the U.S. president and subjects it to domestic institutional factors, including Congress's consent, which result in an outcome that the disputants likely do not know with certainty in advance.

Some alliances also leave signatories the discretion to determine the level of assistance after *casus foederis* has been triggered. Such agreements do not promise or preclude deep transfers such as troops or active participation in defense. Typically, the agreement stipulates that parties can choose their level of military assistance at the time of conflict. An example of this type is the 1916 agreement between Japan and Russia during World War I:

In the event, in consequence of measures taken by mutual consent of Russia and Japan, on the basis of the preceding article, a declaration of war is made by any third power . . . against one of the contracting parties, the other party, at the first demand of its ally, must come to its aid (Art. II).

A Typology of Third-Party Commitments

The conditions under which each of the high contracting parties will lend armed assistance to the other side, by virtue of the preceding article, as well as the means by which such assistance shall be accomplished, must be determined in common by the corresponding authorities of one and the other contracting party (Art. III).

The parties agree to defend each other, but they leave unanswered the question about what will be transferred.

Probabilistic commitments are unique because they contain different consequent promises *y* from any other security commitment. All the other alliances classified in this typology guarantee automatic military support if the respective conditions are activated. However, probabilistic commitments do not guarantee automatic and full third-party assistance even if *casus foederis* has been triggered. The third party's discretion to choose at wartime whether to intervene or how much to transfer causes other players to be uncertain about what will happen in war.

Finally, as mentioned earlier, several alliances contain non-provocation clauses, which specify that signatories are obligated to assist one another if one suffers an unprovoked attack. These commitments are clearly deterrent and contain specific triggers. Thus, they are biconditional commitments in which the promise to defend stipulates that assistance will be provided *if and only if* the adversary initiates conflict with some specified hostile action. As such, they can be classified as a subclass of conditional deterrent alliances, called *pure conditional commitments*.[12] However, because the promise of intervention is also conditional on the protégé's non-provocation of an adversary, these agreements also permit third-party defenders to interpret the circumstances of a conflict involving an ally to determine whether they believe their alliance partner provoked the crisis. The third party's discretion to observe and enforce provocations based on its subjective interpretation of circumstances also gives these agreements a flavor of the uncertainty we find in a probabilistic commitment.

Consider another example in addition to the 1882 Triple Alliance. Article II of the 1905 alliance between Britain and Japan states:

If by reason of unprovoked attack or aggressive action, whenever arising, on the part of any other power or powers, either party should be involved in war in defense of its territorial rights or special interests mentioned in the preamble of this agreement, the other party will at once come to the assistance of its ally, and will conduct the war in common, and make peace in mutual agreement with it.

The wording is unambiguous: third-party defenders are under no obligation to provide military assistance to a protégé if they perceive that the protégé has provoked an "attack or aggressive action." Even though the commitment gives a prospective defender discretion to determine whether it perceives a conflict to be the fault of the protégé, I classify these agreements as *pure conditional*

---

[12] In Chapter 3, I introduce *pure conditional commitments* as a subclass of conditional commitments.

TABLE 2.5. *Cross-Tabulation of Alliance Agreements in the Novel Alliance Typology and the ATOP Dataset*

Novel Typology Alliance Agreements	ATOP Alliance Agreements											
	Offensive Only			Defensive Only			Both			Total		
	No.	Col %	Cum %	No.	Col %	Cum %	No.	Col %	Cum %	No.	Col %	Cum %
UC	3	21.4	21.4	0	0.0	0.0	2	2.9	2.9	5	1.7	1.7
CC	4	28.6	50.0	2	1.0	1.0	0	0.0	2.9	6	2.1	3.8
UD	2	14.3	64.3	22	10.8	11.8	21	30.0	32.9	45	15.6	19.4
CD	3	21.4	85.7	120	58.8	70.6	7	10.0	42.9	130	45.1	64.6
PD	0	0.0	85.7	38	18.6	89.2	1	1.4	44.3	39	13.5	78.1
PCD	0	0.0	85.7	14	6.9	96.1	2	2.9	47.1	16	5.6	83.7
UC & CC	1	7.1	92.9	0	0.0	96.1	1	1.4	48.6	2	0.7	84.4
UC & UD	0	0.0	92.9	0	0.0	96.1	23	32.9	81.4	23	8.0	92.4
UC & CD	0	0.0	92.9	0	0.0	96.1	4	5.7	87.1	4	1.4	93.8
CC & UD	0	0.0	92.9	2	1.0	97.1	3	4.3	91.4	5	1.7	95.5
CC & CD	1	7.1	100.0	1	0.5	97.5	2	2.9	94.3	4	1.4	96.9
CC & PD	0	0.0	100.0	1	0.5	98.0	0	0.0	94.3	1	0.3	97.2
CC & PCD	0	0.0	100.0	0	0.0	98.0	1	1.4	95.7	1	0.3	97.6
UD & PCD	0	0.0	100.0	0	0.0	98.0	1	1.4	97.1	1	0.3	97.9
CD & PD	0	0.0	100.0	1	0.5	98.5	0	0.0	97.1	1	0.3	98.3
PD & PCD	0	0.0	100.0	3	1.5	100.0	2	2.9	100.0	5	1.7	100.0
Total	13	100.0		204	100		70	100		287	100	

Alliance agreement legend: UC = unconditional compellent, CC = conditional compellent, UD = unconditional deterrent, CD = conditional deterrent, PD = probabilistic deterrent, PCD = pure conditional deterrent *commitments*. They fit this definition because they stipulate conditions that obligate *Defenders* to support their *Protégé* if an adversary initiates conflict against the *Protégé* but allow alliance members to escape if the *Protégé* provokes the conflict.

Furthermore, some alliances are both compellent and deterrent. Many unconditional compellent alliances, such as the Pact of Steel, guarantee military assistance under all circumstances, including defense. Agreements that guarantee to preserve territorial integrity against all states or a set of states (a deterrent objective) but also make a demand of a specific state (a compellent objective) are less common but also present. It is also possible for a state to have many different types of alliances with other alliance partners targeting the same state.

Table 2.5 presents a cross-tabulation of ATOP categories with the categories I propose.[13] It shows that the distinction between ATOP offensive and defensive is not the same as the distinction between compellent and deterrent in my typology. It also reveals that commitments that are just probabilistic deterrent types without any overlap in the other categories comprise approximately 19 percent of the ATOP defensive-only alliances. Additionally, commitments that are only pure conditional deterrent represent approximately 7 percent of ATOP defensive-only. Together, those two categories comprise 26 percent of the ATOP defensive-only alliances, which is a sizable percentage of commitments that do not fit the traditional classification of defense pacts. Another notable difference is that there is relatively small overlap in the group of alliances that combine ATOP-offensive-defensive and the alliances that are jointly compellent and deterrent in my typology. Only 38 percent of the joint ATOP-offensive-defensive alliances are also jointly compellent and deterrent. This implies that the refinement of categories disaggregates the broad traditional categories in a way that distinguishes them from one another. Many of the joint ATOP-offensive-defensive alliances, for example, get reclassified as *unconditional deterrent* because the terms of these treaties are clearly designed to defend alliance partners' status quo holdings, but the promises do not specifically rule out active or preemptive defense.

Summary

A theory of third-party commitment design requires an accurate and analytically meaningful specification of different commitment mechanisms. It is possible to infer the structure of the conditional statement of a commitment from the game form of extant formal theories. Extended deterrence theories limit analysis to only one type of third-party commitment. Formal theories of alliance that focus on different alliance types apply to only a modest majority of

---

[13] This table updates the typology of Benson (2011) to include *pure conditional commitments* and additional alliances as well as to reconcile some categorization discrepancies.

alliance commitments in practice, and existing empirical categories of alliances are overly broad. The new typology of alliances and the resultant dataset presented in this chapter yield categories of commitments that are guided by theory and cover historical alliances. These new classifications encompass old categories while also uncovering previously undefined and unexplained commitment mechanisms. The advantage of this typology is that it provides a useful platform for theorizing about the incentives that lead leaders to choose different commitment types. It also permits rigorous testing of theories of alliance formation, because actual historical alliances correspond closely to the categories of the typology.

In the next chapter, I begin to build a theory of commitments and moral hazard in crisis bargaining. The types of commitments classified in the typology developed in this chapter will reemerge as I begin to show how moral hazard and commitment types interact. That process begins toward the end of the next chapter, when I discuss how conditional and probabilistic commitments compare with a generic commitment that precisely specifies the amount of assistance a third party will transfer to its protégé. The categories in the typology come into full force in Chapter 5, when I demonstrate theoretically the conditions under which the different types of deterrent commitments are formed. Finally, in developing the typology in the present chapter, I generated new empirical measures based on these categories. These measures of alliance types will be used in empirical tests in Chapters 4 and 6.

3

Time Consistency and Entrapment

The typology of security commitments presented in the previous chapter shows that leaders make different kinds of promises to allies. The variety of commitments formed in practice suggests that a number of factors, in addition to simple defense, motivate decisions about how to design commitments. One such factor is *moral hazard*, which is an incentive problem that occurs when an actor is emboldened to behave aggressively because it is insulated from the risks of its own actions. An alliance pledging to provide military assistance to an alliance member may deter a prospective adversary from attacking the member, but that same commitment might also embolden the leader of the protected state to take actions that risk provoking the adversary and causing violent conflict, because it knows that the cost of its defense will be shared with its allies. Failing to balance deterrence and the risks of moral hazard can actually lead to the very outcome the third party hoped to prevent. How can the third party resolve this dilemma and design a security commitment that achieves both objectives? In this chapter and in Chapter 5, I develop a contract theory of alliance commitments that explains why a third party's intervention in an international crisis might affect disputants' behavior and how the third party's anticipation of this behavior shapes its choice of the types of promises to make.

The theory generates several predictions about why leaders design different types of security commitments. Chief among them is the conclusion that ambiguous contracts will be selected when the defender's deterrence objectives and policy preferences are at risk because an unambiguous commitment would distort the behavior of the protégé in an undesirable way. A contract that gives alliance members discretion about whether to intervene creates ambiguity about how the third party will respond to the outbreak of war. This uncertainty can discourage adversaries from challenging, while shifting risk about the expected benefits of war back onto the shoulders of the protégé. In addition to achieving deterrence through uncertainty, ambiguous commitments also have advantages if the third party has preferences over the structure of the settlement in addition to its preferences in war. Knowing that the third party might intervene with some probability if bargaining fails causes the adversary and protégé to reach a bargaining settlement that balances their expected benefits of reaching a settlement and their expected benefits of fighting given that probability. Consequently, ambiguous commitments can be effective mechanisms for smoothing the inefficiencies that result from the distortions of moral hazard and time inconsistency, which is a problem of credible commitment introduced in this chapter.

Drawing on the perspective of contract theory and principal–agent models, my theoretical framework focuses on the problem of moral hazard (Bolton and Dewatripont 2005; Arnott and Stiglitz 1988; Hölmstrom 1979). Moral hazard refers to an incentive problem that arises when a party determines how much risk to incur while another party bears the costs if these risks lead to a bad outcome. It has application in many settings, including insurance markets and management. In the insurance industry, for example, the insured can take risky actions that the insurance company will cover if those actions lead to an undesirable and costly result. Consequently, purchasing insurance can distort the insured's behavior by creating the incentive for the insured to behave less cautiously than he or she otherwise would. Moral hazard is also a common "principal–agent" problem in management settings. A principal delegates responsibilities to an agent, who, for a number of reasons, may be insulated from the consequences of his or her actions. If the agent's preferences diverge from those of the principal, then the agent may make choices that are inconsistent with the principal's ideal course of action. The increased measure of riskiness in the insured's and agent's actions can impose high *ex post* costs on the insurance company and principal, leading them to design *ex ante* contracts to minimize the incentives for the insured and the agent to behave recklessly.

In international crises, moral hazard might distort the behavior of state leaders when they expect to receive third-party military assistance if war occurs with their adversaries. Anticipating how the expectation of intervention can affect a leader's behavior toward another state in a crisis can induce a third-party defender to calibrate the kind of commitment it is willing to give its protégé. To see the application of these models to the problem of third-party commitment making, it is useful to think of the third-party defender as the principal and the protégé as the agent. This perspective highlights the potential for the protégé to take actions that do not coincide with what the third party would most prefer. The starting point for this approach is the observation that the protégé and third party may have divergent preferences. For example, say the protégé and an adversary dispute the sovereignty of a piece of territory. The protégé may prefer to possess a greater share of the territory than its third-party ally would like it to have.

Additionally, the protégé may derive greater benefits from fighting for the territory. Such settings with divergent preferences are characterized by a number of significant problems, such as commitment, private information, and, in particular, unobservable actions. As I shall show, if the third party has the ability to commit to particular actions based on how the protégé and adversary interact, then the third party will be able to form a contract that does fairly well at achieving its desired ends. However, when there are constraints on the ability to contract, the third party will have more difficulty obtaining its goals.

Two key constraints will guide the analysis. The first concern is often labeled *credibility* or *time consistency*. Pledges to come to the protégé's aid are credible only if the third party would actually be willing to mobilize troops if the crisis between a protégé and a challenger reaches a critical point. Similarly, third-party pledges to provide *limited* military support are not, in fact, credible if the third party would find it against its interests to refrain from fully supporting the protégé in the midst of a crisis. A treaty that creates the right incentives (avoiding emboldenment but providing sufficient deterrence) may nevertheless not satisfy time-consistency constraints, because the third party's goals in war may not correspond to its goals at the time it forms its commitment. If this is the case, then the contracting environment induces some inefficiencies from the perspective of the third party. As we will see, time consistency can inhibit the third party from obtaining what is sometimes called its "first-best" outcome – that is, its most preferred outcome.

A second concern in contract theory pertains to observability. Treaties are contracts that specify what the third party is obligated to do under different sets of circumstances. For instance, to balance deterrence and restraint, the third party might pledge full support if the protégé is attacked but only weak support if the protégé initiates. In crafting the terms of the treaty, the third party attempts to discourage or to encourage particular actions by the protégé. However, if the third party is unable to observe the disputants' actions and is thus unable to determine why bargaining failed, then some contracts, such as those conditional on the disputants' actions, are infeasible. The constraints of time consistency and observability affect the third party's efforts to design an alliance contract, because they both can exacerbate the problem of moral hazard. The third party's time-inconsistent incentive at the time of war to over-deliver assistance once it has intervened magnifies the amount of the disputed good the protégé believes it can extract from the adversary. Furthermore, the availability of hidden actions distorts both disputants' behavior in crises, because they can avoid blame for the outbreak of war.

The main objective of this chapter is to examine the effects of moral hazard in crisis bargaining. In Chapter 5, I will show how leaders design security commitments to contract around moral hazard. To determine how third-party intervention affects the behavior of the protégé, three questions in the literature on alliances will be addressed. First, it is often claimed that alliances can entrap alliance partners in wars against their interests. What does it mean for allies to have divergent interests, especially when alliance agreements, such as those designed to deter threats and challenges, often spell out the areas of common interest covered by the alliance? Second, how does a third-party ally become entrapped in a war if the war is not covered by the terms of the alliance commitment and the third party has the last clear chance to abandon the alliance? Third, do alliance commitments increase the probability of war, as theories of entrapment suggest, or rather do they induce protégés to behave aggressively in crises in an effort to get a better settlement?

The answers to these questions will be instrumental in assessing how third parties design alliance commitments. This subject is taken up in Chapter 5, along with the related question regarding the possibility that the third party can overcome the limitations imposed by the time-consistency constraint with treaties that are ambiguous because the third party's intervention depends on events that are somewhat out of the control of both the third party and the protégé. Additionally, I will determine whether these types of alliances may actually improve on the "second-best" outcomes that emerge from the model with the time-consistency constraints.

This chapter proceeds according to the following outline. The first section identifies some key questions in the long-standing discussion of emboldenment and entrapment in alliances. The next section presents a theory of entrapment and moral hazard in alliance commitments and crisis bargaining. These arguments are then formalized beginning with a standard game-theoretic bargaining model of conflict, which is then extended to include third-party intervention. In the final section, the theoretical results are illustrated using historical examples.

Emboldenment and Entrapment

A central claim of my theory is that third parties will try to design alliance contracts both to deter adversaries and to restrain opportunistic protégés. Scholars have long discussed whether alliance commitments can serve as mechanisms to restrain allies. Liska (1962), Schroeder (1976), and Weitsman (2004) are often thought to have pioneered the notion of alliances as mechanisms for restraining allies. Much of the focus in these early studies is on the value of an alliance in reducing tensions between alliance members. A potential crisis can be averted, it is argued, by forming an alliance that will improve information flows and facilitate a resolution of disputants' differences. From this perspective, alliances between states decrease the likelihood that they will fight each other. Another central problem related to alliances as restraining devices is the question of whether optimally designed commitments can restrain opportunistic protégés from taking risks that may cause conflict with non-alliance members (Pressman 2008; Crawford 2003; Jervis 1994; Snyder 1984, 1997; Liska 1962). Is it possible that a security commitment may simultaneously prevent an otherwise bellicose non-alliance member from challenging an alliance member while also reducing the risk that an otherwise nonthreatening protégé will be emboldened by the commitment to behave more aggressively toward the non-alliance member? From this perspective, an alliance might succeed in reducing conflict if it can balance deterrence with restraint.

The idea that alliances can embolden allies is not new. By "embolden," I mean that alliance members are incited to behave more aggressively in crises with adversaries. Some theories argue that offensive commitments embolden like-minded allies to provoke conflict (Smith 1995). The more puzzling aspect of moral hazard in alliances, however, is not about offensive alliance treaties; rather, it involves the question of how alliance commitments, which are designed to *deter* challenges to an alliance member, might embolden that alliance member to behave belligerently and risk war (Snyder 1984, 1997). Studies of alliance show that moral hazard distorts the protégé's behavior in a way that might improve deterrence (Yuen 2009; Morrow 1994; Smith 1995).[1] Because the defender is committed to intervene, the protégé is more likely to resist challenges from the adversary. As a result, moral hazard improves deterrence by decreasing the willingness of the adversary to attack the protégé. However, the positive deterrent benefit of moral hazard might wash away if the promise of third-party assistance creates an incentive for the protégé to expand its interests beyond the status quo against the interests and intentions of the third party (Yuen 2009; Zagare and Kilgour 2003, 2006; Snyder 1984, 1997).

The second concern is entrapment, which has also long been discussed by scholars (Christensen and Snyder 1990; Snyder 1984, 1997). From the perspective of the third-party defender, the downside of entrapment exceeds that of the emboldenment effect of moral hazard. In extant studies of entrapment, it typically means that third-party defenders are "dragged by [their] commitment into a war over interests of the ally [protégé] that [the third party] does not share" (Snyder 1997, p. 181). That is, a security commitment to a protégé that insulates it from the risks of its own actions may embolden it not only to attempt to expand its share of a disputed pie, but also to engage in war. With embroiling the third party against its will in a war as the protégé's goal, it must be the case that alliance members' preferences diverge. From this perspective, entrapment also requires that the adversary does not attempt to avoid war by appeasing the more aggressive protégé, and that the protégé would prefer to engage in war than to accept the adversary's conciliatory overtures. This implies that a deterrence commitment leads not only to aggressive crisis bargaining on the part of the protégé, but also to an increase in the probability of war. Additionally, from a standard viewpoint, entrapment occurs if the alliance commitment obligates the third party to fight in the protégé's war, and it cannot renege on its

---

[1] Crawford (2005) and Kuperman (2008) examine moral hazard of third-party intervention in humanitarian crises. Rauchhaus (2005, 2009) and Wagner (2005) raise some of the pitfalls in thinking about the moral hazard in third-party interventions in international and domestic humanitarian and civil conflicts.

commitment if war breaks out. Therefore, the specter of entrapment suggests that the third-party defender may not have anticipated and contracted around being entrapped when designing the alliance and that it values the preservation of the alliance more than it dislikes fighting the war.

These points raise some key questions that a theory of emboldenment and entrapment should address. First, why would preferences about war diverge if the scope of the agreement is deterrence and, therefore, specifically limits allies' war-fighting obligations to defensive wars? In Snyder's (1997) account, the question of entrapment emerges only when a war serves the interests of one ally but not the other. However, because deterrence commitments signal the common intentions of allies to fight defensive wars involving fellow partners, we must be specific about how the interests of parties to such agreements might diverge. There are three ways in which a protégé's interests might run counter to its third-party defender's interests. They may disagree about the degree to which they value defensive wars covered by the alliance agreement, the terms of settlement if war does not occur, and expansionist wars that exceed the scope of the agreement. With respect to defensive wars covered by the alliance agreement, allies may have different preferences regarding how much they benefit from fighting a war against an adversary. That is, even though a deterrence agreement signals commonality of intentions to fight defensive wars, the value of fighting such wars may be more intense for the protégé than for the third party. This is to be expected in many cases in which war is fought in defense of the protégé. One's interest in fighting for an ally is rarely as intense as that in fighting for one's own defense. Many other factors – such as the proximity of the protégé to one's homeland,[2] the commonality of political systems between the third party and protégé,[3] and perhaps even the age of the alliance – may also affect the relative intensity of a third party's interest in fulfilling its alliance obligation to defend its protégé.

In my theory, I build on Snyder's (1997) idea that allies may have divergent interests with respect to fighting wars covered by the alliance agreement. I account for this difference by representing the third party's preferences for war as a weighted value of the protégé's payoff for war. Regardless of the particular factors that contribute to the relative difference in interests, we can think of the overlap as a matter of degree, with the third party more or less agreeing with the protégé. This characterization makes it possible to pin down with some specificity how much allies' relative differences in interests over war affect moral hazard and, ultimately, the type of security commitment that emerges.

---

[2] Many studies assess the role of distance in interstate conflict. See, for example, Boulding 1962; Starr and Most 1976; Diehl 1985; Bueno de Mesquita and Lalman 1986; and Gleditsch and Ward 2001.
[3] For studies on the relationship between domestic democratic institutions and alliances see Lai and Reiter 2000; Leeds et al. 2002; Gibler and Sarkees 2004; Leeds et al. 2009; Simon and Gartzke 1996; and Gibler and Wolford 2006.

Another way in which alliance partners' interests may diverge is that they might have different preferences regarding the settlement between the protégé and adversary if war does not break out. It is natural in practice for third parties to prefer a more moderate settlement than the protégé in crisis bargaining between the protégé and adversary. The Israeli–Palestinian dispute serves as an illustration. Although the United States and Israel do not share a formal treaty, they have a history of tight military cooperation. However, U.S. presidents have tended to favor a more moderate solution to the Israeli–Palestinian dispute than that preferred by Israel. The Obama administration, for example, stated that a solution should be based on the 1967 borders, which did not include the Gaza Strip, the West Bank, or East Jerusalem as part of Israel. Israeli Prime Minister Benjamin Netanyahu bristled at the idea of reverting to the 1967 lines or using them as a starting point for negotiations between Israel and the Palestinians.

I introduce this new dimension by accounting for the possibility that allies may have divergent preferences regarding bargaining settlements. Because preferences over settlements do not factor into the third party's decisions about whether and how to intervene in war once bargaining has failed, they do not directly affect the distortion to the protégé's behavior that results from its expectations about the third party's involvement in war. However, the distortion of moral hazard affects bargaining settlements, and the third party's interests in the settlement influence the type of *ex ante* commitment it designs. Therefore, to the degree that alliance commitments affect allies' bargaining actions, the divergence of allies' preferences over bargaining settlements directly shapes commitment design and also influences the behavior of the disputants when they are involved in crises.

An additional way in which allies' preferences might diverge is that the third party and protégé may have similar preferences on defensive wars but disagree about fighting to expand the war beyond the protégé's borders. This raises a second question that a theory of emboldenment and entrapment should address. In these cases, why would the third party provide assistance in violation of its interests? Snyder (1984, 1997) makes an important point that dependence on the alliance can explain why a third-party ally would rather fight an undesirable war than abandon the protégé. Perhaps the third party is so motivated to preserve the alliance because of its own insecurities or to gain influence over the protégé that it is willing to join an undesirable war. A related explanation comes from Christensen and Snyder (1990), who claim that alliance "chain ganging" occurs when the survival of an ally is indispensable for one's own future security, even if that ally is revisionist and reckless, because its defeat would result in an unfavorable shift in the balance of power. As a result, threats to abandon the reckless ally ring hollow, allowing the ally to drag its unwilling alliance partners into war (1990, 140). It is also possible that the third party believes that its reputation depends on coming to the aid of its allies.

In these accounts, there is an assumption that the alliance contract is null and void or that the third party's reputation is severely damaged if it does not participate in the protégé's war. Dependence on the alliance and fear of losing its alliance partner or reputation help explain why a third party would join in a war covered by the alliance agreement even if it does not place high value on the war. However, in the case of offensive war, it is not clear why a deterrent alliance should be damaged. The protégé may wish to embroil the third party in an expansionist campaign, but the scope of conflict exceeds the obligations specified in an alliance agreement specifically limited to deterrence objectives. As a result, the third party is not in violation of its agreement and consequently should not be at risk of nullifying the agreement and losing its ally if it does not provide military assistance for the offensive portion of the campaign. Given that the protégé knows this, why would a deterrent commitment embolden even a revisionist protégé to do anything more than resist external challenges? A theory that demonstrates how a protégé might succeed in entrapping a reluctant third party in a war that exceeds the obligations of the alliance commitment must identify a mechanism that shows why it is difficult for the third party to limit its military assistance to defensive wars covered by deterrence commitments.

In my theory, I make an effort to address this issue. I show that limiting third-party assistance in war is often subject to a time-consistency problem: third parties that do not want to fight offensive wars on behalf of their protégés may be induced to do so when they cannot commit to limit their assistance once war has broken out. Difficulty fine-tuning the amount of assistance transferred in war results in coarse decision alternatives for leaders when forming promises and delivering assistance to fight wars. Often the boundaries of war are beyond the control of third parties, and a promise to become involved in any part of the war sometimes results in a fight for all of it. When incentives of war cause third parties to be all in or all out, then the moral hazard problem is especially acute. My theory shows how time consistency can result in coarse decision making in war, which in turn may exacerbate the problem of moral hazard in alliance commitments.

Another key question stemming from extant studies of entrapment is: Should an alliance, or the expectation of third-party intervention, increase the probability of war because of the effect of moral hazard? On this point, my theory parts ways with the notion that moral hazard incites the protégé to drag the third-party defender into war. Assuming that an alliance commitment has the effect of increasing the probability that the protégé will win a war, moral hazard should indeed embolden the protégé to behave more aggressively than it otherwise would in crises. This behavior increases the risk of war, but the adversary has an incentive to conciliate the aggressive protégé to reduce the risk of fighting a war. On this point, I follow Yuen (2009), who shows that the disputants may conciliate to avoid war.[4] Adversaries have an incentive to make acceptable offers and accept less in crisis bargaining because the alliance

---

[4] In my account, the adversary knows that the protégé's capabilities increase with an alliance; therefore, it makes concessions to the protégé in bargaining to avoid war. Yuen takes an

commitment increases the protégé's chances of winning a war. My theory, therefore, produces some observable implications that result from the protégé's expectation of third-party assistance in war. These implications include increased belligerence by the protégé; this aggressiveness increases with the size or power of the third party. It also means better settlements for the protégé. Notably, however, we should not expect an increase in the probability of war to follow from alliance commitments that straightforwardly and transparently increase the protégé's military capabilities and, therefore, the probability it will defeat the adversary.

These questions lead to the main focus of the theory presented in this book, which is that of commitment design taken up in Chapter 5. In that chapter I will address the question of whether the specter of moral hazard and entrapment leads third parties to contract around these problems. Fearon (1997) claims that moral hazard may explain "partial" threats and signals. Snyder (1997) claims that the design of alliance commitments often reflects an attempt to balance entrapment with the risk of abandonment – looser and more flexible when fears of entrapment dominate and firmer when fears of abandonment prevail. I build on Snyder's argument by endogenizing the formation of commitment type, given the third party's goals of maximizing deterrence and minimizing undesirable distortions from moral hazard. In so doing, I nail down the conditions, including some novel factors, that affect the design of the commitment. Additionally, I show when and why the optimal commitment for balancing moral hazard and deterrence involves ambiguous or probabilistic treaty terms versus specific conditional stipulations. The factors I identify include the relative interests of the third party and protégé over war and peaceful settlement; the relative capabilities of the defender, protégé, and adversary; and the observability of disputants' actions.

A Theory of Third-Party Intervention and Moral Hazard

Deterring an adversary from challenging a protégé depends on a sufficiently powerful third party making a credible threat of intervention. On the other hand, deterring a revisionist protégé from taking advantage of that threat to challenge the adversary requires that the third party be able to credibly limit its assistance to military campaigns that end at the protégé's borders even when the protégé takes its military adventures abroad. Limiting intervention to defense and finely specifying the level of a limited transfer of assistance can be complicated by factors beyond the third party's control. The main problem is that promises of assistance are realized only if there is war, and the third party's interests after war has begun may be different than before it breaks out. Therefore, even if it was possible to specify a limited transfer *ex ante*, practical

---

additional step and shows that under some conditions, even the protégé will make concessions to the adversary to avoid war.

features of war might impose time-consistency constraints. That is, there may be a gap between what a third party wants prior to war versus what it wants during war. The reason is that in many wars winners gain the entire pie, and losers get nothing. The incentive to win and avoid losing, combined with the fact that the scope and definition of the contest (the size of the pie) are often beyond the control of the third party, creates incentives to over-deliver assistance in war. Consequently, decisions about whether to intervene often clump coarsely into categorical choices between no assistance at all and massive amounts of assistance. This coarsening of options can undermine the credibility of the third party to limit its intervention once the fight has begun. This can be the case even if the third party prefers an intermediate solution to the protégé either receiving or losing the entire pie.

Three conditions can lead a third party's transfer of assistance in war to exceed its prewar goal. First, the structure of war may result in a winner that receives the entire disputed issue or territory and a loser that forgoes the same. Second, the third party may only just favor the protégé's interests in war over those of the adversary. As discussed previously, third parties have interests regarding the outcome of war, and those interests may more or less mirror those of the protégé. For the third party to over-deliver assistance in war, it does not need to completely share the protégé's interests over war; it merely needs to slightly prefer a victory for the protégé over a victory for the adversary. This may be sufficient for the third party to find it in its interests to intervene.

Third, the third party may not completely control and define the boundaries of war, and the boundaries may exceed the third party's ideal division of the proverbial pie. We also said earlier that third parties may have preferences over the prewar settlement that diverge from the protégé's ideal division. This divergence of interests might tempt the third party to promise to transfer a specific amount of assistance in war equivalent to what might induce the disputants to avoid war by agreeing to the third party's ideal settlement. However, when leaders do not control the boundaries, what is required to win a war can exceed what one would ideally like to commit to in advance. Thomas Schelling (1960) made the point that boundaries of war are often beyond the control of the parties to the war because the boundaries arise naturally. Such natural stopping points include preexisting borders; boundaries of ethnically distinct communities; rivers, mountain ranges, or coastlines; and other salient geographical features. Schelling also claimed that boundaries can result from the tacit agreement between disputants. In these circumstances, what disputants in war tacitly agree to fight over may be greater than what a third-party defender would prefer its protégé to have, especially if the stakes involve waging an offensive war to secure concessions from the adversary.

To see how time-consistency problems affect the third party's intervention decision and the *ex ante* contracting decision, suppose a third-party defender favors a protégé against an adversary in a crisis, but the preferences of the third party and protégé diverge on the ideal dispute settlement. For example, the third party may prefer that the protégé's borders remain as they are, whereas the protégé wants to annex a certain amount of territory belonging to the adversary. In many instances, third parties do not participate in the crisis bargaining between the protégé and adversary, and therefore do not directly influence the outcome. Instead, third parties influence the bargaining through the disputants' expectations that the third party might intervene if bargaining fails and war occurs. It is possible, in principle, for the third party to promise *ex ante* to make a wartime transfer of military assistance just sufficient to make the disputants willing to accept the bargaining settlement that the third party prefers. However, at the point at which the third party is called on to transfer the assistance to the protégé, bargaining has failed and any hope of inducing the third party's ideal settlement has passed. Consequently, the third party's *ex post* decision about the amount of assistance it will actually provide depends only on what it gets as a result of war and not what it hoped would occur in bargaining for a settlement before war broke out.

Suppose that the outcome of the war is such that the winner receives the entire pie and the boundaries of the pie are beyond the control of the third party. With war objectives arising naturally or being established by the disputants themselves, third parties are often not able to set their war objectives to be consistent with their *ex ante* goals. Under these circumstances, it may be unreasonable to expect the third party to keep its prewar commitment to limit its amount of intervention. Abstracting away, what is to prevent it from adding one additional tank over what it promised to improve the probability of winning? At the stage where war is underway, the third party is likely to face no such constraints, and may be motivated to transfer as much assistance as it takes to win the war. It is easy to see how its prewar commitment can quickly unravel when the alternatives are to add additional firepower to increase the odds of winning or to refuse to capitalize on its impact and face the risk of losing. Under these circumstances, if the costs for fighting and winning are too high, the third party will not make any transfer at all. Otherwise, it will provide as much support as possible to give it and the protégé the best chance to avoid losing to the adversary.

The incentive to exceed prewar commitments is not an uncommon phenomenon in wars. In third-party intervention campaigns, mission-creep temptations are all too common (Fearon and Laitin 2004). Nor is it limited to third-party intervention. Parties to war with predefined limited objectives often face incentives to add firepower in excess of their original goals. Take, for example, the U.S. war in Iraq. The inconsistency of the U.S. prewar commitment and its incentives during war resulted in an expansion of the U.S. involvement beyond the scope of the original commitment. The 2002 congressional resolution authorizing the war stipulated two objectives: to defend "the national security of the United States against the continuing threat posed by Iraq" and "the enforcement of all relevant United Nations Security Council resolutions regarding Iraq" (Ackerman and Hathaway 2011). The fall of the Iraqi government and deposition of Saddam Hussein met the first objective; the implementation of an interim government in 2004, the elections of a representative Iraqi government in 2005, and expiration of the UN mandate to secure and stabilize Iraq in 2008 fulfilled the second objective (465). However, rather than drawing down U.S. involvement per the original commitment, the Bush administration ordered the troops to remain in Iraq to continue fighting against sectarian violence for at least another three years, and the Obama administration continued along this same path.

Because the objectives of a war are often determined exogenously, the third party's incentive to add resources to meet the objectives of the fight may create discontinuous jumps in the amount of assistance the third party can choose to transfer. In these cases, the third party may do nothing or supply up to the amount necessary to achieve the objective of the contest or the third party's capacity constraint. This creates a coarse set of alternatives. How much the third party will transfer depends on how much is necessary to achieve the objective and how capable the third party is relative to the protégé. That is, the third party can do whatever it takes to help the protégé win the objective up to the limits of its capabilities. If the third party is powerful enough to cover the gap in strength between the protégé and adversary, then the amount of assistance can, in principle, guarantee the achievement of the war objective. This amount might be large if the protégé is weak relative to the adversary. If the third party cannot cover the gap, it can provide as much as it can to increase the odds that the protégé might win. Therefore, the more capable the third party and the less capable the protégé, the more assistance the third party will transfer.

The problem of time consistency and coarse decisions in war came up in the first Quemoy crisis. When deciding how to respond to Chairman Mao's shelling of the island of Quemoy in 1953, President Dwight Eisenhower described how, in reality, the U.S. options for military intervention amounted to two possible extremes. A majority of the Joint Chiefs of Staff advised Eisenhower to authorize Chiang to bomb the mainland in response to the Communist shelling of Quemoy and, if the Communists attacked Quemoy with ground troops, to permit U.S. forces to help defend the island. One dissenting chief of staff, General Matthew Ridgway, argued that such an action would lead to full-scale war. Eisenhower agreed: we are not talking now about a limited, brush-fire war, he said; we are talking about going to the threshold of World War III. If we attack China, we are not going to impose limits on our military actions, as in Korea. Moreover, if we get into a general war, the logical enemy will be Russia and China, and we'll have to strike there (Eisenhower 1963, 463–464). The coarseness of these options presented the United States with, in Eisenhower's words, a horrible dilemma between appeasement and global war (Eisenhower 1963, 463, 483). Eisenhower's identification of a set of discrete and dramatically different alternatives stemmed from his recognition that, in the particular crisis faced in 1953, the immediate desire to supply a limited amount of military assistance to the Chinese Nationalists if war broke out between the Nationalists and Communists was inconsistent with the future incentive in war to escalate to a significantly larger transfer of assistance by the United States.

The third party's difficulty in limiting transfers in war can be thought of as a type of entrapment problem, because the protégé may recognize that the third party, once involved in a war, may feel pressure to provide significantly more support than it would ideally prefer to contribute prior to the war. Importantly, the protégé may further understand that the third party may even be induced to supply wartime support in excess of the scope of a deterrence commitment to include offensive campaigns that benefit only the protégé. Consider the following scenario: Suppose two disputants both want to rule a territory. The status quo distribution of the territory is as follows: three-fourths of the territory is held by disputant B and one-fourth controlled by disputant A. A powerful third party's ideal division is the status quo. Its least preferred outcome is for disputant A to gain control over the entire territory. Further, assume that the third party's second choice is for B, its protégé, to rule the entire territory. To influence the outcome, the third party might wish to precommit to defend B by providing just enough military assistance to defend the three-fourths line. However, this precommitment may unravel if bargaining fails. If a war breaks out because A challenges with a demand that goes beyond the three-fourths line into B's territory, then the third party's deterrence obligation is activated. It then chooses whether to intervene and how much military assistance to transfer. If it intervenes and the disputants are committed to fighting for the entire territory, it makes sense for the third party to use its resources to yield the best chance of winning to avoid its least preferred outcome. As long as winning with B is preferred to losing and the natural outcome is one or the other, then the third party will give up its hopes of receiving its first-best outcome and will give B as much assistance as possible to prevent obtaining the third party's least preferred outcome.

Although these wartime incentives can cause the reluctant third party to become entrapped in an offensive war for the entire territory, the reason for becoming entrapped is not because the protégé dragged it into a war. It becomes entrapped when it intervenes in a broader war than it would ideally prefer to fight, and losing to the adversary is worse than winning for the protégé. In fact, even when the protégé knows that the third party will become entrapped if war breaks out, the protégé will not automatically choose to engage in war. Its expectation that the third party will intervene to boost its chances in war induces the protégé to bargain aggressively for a favorable settlement at least as large as what it expects to receive by going to war against the adversary with the full support of the third party. Therefore, the expectation of third-party intervention gives rise to moral hazard in crisis bargaining. By insulating the protégé from the risks of its actions (by increasing the probability it will win the war if bargaining fails), the protégé is induced to behave more aggressively in bargaining by either rejecting many offers it would otherwise accept or challenging the adversary for concessions that it otherwise not dare demand.

At this point, it is worthwhile to summarize some of the key conclusions from this discussion about time consistency in third-party intervention. We can also draw some implications for the protégé's behavior. First, exercising restraint in war is often problematic from the third party's perspective, for if it intervenes it may not make sense to leave resources on the table that can be used to increase the likelihood of winning. Second, the incentive to add resources in war leads to a coarsening of options in war. Although, in theory, the third party's options consist of the two extreme alternatives of providing no assistance and transferring whatever possible to win the war, the broader intuition is that wartime decisions often clump around discontinuous amounts of assistance. The reason is that military resources are committed to achieve certain objectives and it pays to supply what is sufficient to achieve them. Third, the coarseness of the choice exacerbates moral hazard. Just knowing the third party will intervene with assistance creates incentives for the protégé to push aggressively for outcomes that would not be feasible without the third party's assistance. That the protégé might expect the amount of that assistance to be very large only intensifies the distortion of its behavior. Fourth, because the amount of assistance corresponds both to the war objective and the capability of the third party, the moral hazard distortion increases the more powerful the third party is. Fifth, the protégé's aggressiveness can be observed in the crisis bargaining phase. This aggression can take the form of hostile military posturing, for it is better for the protégé if the adversary makes concessions equivalent to what a protégé expects to receive in a war in which the third party provides unlimited assistance. Finally, the coarseness of war options calls into question the credibility of any prewar promise on the part of the third party to limit its intervention short of the war objective. As a result, the ability of the third party to select the promise that creates the right incentives is also in question. This last point is the subject matter of Chapter 5.

It is important to offer some qualifications to clarify when we might observe exceptions to these predictions. First, the incentive to add support in war does not imply that state leaders necessarily have incentives to press for unlimited war, by which we often think of something such as World War II. States often fight "limited wars." For example, the Korean War and the Vietnam War were limited in the sense that the United States stopped short of using nuclear weapons and, in the case of the Korean War, did not expand the conflict into China. This point underscores the importance of the discussion of boundaries, because many "limited wars" have naturally occurring or agreeable boundaries that prevent war from escalating to unlimited war. A key factor that drives the time-consistency problem is whether the combatants' objectives in war are beyond their control and exceed what they would ideally like to fight for. Third parties are especially susceptible to this problem, because they are typically joiners to someone else's war.

Second, why do some alliance agreements formed in practice specify *ex ante* precisely the amount of support that will be provided in war? The answer to this question is related to the previous point. The time-consistency constraint does not afflict every third-party deterrence problem, because prewar goals and wartime goals can be consistent when the objectives of war correspond with what the third party wants. In many wars, including some limited wars, the objectives happen to match the goals of the third party or can be clearly established in advance, so what a state wishes to achieve before the war is consistent with its goal of winning during war. This is most likely to occur when the third party and protégé have identical goals regarding how the disputed issue or territory should be apportioned between the protégé and adversary. The most common case in which this might apply occurs when the protégé controls a territory and does not wish to expand into an adversary's territory. When the third party and the protégé agree on how a dispute should be settled, then the third party can form a credible commitment that clearly specifies the amount to be transferred without fear that it will induce the protégé to behave overly aggressively in bargaining.

Third, there remains a question about other commitments, which were introduced in the typology presented in Chapter 2. Are conditional and probabilistic commitments also susceptible to entrapment in the same way alliance commitments that specify a precise amount of assistance are? In Chapter 5, I offer theoretical conditions under which a third party will prefer to form these different types of commitment, but it is worthwhile to address briefly the question of how these different commitments affect war and bargaining decisions. This is important because it raises a key point about credibility of commitments, which I do not formalize in my theory because it has been thoroughly addressed in the literature. However, going forward, I assume that these other commitments are credible while maintaining here that it is often not credible that third parties will limit wartime assistance to an amount specified in a commitment. This requires some explanation.

In constructing my theory, I build on the credible commitments literature (Fearon 1997; Smith 1995; Morrow 1994), which demonstrates that commitments are credible when third parties suffer *ex post* costs if they fail to deliver what they have promised. In reality, third parties suffer costs if they underdeliver on their promises. Thus, if a commitment says that state A will defend state B, then A suffers a credibility cost if it fails to defend B's borders. It does not, however, suffer a credibility cost if it exceeds the commitment to assist B in an offensive war unless the commitment specifically precludes such behavior. Therefore, if a third party is bound by a deterrent commitment, it incurs costs if it does not defend. However, it does not incur costs if it assists beyond defense. In a conditional deterrent commitment, a third party incurs costs if an adversary initiates the challenge specified in the commitment and the third party does not at least provide defense. In a pure conditional commitment, in which a third party promises to intervene if and only if an adversary initiates a challenge, the third party suffers a cost if it fails to defend when the adversary initiates the challenge *and* it pays a credibility cost if it provides military assistance when the adversary does not initiate the challenge. In a probabilistic commitment, which I describe in much greater detail in Chapter 5, the third party suffers a credibility cost if it does not subject its decision to intervene to the randomization mechanism specified in the commitment. Furthermore, in the case of a commitment that precisely specifies the amount of assistance, a third party would suffer a cost if it under-delivered, but it is difficult to believe that it would also incur a loss of credibility if it supplied the amount promised in the contract and then added more to it. From this perspective, it is easy to see that delivering *at least* on the promise contained in all types of commitments can be made credible. However, it may be problematic for third parties to form a credible commitment to *limit* the amount of assistance they provide to a protégé. Only probabilistic commitments and certain types of pure conditional commitment are not vulnerable to the problem of over-delivering the promise without suffering a loss in credibility. A probabilistic commitment avoids the problem, because the commitment is to randomize between the extreme possibilities of doing nothing and going all in. Pure conditional commitments, which specifically limit intervention only to defense and nothing more, are also credible against over-delivery because a cost would be incurred for taking offensive actions as well as not taking defensive actions when an adversary challenges.

The final point that needs to be explained is the fact that sometimes third-party support is, in fact, limited in the sense that it falls short of any obvious wartime objective. How might we explain such anomalies? In China's civil war, the United States originally provided limited assistance to Chinese Nationalist troops by airlifting them into areas vacated by Japanese troops and some areas held by Chinese Communist forces. It also supplied financial assistance but would not commit massive troop deployments or weaponry. Some such activities in wars might be explained by motives that go beyond the scope of my theory. For example, in the case of airlifting Nationalist troops, it is reasonable to view this as an effort to conclude the war against Japan and put the Nationalists on as strong a footing as possible to secure China in the aftermath of the Japanese occupation. The limited financial assistance to the Nationalists was widely viewed as a way of appeasing the powerful pro-China lobby in the U.S. Congress and domestic anti-Communist pressures (Christensen 1996). In fact, the financial support from the United States continued long after the Truman administration reconciled itself to the fact that the Nationalists would lose to the Chinese Communists, suggesting that it was not intended to help the Nationalists win the war.

In spite of the trickle of support that the United States provided to the Chinese Nationalists for reasons that do not factor into my analysis, the logic of my theory nevertheless explains the U.S. recognition that meaningful intervention implied a decision between a coarse set of alternatives, and that fighting for the most extreme alternative did not match the primary goals of U.S. officials. As hostilities in the civil war began, the United States considered whether it should commit its troops already on the ground from the war against Japan to the Nationalist cause, expand its support, or prevent U.S. troops from fighting in China's civil war. One option discussed by some U.S. officials was for the United States to commit to bringing about a divided China by allowing the Chinese Communist Party (CCP) to rule Manchuria and parts of north China and the Guomindang (GMD) to rule everything else. A prominent proposal along these lines included freezing hostilities between the GMD and CCP, establishing a UN trusteeship to be established over China, and making a firm U.S. defense commitment to the Nationalist position *only* for Nationalist-occupied regions. General Albert Wedemeyer, the U.S. commanding officer in China after World War II, recognized that committing to a partition of China was not likely sustainable in war because the Nationalists and Communists were resolved to fight for the fate of all China. Accordingly, he requested that U.S. troops either be withdrawn or be given unlimited latitude to fight to win China (Schaller 1979, 282–283, 284, 286). Ultimately, the United States decided against fighting for both a divided China and all of China, largely because of the fear of being drawn into a protracted conflict beyond its goals.

Having explained how time-consistency constraints in third-party intervention may give rise to moral hazard in crisis bargaining, it is also possible to construct a game-theoretic model to analyze this effect on the protégé's behavior. To capture the intuition, let us first consider a standard two-player conflict bargaining model found in Fearon (1995). Analysis of this model will establish baseline expectations of the protégé's behavior when the third party is uninvolved in the interaction between the protégé and the adversary. Then, I extend the basic conflict bargaining model to account for the third party's decision to intervene.

In keeping with the preceding discussion, the third-party intervention model allows for the possibility that the third party and protégé may have different utilities for war. This contrasts with previous models, such as that of Smith (1995), which assume that the third party and protégé have identical preferences. As a result, the model is flexible enough to provide insights about a range of possible third-party preferences with respect to fighting on the protégé's behalf. Therefore, the analysis concentrates on the third party's decision to make transfers to the protégé given that it may not have the same utility for war. It is then possible to assess the protégé's behavior in conflict bargaining as it anticipates the third party's transfer of assistance if war occurs.

Baseline Conflict Bargaining Model

In the baseline conflict bargaining model, two governments, A and B, bargain over a divisible pie of value 1, which represents a disputed issue or territory in

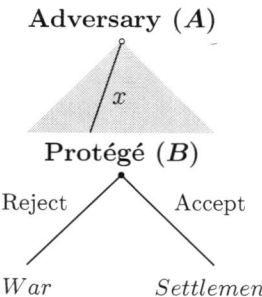

FIGURE 3.1. Sequence of moves in the baseline game.

international politics. Government A, the adversary, is the proposer and makes some demand of Government B, the protégé. In the baseline model, there is no possibility for the third party to intervene.

One of the primary risks in conflict bargaining is that players are not fully informed about some aspect of their opponent's payoffs. War can occur as a result of this uncertainty. Following Fearon (1995), I assume that B has private information about its war costs, c_B. Consequently, when A makes its offer, it is uncertain about B's war costs.

At the beginning of the game, B's war costs are drawn from the uniform distribution on $[0, p]$ and B then learns its cost prior to bargaining, but A does not. A then makes some demand $x \in [0, 1]$. B can accept, in which case the pie gets divided according to the agreement and settlement payoffs are $(1 - x, x)$, where x is the amount allocated to B. Alternatively, B can reject the demand and fight a war against A. Figure 3.1 depicts the sequence of players' moves in this game. Note that the extensive form game, which I do not show here, would have nature moving first and then A's decision nodes would belong to one information set. Because subgames do not cross information sets, this game, as well as all subsequent models in this chapter and in Chapter 5, does not have proper subgames. Consequently, every Nash equilibrium is subgame perfect. The appropriate equilibrium concept is perfect Bayesian equilibrium (PBE), which requires players to have posterior beliefs at every information set and that strategies are sequentially rational. In each of the games considered here, the veto player in bargaining is always the player with private information. Because the veto player always moves after the proposer, which is the player that does not know the veto player's war costs, players do not update their beliefs in any of the models. Consequently, in solving for PBE, it is not important to focus on the consistency of players' beliefs, and equilibrium depends only on sequential rationality. Sequential rationality requires that at every information set a player uses its best response given the strategies of other player(s). Accordingly, to solve the baseline game and the other models in this theoretical part of the book, I will solve for each player's best response at each information set.

Time Consistency and Entrapment

Player A's utility for settling the dispute without fighting is $U_A(x) = 1 - x$, and B receives $U_B(x) = x$. The outcome of war is settled by a lottery, and the winner receives the entire pie. Let $p \in (0, 1)$ denote the probability that B wins the war. War is costly. Players pay c_i to fight, where $i \in \{A, B\}$ identifies the player. A's utility from war is $U_A(war) = 1 - p - c_A$, and B receives $U_B(war) = p - c_B$.

Government B is willing to accept any offer that yields a payoff at least as high as what it can expect to receive in war. Therefore, B accepts if $x \geq p - c_B$, and A will try to make an offer just high enough to entice B to accept. However, there is some risk associated with A's offer, because A is uncertain about B's war costs. Too high an offer will result in A giving up more than necessary to reach a peaceful settlement. Conversely, if A's offer is too low, then it is not enough to offset B's expected payoff if it chooses to fight. B will reject any offer if $c_B < p - x$. This implies that the probability that B rejects an offer and starts a war is $pr(war) = \frac{p - x^*}{p}$, where x^* is A's equilibrium offer to B. It is now possible to find A's optimal offer, given that with any offer it makes there is some probability it will result in war and some probability it will be accepted. Therefore, A chooses an offer x that maximizes

$$EU_A(x) = \left(\frac{p-x}{p}\right)(1 - p - c_A) + \left(\frac{x}{p}\right)(1 - x).$$

The first product in the expression is A's expected payoff if its offer is rejected and war occurs. The second denotes A's expected payoff from making an offer that is accepted. A will choose the offer that yields the highest payoff given that it expects higher offers to decrease both the probability of war but also A's own share of the pie. On the other hand, lower offers allocate more pie to A if accepted, but also increase the probability that A will end up fighting a war over the entire pie.

The offer x^* that maximizes A's expected utility is

$$x^* = \frac{1}{2}p + \frac{1}{2}c_A.$$

Because A is uncertain about B's war costs, it does not pin its offer to B's expected utility of war, as it would in a game of complete information. Instead, A's offer is made in anticipation that its offer might be rejected and return its own war payoff. The amount A expects to receive from a peaceful agreement is bounded on the lower end by its war payoff and, on the upper end, by what it demands for itself subject to the probability that B will not reject that demand. In other words, A's proposed agreement gives it more than it would receive in war, which is evident from that fact that $1 - x^* > 1 - p - c_A$ because $p + c_A > \frac{1}{2}(p + c_A)$. Moreover, its optimal choice of x^* is a function of its own rather than B's war costs. The higher A's costs, the more it offers to B, because it stands to lose more if the offer is rejected. If $p - c_A < 2c_B$, then A can expect to get a share of the pie that is smaller than what it would demand if it knew B's war costs, which implies that under this condition A pays a cost for not having complete information.

The equilibrium offer can be used to calculate the probability of war at that offer. Substituting x^* into the equation for the probability of war results in the following:

$$\Pr(war) = \frac{p - c_A}{2p}.$$

This equation captures the intuition that as it becomes more expensive for A to fight a war against B and as the likelihood that B will win the war increases, then the probability that war will occur decreases. The model provides some baseline expectations in conflict bargaining without a third party. Notably, as long as there is some positive probability that B will win in war ($p > 0$) and that probability exceeds A's war costs ($p > c_A$), then A will always make some positive offer to B.

It is possible to compare these results to those from a model in which the third party can intervene to assist B in war. In the next section, I present a model in which C can choose some amount of military assistance to transfer to B if bargaining fails and war breaks out. This model will allow us to evaluate whether C's involvement has an effect on the bargaining process between A and B: if B now receives more of the pie in a prewar settlement than in the baseline model, we can conclude that C's assistance does have an effect. The model presented in the next section shows that the probability with which the protégé will reject and escalate to war increases with the amount of assistance the protégé expects to receive from the third party.

Model with Third-Party Intervention

Consider a simple extension to the baseline conflict model. If B rejects A's offer, then war results and a third-party defender C can make a transfer $\theta > 0$ of military assistance to its protégé, B. Figure 3.2 depicts the sequence of players' moves in the third-party intervention game. As before, the equilibrium concept is PBE.

The parameter θ represents any form of military transfer C can make to assist B in war. For example, C may give B troops, armaments, funding, or logistical support. In practice, C's transfer can both improve B's probability of winning and reduce its war costs. In the model, I assume that transfers increase B's probability of winning so that θ has an impact on war payoffs for both A and B. Therefore, the expected utilities of war for players A and B given θ are

$$U_A(war) = 1 - p - \theta - c_A$$
$$U_B(war) = p + \theta - c_B.$$

Time Consistency and Entrapment 63

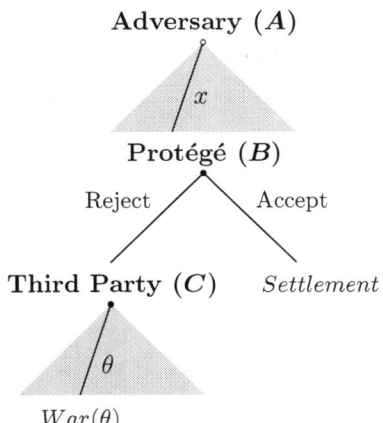

FIGURE 3.2. Sequence of moves in the third-party intervention game.

Government C's capabilities are denoted by μ, and it cannot transfer an amount of resources exceeding its capabilities. Therefore, $\theta \in [0, min\{1 - p, \mu\}]$, which is to say that C can choose any level of transfer from no support to the minimum of either its total resource capacity μ or what is required to top off B's strength to guarantee victory. If $\mu + p \geq 1$, then C is decisive in any conflict against A. The amount of transfer necessary to win is the difference between the total value of the pie and the probability that B wins if it fights without C's assistance. Hence, for C to be decisive, it must be capable of guaranteeing victory for B by transferring $\theta = 1 - p$ regardless of the value of p. On the other hand, if $\mu + p < 1$, then C is not decisive in the war; its assistance increases the probability that B wins, but does not guarantee victory. In this case, the maximum amount of assistance C can transfer is $\theta = \mu$. For the remaining analysis, two cases will be considered. Case 1 is when $\mu + \theta \geq 1$, and case 2 is when $\mu + p < 1$.

Because the level of C's commitment to B is public knowledge, A and B's bargaining takes into account how C's transfer will affect a potential war. Therefore, let us begin by assessing C's decision to transfer military assistance to B. A unique feature of this model is that the third party's war payoffs are not necessarily identical to those of the protégé. To capture the allies' divergent preferences, C's value of B's war utility is weighted by a parameter $\lambda \in [0, 1]$, which can be interpreted to represent the amount that C shares B's preferences. The less C identifies with B in war, the more it worries about the cost of making transfers to B. Therefore, C's utility for war is as follows:

$$U_C(war) = \lambda(p + \theta - c_B) + (1 - \lambda)(-\theta).$$

The interpretation of this expression is straightforward. C weights its value of B's war payoff, $p + \theta - c_B$, by some amount λ, and it weights its costs for transferring θ to B by $1 - \lambda$. C's utility is linear in θ, although it is not immediately obvious whether it is increasing or decreasing in the amount of the transfer. Whether military transfers have a positive or negative impact on C depends on how much C identifies with B. The third party C's optimal transfer is a function of λ, which is how much it shares the protégé's preferences in war. C's utility is strictly increasing in θ if $\lambda \geq \frac{1}{2}$, but is decreasing if $\lambda < \frac{1}{2}$. In other words, if C leans toward sharing B's goals, then it will prefer transferring as much military assistance as possible to B. However, if it tends not to identify with B's preferences, then C is better off giving as little assistance as possible. Therefore, if $\mu + p > 1$,

$$\theta^* = \begin{cases} 0 & \text{if } \lambda < \frac{1}{2} \\ 1 - p & \text{if } \lambda \geq \frac{1}{2}. \end{cases}$$

If $\mu + p < 1$, then

$$\theta^* = \begin{cases} 0 & \text{if } \lambda < \frac{1}{2} \\ \mu & \text{if } \lambda \geq \frac{1}{2}. \end{cases}$$

In each case, there are only two feasible levels of military assistance chosen by C. Either it transfers the minimum of whatever is sufficient to top up B's resources to guarantee victory or the maximum amount it is capable of providing, or it gives no assistance at all. It is, in fact, unable to choose a level of military transfer just high enough to make A and B prefer a given peaceful bargaining solution to war, because it is unable to commit not to add more resources to the war if it has them. Consequently, C's decision of military transfers is a coarse decision between going all in (by which I mean providing as much as possible or as is required to achieve the military objective) and not going in at all.

Interestingly, C will go all in even when it does not fully share B's goals. That is, C will make the equilibrium transfer θ^* even if $\frac{1}{2} < \lambda < 1$. The motivation for doing so stems from the fact that C benefits when B wins the war. Therefore, if C is just partial enough to B that it prefers to intervene, then it will do whatever it can to maximize the likelihood of winning the contest. Otherwise, it does not pay to become involved at all.

These insights about C's incentives have dramatic effects on B's equilibrium behavior in bargaining. On the one hand, if $\lambda < \frac{1}{2}$, then A's optimal offer is identical to that in the baseline game described earlier. C will not transfer assistance to B in war; knowing this, B is not emboldened to reject offers that it would otherwise find unacceptable if it expected assistance. However, if $\lambda \geq \frac{1}{2}$, then B anticipates receiving θ^* in military assistance and is, therefore, more willing to refuse many potential bargaining settlements.

To see this, consider the bargaining game in both cases when $\lambda \geq \frac{1}{2}$. First, consider case 1 when $\mu + p > 1$. If $\theta^* = 1 - p$, then the expected utilities of war for players A and B given θ^* are

$$U_A(war) = -c_A$$
$$U_B(war) = 1 - c_B.$$

War gives A a strictly negative payoff. To avoid it, A must offer B at least what B expects to receive in war. Compared with the baseline model, B's expected war payoff is greater as a result of its expectation of help from C. As in the baseline model, government A's optimal offer is shaped by its uncertainty about B's costs of war. If A knows B's private values, then it will offer $x \geq 1 - c_B$. However, because A knows only the distribution from which c_B is drawn, its choice of x is a function of what it expects to receive given that the offer will be rejected with some probability and accepted with some probability. As in the baseline model, assume that c_B is drawn from the uniform distribution with support $[0, p]$ and that $c_A \in [0, 1 - p]$ is commonly known. Given that B accepts any offer satisfying the inequality

$$c_B \geq 1 - x,$$

then A chooses its offer to maximize the following utility:

$$U_A(x|\theta^*) = \left(\frac{1-x}{p}\right)(-c_A) + \left(\frac{p-1+x}{p}\right)(1-x).$$

The optimal offer, then, is

$$x^* = 1 + \frac{1}{2}c_A - \frac{1}{2}p.$$

The probability of war given this offer can be found by substituting x^* into the cutoff that determines whether B will accept or reject an offer:

$$\Pr(war|x^*, \theta^*) = \frac{p - c_A}{2p}$$

Now it is possible to assess the effect of the third-party defender's intervention on the protégé's behavior in conflict bargaining. Does knowing that the third party will intervene by transferring military assistance affect how receptive the protégé is to the adversary's offers? Comparing the adversary's optimal offer in the baseline model to the third-party intervention model reveals how aggressive the protégé is when it expects assistance. When A expects C to intervene, its offer of x^* is $1-p$ larger than when C does not intervene. Notably, however, including third-party intervention does not affect the probability of war from the baseline model.

In case 2, when $\mu + p < 1$, the analysis is similar to that of case 1, except that now the calculation for A involves risk that is related to C's capabilities. The offer will be rejected if it is not large enough to satisfy the constraint

$c_B < p + \mu - x$. This cutoff captures the moral hazard created by C's intervention. Given that B knows that C will intervene by transferring μ if there is a war, then the greater μ is, the more likely B will reject A's offer of x. In other words, B recognizes that C cannot restrain itself when it intervenes, and, therefore, the more powerful C is, the more likely B is to reject A's offer and instead fight a war.

The optimal offer A makes to B is

$$x^* = \frac{1}{2}c_A + \frac{1}{2}p + \mu.$$

The probability of war given this offer can be found by substituting x^* into the cutoff that determines whether B will accept or reject an offer:

$$\Pr(war|x^*, \theta^*) = \frac{p - c_A}{2p}.$$

As in case 1, the equilibrium probability of war is unchanged from the baseline model, but the promise of third-party intervention creates moral hazard. In cases in which $\mu + p < 1$, the protégé expects to receives offers of at least μ units greater than it does without third-party intervention. Therefore, its behavior in crisis bargaining should be more aggressive in the sense that it will drive harder for a larger amount of pie. We would expect the same aggressiveness in bargaining if the protégé acted as the proposer rather than the veto player. The reason the probability of war does not change is because A makes a more conciliatory offer in response to the protégé's aggressive bargaining behavior. Therefore, when intervention increases the probability the protégé will win the war, it is possible to conclude that promises of assistance from powerful third-party defenders do not induce the protégé to drag third-party defenders into wars but do create a distortion in the protégé's behavior in crises.

Applications

The model of third-party intervention demonstrates that, in some cases, third parties that do not necessarily share a protégé's preference for war will intervene to make transfers on the protégé's behalf in war. Significantly, if the third party does intervene, it will transfer as much as it can to improve the chances of winning. This has the effect of increasing the probability that the protégé will prevail. The impact on the protégé is significant, causing it to bargain harder by rejecting a larger range of offers from A. This aggression can take the form of hostile military posturing in crisis bargaining including initiating and engaging in conflicts short of war for the purpose of extracting a better deal.

Are there historical examples in which anticipating third-party support emboldened protégés to behave aggressively, as predicted in the model? Russian President Dmitry Medvedev and other Russian officials made such an argument about the cause of Russia's war with Georgia in 2008. They claimed that

Georgia's expectation of U.S. and NATO assistance emboldened Georgian President Mikheil Saakashvili to attack South Ossetia on August 8, 2008 (Dyomkin 2008). Although the United States did not, in fact, come to Georgia's aid, the broader intuition that is important to capture is the effect of the protégé's perception that it will receive aid. Some analysts claim that promises of NATO commitment and ongoing support caused Georgia to believe it would also receive U.S. support, leading Saakashvili to move against South Ossetia (de Waal 2010).

As another example, consider the effect of both Russian military aid and a formal military alliance signaling Russia's commitment in the 1990s to make transfers to Armenia in the event of future conflict. Throughout the 1980s and early 1990s, Armenia and Azerbaijan disputed the disposition of the Nagorno-Karabakh region in Azerbaijan. Armenia supported the Karabakh Armenian majority, who sought to be united with Soviet Armenia and maintained that desire after Armenia and Azerbaijan both gained independence from the Soviet Union in 1991. Azeri leaders opposed Nagorno-Karabakh secession and attempted to suppress Karabakh Armenian protests. Ethnic violence led to full-scale war between 1991 and 1994. Despite a cease-fire that year, disagreements persisted. In 1997, Armenian troops violated the cease-fire and attacked Azeri forces along the northern border. Russia was widely viewed as supporting the Armenian position. Much of this perception stemmed from the fact that Russia transferred military support to Armenia during the Nagorno-Karabakh War. However, increased Russian support after the war reinforced the belief of a deepening relationship. Russia provided arms to Armenia and established military bases there in 1995. In August 1997, Russia and Armenia signed an official alliance committing mutual military assistance. With Russian support assured, Armenia initiated further conflicts beginning in February and March 1998. Armenia continues to station troops inside the Nagorno-Karabakh region, controlling Azeri territory, and has violated the 1994 cease-fire agreement on several occasions. Armenia's subsequent refusal to accept the 1994 status quo is arguably the result of sustained Russian military assistance – a protégé acting aggressively because it knows it has a powerful third party on its side.

In fact, there are many historical examples of the effects that promises of military assistance have on leaders' crisis behavior. Another example is the Chinese Nationalist government (GMD) reaction to U.S. support in World War II. The GMD was emboldened by U.S. transfers to behave aggressively in their interaction with the Chinese Communists (CCP).[5] The example does not illustrate the third-party incentives in the model, as the United States intended to assist the GMD against Japan and not the CCP. However, it does effectively depict the problem of moral hazard on the part of the protégé, the GMD, that

---

[5] Some of the following discussion about the effect of U.S. support on the Chinese Nationalists' behavior toward the Chinese Communists draws on Benson (2006, 73–75).

resulted when it received and expected to continue receiving large, lump-sum transfers from the United States.

In 1937, Japan invaded China. Although Japanese forces had been encroaching on Chinese territory since 1931, full-scale invasion occurred in 1937. By the end of the year, it occupied major urban centers in northern and coastal central China, including Beijing, Shanghai, and the capital city of Nanjing. By 1941, Japanese forces controlled most of China's east coast and significant portions of southeast China. China's ability to defend itself was complicated by the fact that Japan's military was superior to China's and the GMD was preoccupied with an ongoing civil war against the CCP. To address the first concern, the Chinese government received military aid from the Soviet Union during the first few years of the war. The second problem was temporarily resolved at the end of 1936, when the GMD and CCP agreed to form a united front to oppose Japanese encroachment on Chinese territories. The fragile truce, brokered between the GMD and CCP as part of a deal to free kidnapped GMD leader Chiang Kaishek, was sustained by the presence of invading Japanese forces and the GMD's dependence on the Soviet Union, which also supported the CCP.

As Soviet assistance to the GMD declined, Chiang stepped up his lobbying efforts for substantial U.S. support. The GMD received its first major boost from the United States in November 1940 when President Roosevelt approved a $100 million loan to China. The loan, intended as a transfer to assist China in its war against Japan, had immediate – and, from the U.S. perspective, unexpected – consequences. Within days of receiving the loan, an emboldened Chiang demanded that the Communist Eighth Route Army and the New Fourth Army withdraw from Anhui and Jiangsu provinces. To enforce the demand, Nationalist troops attacked the Communist forces and forcibly pushed them back. Chiang then diverted as many as 400,000 of his best troops away from the war against Japan to blockade Communist areas. The purpose of this maneuver was to prevent the Communist Eighth Route army from penetrating into southern China. Although civil war between the Nationalists and the Communists did not officially resume until after the Japanese surrendered, the transfer of U.S. aid to the Nationalists gave rise to their aggressive crisis bargaining behavior toward the Communists.

There is no question but that Chiang hoped for and anticipated receiving massive ongoing transfers of assistance from the United States to further its objectives vis-á-vis the Communists. Although U.S. leaders expressed their desire for the GMD and CCP to unite against the Japanese (Tao 1989), U.S. diplomats worried that the Chinese Nationalists would actually use U.S. aid and military transfers to gain an advantage against the CCP. In fact, many diplomats reported hearing Chiang and other Nationalists boast that U.S. commitment in the war against Japan would free their hands to deal with the Communists (Tao 1989, 46).

When the United States entered World War II after the Japanese attack on Pearl Harbor, its level of support for the GMD against Japan increased dramatically. As U.S. forces were ramping up preparations to deploy to the

Pacific theater, the federal government immediately issued a $500 million loan to Nationalist China. Government officials again expected Chiang to use these funds to advance the war effort against the Japanese. However, many American officials opposed granting unregulated, lump-sum money transfers to the GMD, because they believed Chiang would divert significant shares of the assistance to fight the CCP. The U.S. ambassador to China, Clarence Gauss, warned against extending a blank check to Chiang. General Joseph W. Stilwell, who was the commander of the China–Burma–India theater and also responsible for administering U.S. Lend-Lease support to China, claimed that Chiang intended to use U.S. assistance not to fight the Japanese, but to gain an advantage over the Chinese Communists. Nationalist misuse of Lend-Lease funds was a constant source of aggravation for Stilwell. The Chinese Communists also warned that Chiang would use U.S. money against them (Schaller 1979, 89, 111). U.S. Treasury Secretary Henry Morgenthau favored conditioning aid on the performance of Chinese troops in the war against Japan. Stilwell also warned against becoming entrapped by Chiang and consistently pushed for aid to be tied to Chiang's commitment of Chinese troops to fight the Japanese, Nationalist concessions on military and political reforms, and the integration of the Chinese Communist troops in China's government and military (Tuchman 1971).

Nevertheless, the continued Lend-Lease support affected GMD actions toward the CCP. Not only did the Second United Front collapse, but Chiang was also intransigent in bargaining. In 1945, Ambassador Patrick Hurley attempted to broker a truce between the GMD and CCP. The goal was to unite China. However, Chiang firmly demanded that the Communist armies disband and all groups in China subordinate to Nationalist command. Mao saw in Chiang's demand a threat to the survival of the CCP. Consequently, the negotiations failed.

The account of U.S. aid to China supports the moral hazard aspects of the theory. Before U.S. aid began, the GMD and the CCP were joined in a tenuous united front against the Japanese. Once the United States became involved, however, Chiang's expectation of large ongoing transfers of support from the United States emboldened him to deal more aggressively with the CCP. The New Fourth Army incident, the Nationalist's permanent blockade of CCP forces, and Chiang's extreme and unwavering bargaining positions in negotiations with the CCP resulted from Chiang's belief that such support would continue.

Summary

This chapter began by posing some questions about the externalities of protégé emboldenment and entrapment in third-party commitment making. One question asked why deterrent commitments embolden if they imply a commitment to defend the status quo but not to support protégé aggression. An answer to this question is that decisions in war are often coarsely arranged so that finely specified commitments of limited military assistance may not match the realities of war. If the third party intervenes, it will often have to transfer as much assistance as it can to achieve the given war objective, even if that amount exceeds what the third party preferred to transfer before the war.

Another question is how protégés can entrap third parties that always have the *ex post* option of abandoning the protégé in war. Previous research argued that entrapment is possible when the third party cannot risk quitting the alliance for fear of losing an ally necessary for its own security benefits or reputation. The answer provided here offers another perspective. One type of entrapment does not actually induce the protégé to drag the third party into a war. Rather, the conditions of war are often such that the third party has no choice but to supply the protégé with a great deal more than it would prefer. Even third parties that only weakly share the protégé's preferences for war outcomes will converge on a decision to do whatever it can to improve the protégé's chances of winning. This may even include fighting in offensive wars. If the contest is over the boundaries of the *status quo ante* partition, as may be the case if neither the third party nor the protégé is revisionist, then the third party can go all in to defend the status quo. However, if the pie contested by the disputants includes more than what the third party is willing to fight for, then it is possible to entrap the third party in an offensive war that it is willing to fight only because it cannot tolerate the prospect of losing the entire pie to the adversary.

To be sure, third parties may decide not to intervene at all when protégés become overly aggressive. The example of Chiang Kaishek's attempt to entrap the United States in China's civil war after the conclusion of World War II illustrates this point. Many U.S. officials described their dilemma as having to choose between becoming completely embroiled in a fight for all of China or to abandon the Nationalists entirely. The coarseness of the options and the framing of the boundaries of the contested pie made the problem irreducible to intermediate solutions. As a result, the United States determined that it was too costly, on the heels of World War II, to fight for all of China. Without U.S. assistance, the Nationalists were eventually forced to retreat to Taiwan, ceding all of mainland China to the Communists.

This chapter has dealt with the downstream problems of emboldenment and entrapment; however, as discussed at the beginning of the chapter, these issues have important implications for upstream decisions about the optimal design of a security commitment. Because coarse intervention decisions might embolden protégés to behave aggressively in a way that makes third parties worse off, third parties may have strong incentives to design *ex ante* commitments to offset moral hazard by pushing some of the risk back onto the protégé. The question of commitment design is taken up in Chapter 5. First, I turn to an empirical exercise to establish a moral hazard effect in crises in the observational data. This analysis is presented in the next chapter.

4

Evidence of Moral Hazard in Military Alliances

This chapter investigates the empirical data on alliances and conflict to determine whether a moral hazard effect exists with alliance agreements. One key result derived from Chapter 3 is that leaders will bargain more aggressively with adversaries when they anticipate that a third-party defender will assist them if bargaining breaks down and war results. This finding informs us how world leaders will likely respond when they receive promises of military assistance such as those formalized in military alliances. Compared with states that do not have any external assurances, countries that have military alliances in crises might be more likely to reject adversaries' challenges and make aggressive demands from adversaries. These results imply good news and bad news for international conflict: alliances may both enhance deterrence and lead to conflict. That is, moral hazard generated by an alliance commitment might improve deterrence, because adversaries are less likely to challenge countries when they expect those countries to be unwilling to concede to their demands. On the other hand, an alliance may also embolden protégés to challenge their adversaries in crisis bargaining. According to the theory, the key to understanding how military alliances affect conflict lies in the design of the commitment. Commitments affect how the protégé bargains with the adversary and then the adversary modifies its bargaining behavior accordingly.

This chapter examines the broader intuition, established in Chapter 3, that expectations of third-party intervention, such as we might expect in wars involving an alliance member, can give rise to a moral hazard effect observable in the alliance member's decision to initiate a conflict against a non-alliance member who is targeted in the terms of the alliance agreement. The chapter begins with a discussion about the empirical implications derived from Chapter 3. The following section in this chapter explains the research design and introduces a dataset of alliance agreements, which is generated from the categories in the typology from Chapter 2. I then estimate statistical models to determine whether different types of deterrent alliances affect the likelihood that a revisionist leader of the state holding the alliance will initiate a conflict against a targeted adversary. The chapter closes with a section that summarizes the evidence and major findings.

The Relationship between Military Alliance Commitments and Moral Hazard

The main result from Chapter 3 is that when protégés, which are revisionist because they wish to expand their share of a disputed pie through conflict bargaining, receive a commitment of military support from a third party, they are emboldened to behave aggressively toward their opponents. We should expect this aggression to depend on the type of military commitment shared by the third party and protégé as well as their relative capabilities. When protégés receive unconditional commitments, they are especially aggressive, because the protégé engages in the bargaining process with the belief that it will receive full support from the third party if there is a war. The level of aggressiveness depends on the strength of the third party relative to the protégé. If a third party is capable of making only a modest contribution in war, then we might expect the protégé to be relatively humble when bargaining with the adversary. However, if the third party is so powerful that its support may decide the outcome of a war, then the protégé will be dramatically bolder and its behavior in crisis bargaining will reflect this fact. If the theory is correct, unconditional deterrent alliances in the hands of revisionist alliance members will be more likely than the absence of an external alliance to result in conflict because of these incentives, and the more powerful the third party, the higher the likelihood is that the protégé will behave aggressively.

Unlike unconditional commitments, conditional deterrent agreements stipulate that the third party will transfer assistance if the adversary takes an enumerated observable hostile action against the protégé. Because this type of commitment creates disincentives for either side to initiate a conflict, it would seem that it would eliminate the negative effects of moral hazard while retaining the desirable deterrent benefits. However, protégés still have incentives to behave aggressively. Because the protégé expects full support if the adversary initiates conflict bargaining, it will reject more offers of peaceful settlements than it would if there was no commitment. Consequently, although a conditional commitment may deter the adversary from initiating an overtly hostile action that would trigger the third party's defense obligation, the protégé will be unwilling to accept many settlements that it would otherwise find acceptable. Therefore, compared with having no commitment at all, we should expect to observe that the protégé's increased intransigence will result in more conflicts when revisionist protégés have conditional deterrent alliances. However, compared to unconditional deterrent commitments, conditional agreements clearly exempt the third party from its obligation to intervene in at least some crises.

TABLE 4.1. *Likelihood the Protégé Will Be Aggressive Given Different Types of Alliance*

	Unconditional Alliance	Conditional Alliance	Probabilistic Alliance
Protégé is aggressive*	No effect	No effect	No effect
Revisionist Protégé is aggressive	+	+	No effect
Revisionist Protégé is aggressive when its alliance partner is a major power	+	+	No effect

* No distinction is made as to whether the protégé is revisionist or not.
Note: The comparison case is no alliance.

Therefore, the comparison of conditional alliances with no-agreement cases will likely not result in as dramatic emboldening effects as the comparison of unconditional alliances with the no-agreement cases.

Probabilistic alliance commitments, on the other hand, will not be as likely to lead the protégé to behave aggressively. The uncertainty about whether the third party will intervene leads the protégé to accept more offers and to make less aggressive demands. Depending on how the probability of intervention affects disputants' expectations about their payoffs in war, the adversary or protégé might make a demand, or both may leave the status quo allocation as is. Additionally, because the uncertainty tempers disputants' expectations about their war payoffs, their demands, which are made in anticipation of the likelihood that conflict might break down, should be relatively moderate. Therefore, we should not expect there to be a significant difference in the aggression of protégés that have probabilistic alliances versus those that do not have any external alliance.

Table 4.1 summarizes the relationships that are examined in this chapter. The expected effects of alliance commitments on the likelihood the protégé initiates a conflict depend on the type of commitment, how powerful the third party is, and whether the protégé would like to make gains at the expense of a state targeted by the alliance. I call protégés who prefer to make gains at the expense of a state targeted by the alliance "revisionist." The theory makes no prediction about the behavior of nonrevisionist protégés. Thus, as can be seen in the first row of Table 4.1, there is no predicted effect for any type of alliance commitment when protégés are not identified as being either revisionist or nonrevisionist. When protégés are revisionist, however, unconditional and conditional alliance commitments are more likely than the cases in which there is no alliance to lead to aggressive behavior. These effects are indicated in the second row of Table 4.1. The third row summarizes the expectations when the protégé has a militarily powerful third-party alliance partner. The likelihood that the protégé will be aggressive is even greater if the third-party alliance partner is a major power. However, probabilistic alliance commitments should not be more likely than having no alliance to create incentives for the protégé to behave aggressively regardless of whether the protégé is revisionist or its alliance partners are major powers. I estimate a series of statistical models to test these relationships.

Research Design and Data

To examine the relationships summarized in Table 4.1, I estimate four statistical models. Model 1 estimates the effect of any kind of alliance on the behavior of the protégé. This model gives a sense of the impact of alliance commitments before the category is disaggregated by type. In Model 2, I unpack the alliance variable according to categories defined in the typology in Chapter 2. From this model, it is possible to observe the effect of *compellent alliances, unconditional deterrent alliances, conditional deterrent alliances,* and *probabilistic deterrent alliances* on the protégé's behavior. Extant studies of alliances have shown that leaders of countries holding offensive alliances (Leeds 2003b) or unconditional compellent alliances (Benson 2011) are likely to initiate conflicts. These studies highlight the impact of moral hazard when alliance members explicitly stipulate in an agreement their offensive goals to expand their share of a disputed pie at the expense of a common adversary. Because alliance members specify in the agreement their common interests for revising the status quo, we should not be surprised that they are likely to follow the formation of the alliance with aggressive actions to extract concessions from the adversary.

Benson (2011) and Leeds (2003b) also analyze the effect of deterrent alliances but only on the likelihood that states initiate militarized dispute against states holding such alliances. They do not assess the likelihood that states holding these types of alliances will initiate a militarized dispute against another state. Johnson and Leeds (2011) and Benson et al. (forthcoming) take up this latter question, examining the effect of deterrent alliances on the behavior of states holding these types of alliances. Model 2 explores the consistency of these findings when deterrent alliances are disaggregated into categories of unconditional, conditional, and probabilistic commitments.

What about the effects of different types of deterrent alliances when the protégés holding these alliances are revisionist? The predicted relationships are described in the second row of Table 4.1. Benson et al. (forthcoming) estimate the relationship between unconditional and conditional deterrent alliances on the behavior of revisionist dyad initiators. In Model 3, I similarly analyze these relationships and also examine the effect of probabilistic commitments in addition to the unconditional and conditional types.

Model 4 is designed to determine whether the strength of the third party accentuates the problem of moral hazard, as described in row 3 of Table 4.1. I, therefore, specify the model to see whether protégés are even more aggressive when they share these types of alliances with at least one major power. Alliances with such powerful partners should further increase the likelihood that the protégé will be aggressive.

For the variables designating types of alliance commitments in Models 1 through 4, I construct a directed dyad-year alliance dataset. To do so, I merge directed dyad-year conflict data from the years 1816 to 2000 retrieved from the EUGene software package (Bennett and Stam 2008) with a dataset of alliance types based on the typology presented in Chapter 2. A directed dyad design makes it possible to distinguish between prospective initiators and targets of a conflict. This is important for the analysis in this chapter, as the question being examined here is whether particular alliances cause states holding particular alliances to direct aggression toward an adversary targeted by the alliance agreement.

The data consist of all politically relevant directed dyads if they include pairs of states that are either contiguous, are separated by less than 25 miles, or include a major power.[1] Using politically relevant dyads excludes only cases in which states are substantially less likely to become involved in an interstate conflict. The model is estimated using a logistic regression with Huber-White robust standard errors and standard errors clustered on the directed dyads.

Table 4.2 lists and explains all the dependent and independent variables used in the analysis along with their coding rules. The main variable of interest is the initiation of *militarized interstate disputes* (MIDs), as this is a proxy for aggression. The theory predicts that guaranteed promises of *ex post* military support will lead revisionist states to behave more aggressively in conflict bargaining. No prediction is made about the likelihood of war, as the probability of war does not increase in the theoretical model. We may think of moves in conflict bargaining as including hostilities such as demands, threats, mobilizations, occupations, and other aggressive actions that could escalate to war if the leader of the targeted state does not capitulate. These acts of aggression are classified as *militarized interstate disputes* in Zeev Maoz's dyadic dataset (Maoz 2005).

The key explanatory variables are indicators for each of the categories of deterrent commitments based on the typology of Chapter 2: *compellent, unconditional deterrent, conditional deterrent*, and *probabilistic deterrent alliances*. With some minor exceptions, the coding rules follow Benson (2011) and are summarized in Table 4.2. Unlike Benson (2011), I do not include non-provocation agreements in the category of probabilistic deterrent alliances here, because non-provocation agreements are analyzed as a distinct type of alliance commitment called a pure conditional commitment in later chapters. To create each alliance category, I apply the qualitative distinctions presented in Chapter 2 to the actual wording of relevant alliance provisions recorded in ATOP code

---

[1] The results are unchanged using several different measures of contiguity (direct land, 24 miles of water, 150 miles of water, 400 miles of water, and many combinations thereof).

TABLE 4.2. *Variable Concepts and Measurement*

Variable Name	Concept	Measurement
Outcome Variable		
MID initiation	Dispute occurrence	Coded 1 if there was a MID initiated by state A against state B in the dyad year; 0 otherwise.
Control Variables		
Joint democracy	Joint democracy	Coded 1 if both members of the dyad score > 6 on the dyad's POLITY IV scale; 0 otherwise (Marshall, Jaggers, and Gurr 2002).
Contiguity	Direct contiguity	Coded 1 if the dyad members either share a land or river border or are separated by less than 25 miles of water; 0 if they are separated by more than 25 miles of water.
Capabilities ratio	Power parity	Scored on a 0 to 1 scale using CINC scores from the Correlates of War project (Singer 1988), with 0 indicating total preponderance and 1 indicating total parity.
s-score	Foreign policy similarity	Measured on continuous interval [−1,1] with 1 indicating similar revealed policy positions between dyad members and −1 being the most dissimilar (Signorino and Ritter 1999).
Peace years	Peace years' duration	Years since last MID (Beck, Katz, and Tucker 1998; Carter and Signorino 2010).
Key Explanatory Variables		
Compellent or deterrent alliance	Prospective initiator has a compellent or deterrent alliance	Coded 1 if initiator in dyad has at least one alliance promising any kind of military support against the dyad target state; 0 otherwise.
Compellent alliance	Prospective initiator has an unconditional or conditional compellent alliance	Coded 1 if initiator in dyad has at least one unconditional compellent alliance targeting the dyad target state; 0 otherwise.
Unconditional deterrent alliance	Prospective initiator has an unconditional deterrent alliance	Coded 1 if initiator in dyad has at least one unconditional deterrent alliance targeting the dyad target state; 0 otherwise.

TABLE 4.2 (cont.)

Variable Name	Concept	Measurement
Conditional deterrent alliance	Prospective initiator has conditional deterrent alliance	Coded 1 if initiator in dyad has at least one conditional deterrent alliance targeting the dyad target state; 0 otherwise.
Probabilistic deterrent alliance	Prospective initiator has probabilistic deterrent alliance	Coded 1 if initiator in dyad has at least one probabilistic deterrent alliance targeting the dyad target state; 0 otherwise.
Revisionist initiator	Prospective initiator has revisionist preferences in ongoing crisis	Coded 1 if initiator in dyad has announced preferences to revise the status quo in ongoing conflicts (COW data); 0 otherwise.
Alliance × Revisionist Interaction*	Three separate interaction terms for each of the different deterrent alliances above interacted with revisionist initiator	Coded 1 if initiator in dyad is both revisionist and holds the deterrent alliance type in question; 0 otherwise.

* Model 4 substitutes the *unconditional, conditional deterrent,* and *probabilistic deterrent* variables in these interaction terms with variables for *unconditional* and *conditional deterrent alliances with at least one major power alliance partner.*

sheets (Leeds et al. 2002). These categories are then converted to the directed dyad-year format. For each alliance, all signatories are coded as prospective initiators, and the states targeted by the alliance are coded as prospective targets in the dyad.

To identify the effects of the alliances on the probability of a militarized dispute, each agreement is coded to identify its type, the states that are party to the agreement, the obligations each ally has under the agreement, and a list of the states that are targeted by the agreement. With this information, it is possible to determine whether the initiator in each dyad observation is party to a compellent or deterrent alliance and the target in the dyad is also targeted by the alliance. Therefore, variables of commitment types indicate whether the dyad initiator holds the respective type of alliance against the dyad target state. Columns 1 and 2 in Table 4.3 summarize the breakdown of the number of agreement types across categories between 1816–2000. There are 34 *unconditional compellent commitments*, 19 *conditional compellent commitments*, 74 *unconditional deterrent commitments*, 139 *conditional deterrent commitments*, and 46 *probabilistic deterrent commitments*.

It is possible for a state to possess multiple types of commitments against the other member of the dyad. Consequently, disentangling the effect of a state's alliance portfolio with multiple different promises may be problematic,

TABLE 4.3. *Frequency of Commitment Categories, 1816–2000*

Commitments Type	Frequency of Commitments		Frequency of Commitments, Directed Dyad Observations	
	No.	Col %	No.	Col %
Unconditional compellent	34	0.10	2,661	0.02
Conditional compellent	19	0.06	35	0.00
Unconditional deterrent	74	0.24	10,199	0.09
Conditional deterrent	139	0.45	75,941	0.66
Probabilistic deterrent	46	0.15	26,829	0.23
Total	312	1.00	115,665	1.00

The first two columns contain the number and percentage of each type of commitment in the time period. The third and fourth columns contain the number and percentage of directed dyad-year observations each type of commitment represents in the dataset when cases containing compellent agreements are excluded from the conditional and unconditional deterrent categories (but are still left in the compellent categories).

as it is possible to mistakenly credit an alliance type with an effect that is actually driven by another alliance held by the same state. Especially worrying is the possibility of drawing the mistaken conclusion that unconditional deterrent alliances create significant incentives for moral hazard when, in fact, compellent alliances held by the same state are responsible for the observed aggressiveness. To minimize confounding effects of multiple types of alliances, a prospective initiator in a dyad is coded as possessing an unconditional or conditional type of deterrent commitment only if it does not also hold a compellent commitment targeting the other state in the dyad. Therefore, if the state holds one of these deterrent types of commitment and *does not* hold a relevant compellent agreement, then the respective deterrent variable is coded 1. Isolating the observations with deterrent alliances focuses the analysis on the claim that unconditional deterrent alliances might create incentives for moral hazard. Distinguishing compellent from probabilistic commitments is less important, because probabilistic commitments stipulate that allies may or may not intervene regardless of the objective or conditions of the alliance.

Columns 3 and 4 in Table 4.3 show the frequency of the different types of agreements in directed dyad-year observations when the coding rules just described are applied. Note that the proportion of directed dyad-year observations generated by each alliance category differs markedly from the corresponding proportion of agreements. The 34 *unconditional compellent commitments* generate 2,661 directed dyad-year observations, but the 19 *conditional agreements* generate only 35 directed dyad-year observations. This disparity in directed dyad-year observations results because *conditional compellent commitments* contain specific demands, which typically result in the termination of the alliance once the demands have been satisfied. Because the longest duration of a conditional compellent agreement was six years, there are relatively few associated directed dyad-year observations. By contrast, many *unconditional compellent commitments* target all states in the system, and some endure for decades.

Table 4.3 also reveals some differences between compellent and deterrent types of alliances. Compared to all the deterrent types of agreements, both types of compellent agreements represent a smaller fraction of directed dyad-years. An explanation for this difference may be given by Schelling, who observed that there are "limits, probably, to how long the compellent action can be sustained without costing or risking too much, or exhausting itself or the opponents so that he has nothing left to lose" (Schelling 1966, 76). By contrast, deterrent threats, which commit alliance partners only to waiting and reacting, can survive for a long time. The longest enduring alliance, for example, is the North Atlantic Treaty Organization, a deterrent alliance lasting 53 years in the dataset.

The most common type of agreement is the conditional deterrent category, which consists of 139 agreements from 1816 to 2000, resulting in 75,941 directed dyad-year observations. Comprising 45 percent of all alliances and 66 percent of directed dyads, not only is this the most common type of alliance, but it is also the type of agreement that occurs most frequently in directed dyad-year observations.

For Model 1, I combine all compellent and deterrent categories to form an aggregate alliance variable. For Models 2 through 4, I disaggregate deterrent types of alliances. In these models, I combine conditional and unconditional compellent alliances to create one variable of *compellent alliances*. This variable is included primarily to confirm extant literature on the effects of offensive and compellent alliances. The variables for deterrent types of alliances directly correspond to those categories in the typology described previously. In Model 4, I replace the variables of *conditional* and *unconditional deterrent alliances* with variables that are coded to indicate whether the initiator in the dyad shares these respective types of alliances with at least one major power.

The counterfactual for the effect identified by each alliance variable in each of the models is the likelihood of conflict given that a prospective initiator has none of the specified types of alliances whatsoever. Consequently, the estimated results reveal the effect of the alliance type relative to the counterfactual category; coefficients can also be compared with estimations of other alliance types to determine the relative effect of comparisons with the baseline case.

The *revisionist* variable from the Correlates of War (COW) dataset is used to indicate whether the prospective initiator is revisionist. As in Benson et al. (forthcoming) and Senese and Vasquez (2008), the variable is coded 1 if the initiator state in the directed dyad has made any public statements regarding its desire or intention to revise the status quo in areas belonging to the target state.

My approach builds on Benson et al. (forthcoming), which examines the effect of conditional and unconditional types of alliances on the behavior of revisionist dyad initiators. They find that revisionist states in unconditional deterrent commitments are more likely than states with no alliance or a conditional deterrent alliance to initiate militarized conflict with a target of the alliance. Their analysis provides some evidence that unconditional deterrent alliances are especially likely to give rise to moral hazard.

I extend their analysis in two directions. First, I add probabilistic deterrent alliances so that it is possible to compare their effects to those of conditional deterrent, unconditional deterrent, and no alliance alternatives. Comparisons across these types of commitments will paint a broader picture of the extent to which different types of commitments give rise to moral hazard. Second, I then consider the effect of these types of alliance commitments if one or more of the prospective initiators' allies are a major power.

To examine these relationships, I introduce interaction terms for different types of alliance agreements held by revisionist states. The method for constructing these variables follows Benson et al. (forthcoming), except I add an additional variable interacting probabilistic alliance commitments on the initiator side with the variable that indicates whether the initiator is revisionist. In Model 3, I estimate the effect of three interaction terms: one is the product of unconditional deterrent alliances on the initiator side with revisionism, the second interacts conditional deterrent alliances with revisionism, and the third interacts probabilistic deterrent alliances and revisionism. With these variables it is possible to estimate the effect of each type of alliance commitment on the dyad initiator's likelihood of initiating an MID with a target of the alliance when the initiator is revisionist.

The next step is to examine the claim that the strength of alliance partners might exacerbate moral hazard (row 3 of Table 4.1). Model 4 is designed to determine whether commitments from more powerful third-party allies increase the aggressiveness of the protégé in crises. To examine the effect of alliance partners' strength on a prospective initiator's behavior, I create an additional set of interaction terms for the three types of alliance agreements in the analysis. I generate variables for each of these types of commitments held by revisionist dyad initiators where at least one of the alliance members (not counting the prospective dyad initiator) is a major power. I then estimate the effects of these variables on the likelihood that the dyad initiator initiates a militarized dispute with a state targeted by the alliance.

I also include several standard control variables. The coding for these variables come from Benson et al. (forthcoming) and are summarized in Table 4.2.

Analysis

I now present the analysis of the statistical estimations. Throughout, the objective is to determine whether alliance commitments create moral hazard among alliance members. Therefore, in the logistic Models 1 through 4, I examine the

TABLE 4.4. *Effects of Third-Party Alliance Commitments on the Protégés' Initiation of Militarized Interstate Disputes, 1816–2000 (Models 1 and 2)*

	Model 1 Coefficient (Standard Error)	Model 2 Coefficient (Standard Error)
Joint democracy	−0.7316** (0.132)	−0.6801** (0.131)
Contiguity	1.4682** (0.110)	1.4800** (0.109)
Capabilities ratio	0.9841** (0.139)	0.9888** (0.137)
s-score	−0.6900** (0.111)	−0.6864** (0.112)
Compellent or deterrent alliance	0.2070** (0.070)	
Compellent alliance		1.2092** (0.121)
Unconditional deterrent alliance		0.1410 (0.172)
Conditional deterrent alliance		0.0957 (0.080)
Probabilistic deterrent alliance		0.0311 (0.120)
Constant	−3.8114** (0.093)	−3.8223** (0.096)
N	172196	172196
Log-Lik intercept only	−11477.2008	−11477.2008
Log-Lik full model	−9981.0462	−9923.3727

*$p < 0.05$; **$p < 0.01$

estimated relationships to identify whether prospective initiators in a directed dyad design are more likely to initiate an MID against the dyad target if the initiator holds a particular type of alliance compared with protégés that do not have that alliance. Model 1 is the most basic regression, as it contains only one alliance variable, which simply indicates whether the dyad initiator holds *any* compellent or deterrent alliance in which alliance members promise military support if there is a conflict against the dyad target. This model depicts a broad view of moral hazard, because alliances are considered in aggregate. From the results of the model, which are presented in the first results column of Table 4.4, it is immediately clear that the broad category of *compellent or deterrent alliance* increases the likelihood that a state holding such an alliance will initiate an MID against a state targeted by the alliance. The coefficient for this variable is 0.2070, and it is statistically significant at the $p < 0.01$ level. Consequently, it may be possible that states that are party to any type of alliance promising military assistance in a conflict are more likely to be aggressive and initiate challenges against states targeted by that alliance than protégés not holding any kind of alliance at all. However, before concluding that alliances have a potentially destabilizing effect for those that possess them, it is important first to disaggregate alliances by type.

Before proceeding to Model 2, I first note that the control variables in Model 1 have the expected effects. The variable for *joint democracy* reduces the likelihood that the initiator will initiate an MID, and *contiguity* increases the likelihood of conflict. The coefficient for the *capabilities ratio* variable, which is a measure of uncertainty in the dyad, is positive and insignificant. The *s-score* variable is negatively associated with *MID initiation*. This implies that the more congruent are dyad states' foreign policy preferences, as measured by shared alliances, the less likely they will be to engage in conflict. As we will see, the effects of the control variables are mostly consistent in all the models in this chapter.

Because the focus of the theory in this book is to understand how commitment mechanisms affect alliance members' incentives, and, in particular, their likelihood to behave aggressively, the next step is to disaggregate the broad variable of alliance commitment into separate categories reflecting some of the classifications in the typology in Chapter 2. Accordingly, in Model 2, alliances are broken into *compellent alliances, unconditional deterrent alliances, conditional deterrent alliances*, and *probabilistic deterrent alliances*. The results of the analysis are detailed in the second column of results in Table 4.4. In this model, only compellent alliances generate dangerous incentives for alliance members. Of the alliance categories, the category of compellent alliance alone is associated with a statistically significant increase in the likelihood that an alliance holder will initiate an MID. Moreover, with a coefficient of 1.2092, the effect is sizable and swamps the other types of commitment. These results are in line with the expectations given in the first row of Table 4.1 and are broadly consistent with Johnson and Leeds (2011).

Can we infer from Model 2 that moral hazard is problematic only when alliance members explicitly write compellent types of agreements? There is a missing piece in the empirical model. The theory predicts that extending an alliance commitment to a revisionist government will lead that government to be more likely to initiate an MID against the dyad target state.

Model 3 is designed to incorporate into the analysis the possibility that protégés may have revisionist preferences. The expectation (summarized in row 2 of Table 4.1) predicts that revisionist protégés holding *unconditional deterrent alliances* and *conditional deterrent alliances* will be more likely to initiate conflict against the target of the alliance. Additionally, probabilistic deterrent alliances should have no such effect because they do not promise guaranteed transfers of military assistance to the protégé. Therefore, there should not be a significant difference between a revisionist protégé's likelihood to initiate a conflict when it has a probabilistic commitment as opposed to when it has no commitment.

The results of the model are presented in Table 4.5; they are consistent with the theory provided in Chapter 3. First, it is unsurprising that the *revisionist initiator* variable is, by itself, a powerful determinant of conflict. It has the largest coefficient of any covariate (4.9357). The substantive impact of the independent variables on the predicted probability of conflict can be seen in the second column of results in Table 4.5. This column reports the change in predicted probability when each continuous variable is increased one standard deviation and the dummy variables are increased from 0 to 1. These discrete changes in the predicted probability are calculated when all the continuous

TABLE 4.5. *Effects of Third-Party Alliance Commitments on Revisionist Protégés' Initiation of Militarized Interstate Disputes, 1816–2000 (Model 3)*

	Model 3	
	Coefficient (Standard Error)	Discrete Change in Predicted Probability
Joint democracy	−0.2943** (0.110)	−0.0009
Contiguity	0.8082** (0.117)	0.0025
Capabilities ratio	0.1721 (0.162)	0.0005
s-score	−0.4251** (0.155)	−0.0013
Compellent alliance	0.3529+ (0.187)	0.0011
Unconditional deterrent (UD) alliance	−0.3961 (0.317)	−0.0012
Revisionist × unconditional deterrent alliance	1.0926** (0.384)	0.0034
Conditional deterrent (CD) alliance	−0.4340** (0.133)	−0.0014
Revisionist × conditional deterrent alliance	0.6369** (0.184)	0.0020
Probabilistic deterrent (PD) alliance	0.1751 (0.182)	0.0005
Revisionist × probabilistic deterrent alliance	−0.1476 (0.298)	−0.0005
Revisionist initiator	4.9357** (0.134)	0.0154
Constant	−5.2561** (0.141)	
Baseline predicted probability of conflict		0.0031
Predicted probability of conflict when UD alliance to revisionist initiator		0.0207
Net change		0.0176
Predicted probability of conflict when CD alliance to revisionist initiator		0.0191
Net change		0.0160
Predicted probability of conflict when PD alliance to revisionist initiator		0.0187
Net change		0.0156
N	172196	172196
Log-Lik intercept only	−11477.2008	−11477.2008
Log-Lik full model	−5864.5183	−5864.5183

+$p < 0.10$; *$p < 0.05$; **$p < 0.01$

variables are held at their mean values and the indicator variables are set to equal 0. When a state is revisionist with respect to the dyad target, the predicted probability it will initiate a conflict against the target state increases 0.0154, which results in a change from the baseline predicted probability of conflict of 0.0031 to 0.0185. This is the single largest predictor of conflict in the model by a large margin, but unsurprising given that revisionism is measured by states' publicly stated policy announcements during ongoing crises.

Next, consider the effects of the variables of interest. Compared with Model 3, the effects of alliances are dramatically different when the prospective initiator has revisionist preferences. To see this, note the positive and significant coefficients on the interaction terms for *unconditional* and *conditional deterrent alliances* to *revisionist initiators*. These coefficients signify the amount of the increased effect of a certain alliance when the prospective initiator is revisionist as opposed to nonrevisionist. The resultant predicted probability of conflict can be found by summing the baseline predicted probability with the change in predicted probabilities that correspond to the respective interaction term and the indicator variables for a *revisionist initiator* and the alliance commitment in question. These substantive effects are provided in the bottom half of Table 4.5.

The combined effect on the probability of conflict due to a revisionist initiator holding an unconditional deterrent alliance is a net positive change in the predicted probability of conflict from 0.0031 to 0.0207, which represents a dramatic change in the predicted probability that the dyad initiator will initiate a militarized dispute against the dyad target. To be sure, much of this effect is driven by the fact that the initiator in the alliance is revisionist, but the combination of the type of alliance commitment and the protégé's revisionism increases the chances of conflict even more. The increase in the probability of a militarized dispute confirms the theory's implication that an unconditional deterrent commitment to provide military assistance creates a powerful incentive for moral hazard, which revisionist protégés can then exploit in crisis bargaining.

Conditional deterrent alliances in the hands of revisionist allies can also lead to conflict, although neither the magnitude of the effect nor the significance of the result is as pronounced as the finding on unconditional deterrent alliances. Table 4.5 reveals that conditional deterrent alliances to revisionist initiators are positively associated with conflict. These types of alliance commitments in the hands of a revisionist protégé have a net impact of increasing the predicted probability of conflict from 0.0031 to 0.0191. This finding provides evidence that even a mechanism that conditions military intervention on observable initiations of conflict by the adversary will create a moral hazard distortion. However, the protégé's behavior is more restrained in this alliance than in an unconditional deterrent alliance. The theory shows that in a conditional deterrent commitment the protégé expects assistance from an alliance partner as long as the adversary initiates an attack. Thus, the commitment distorts behavior because it induces aggressive behavior in crisis bargaining as long as the protégé stops short of nullifying the defender's obligation to defend by attacking the adversary. Consequently, these mechanisms are likely designed by alliance members who are willing to trade off some restraint of fellow alliance members in exchange for enhanced deterrence of an adversary's challenges. In the next chapter, I will take up the analysis of the upstream decision to form such alliances given leaders' anticipation of the effect of moral hazard.

Finally, the effect of probabilistic deterrent alliances to revisionist initiators is not significantly different from cases in which protégés do not have any alliance commitments. This result is also consistent with expectations, as probabilistic commitments likely induce protégés to be cautious in conflict bargaining. In sum, the analysis in Model 3 confirms the relationships summarized in Table 4.1. Unconditional deterrent alliances and conditional deterrent alliances increase the likelihood that revisionist alliance members will be aggressive. Moral hazard in the case of conditional deterrent alliances is relatively moderate compared with the emboldening effect of unconditional deterrent alliances. Probabilistic deterrent alliances do not have a significant effect on the likelihood that protégés will behave aggressively.

Before proceeding to Model 4, first note that the indicator for compellent alliances is positive, but the coefficient is significantly smaller than its counterpart in Model 2 and the finding is significant at $p = 0.059$. The reason for this shift is the inclusion of the *revisionist* variable in the model. Once revisionism is controlled for, much of the positive effect seen in the previous model gets soaked up. It is, nevertheless, clear that compellent alliances embolden alliance members to behave aggressively toward the adversary targeted by the agreement.

Note also that unconditional and probabilistic deterrent alliances on the initiator side by themselves are not statistically distinguishable from zero, and the effect of a conditional deterrent alliance is negative and significant. Because of the presence of the interaction terms in the model, these indicators should be interpreted as the effects of the alliance commitment when held by nonrevisionist prospective initiators. The negative signs on the coefficient for unconditional deterrent alliances suggest the possibility that these alliances may, in fact, reduce the likelihood that nonrevisionist protégés will be aggressive, but it is impossible to infer this from the model. It is possible to conclude, however, that such alliances do not lead nonrevisionist states to behave aggressively.

On the other hand, conditional deterrent alliances clearly decrease the likelihood that nonrevisionist states holding them will initiate militarized conflicts with non-alliance members. The indicator is both negative and statistically significant at the $p < 0.01$ level. To assess the substantive effects of this relationship, again note the change in predicted probability in the second column of Table 4.5. Conditional deterrent alliances decrease the probability of conflict by 0.0014, reducing the baseline predicted probability from 0.0031 to 0.0017. As a result, we might expect that signatories will tend to form these types of commitment when they are not revisionist and wish only to signal deterrent intentions.

Finally, the control variables are mostly consistent with expectations. An exception is the non-finding on *capabilities ratio*. This variable is highly sensitive to the inclusion of the *revisionist initiator* variable. Excluding the *revisionist* variable results in a positive and significant finding, whereas including it makes the finding insignificant. A reason for this sensitivity may be that uncertainty about the relative capabilities between the dyad members by itself might not lead to conflict if the initiator is not revisionist and therefore is not motivated to make gains at the expense of the dyad target state.

Now I analyze Model 4, which is identical to Model 3 except that the variables for *unconditional* and *conditional deterrent alliances* are replaced with variables indicating whether those alliances include at least one major power. As discussed previously, the objective of this modeling strategy is to determine whether commitments from powerful third-party allies exacerbate the problem of moral hazard. According to the theory, the amount protégés expect to receive in conflict bargaining is increasing in a third-party ally's power or military capacity, causing them to be willing to reject offers they would otherwise find acceptable and to demand more than they would otherwise. Therefore, commitments from more powerful third-party allies should increase the aggressiveness of the protégé in bargaining crises.

To analyze the effects of unconditional commitments from powerful allies, I create a variable indicating whether the initiator has an unconditional deterrent alliance with a major power. The variable is coded 1 if the prospective initiator has an unconditional deterrent alliance with a major power targeting the target state in the dyad and it does not have any compellent alliances targeting that same state. As described earlier, I create an interaction term for the product of this indicator and the revisionist initiator variable.

Table 4.6 presents the results from the statistical model. Because the results for the control variables and the indicator variables for *compellent* and *probabilistic alliances* are approximately the same as in Model 3, I focus the discussion on the effects of the *unconditional* and *conditional deterrent alliances with major powers*. There is a sizable effect when an unconditional deterrent alliance is held by a revisionist power. The coefficient on the interaction term is both large (1.5760) and distinguishable from zero ($p = 0.04$). A coefficient of this magnitude is more than sufficient to overwhelm the negative value estimated for the indicator variable of unconditional deterrent alliances. As the predicted probabilities shown in the bottom half of Table 4.6 reveal, the overall change in the predicted probability of conflict that occurs as a result of a revisionist prospective initiator possessing an unconditional deterrent is 0.0169. That is, the predicted probability that a state, which shares such an unconditional alliance with a major power, initiates a militarized dispute with a state targeted by the alliance increases from 0.0029 to 0.0198. The overall impact of the presence of the major power makes the initiator more aggressive.

Similarly, increases in the third party's power also intensify the aggressiveness of the protégé when the third party extends a conditional deterrent commitment. The predicted probability of conflict increases when the prospective initiator in the dyad is revisionist and holds a conditional deterrent alliance with a major power. The predicted probability of conflict changes from the baseline predicted probability of 0.0029 to 0.0181. Again, the revisionism of the initiator drives most of this effect. However, it is clear that the interaction of

TABLE 4.6. *Effects of Major Power Third-Party Alliances on Revisionist Protégés' Initiation of Militarized Interstate Disputes, 1816–2000 (Model 4)*

	Model 4	
	Coefficient (Standard Error)	Discrete Change in Predicted Probability
Joint democracy	−0.2990** (0.110)	−0.0009
Contiguity	0.8266** (0.118)	0.0024
Capabilities ratio	0.1858 (0.164)	0.0005
s-score	−0.4401** (0.154)	−0.0013
Compellent alliance	0.3449+ (0.189)	0.0010
Unconditional deterrent (UD) alliance with a major power	−0.7360 (0.693)	−0.0021
Revisionist × UD alliance with a major power	1.5760* (0.769)	0.0045
Conditional deterrent (CD) alliance with a major power	−0.3482* (0.153)	−0.0010
Revisionist × CD alliance with a major power	0.6103** (0.214)	0.0017
Probabilistic deterrent (PD) alliance	0.0955 (0.172)	0.0003
Revisionist × PD alliance	0.0187 (0.293)	0.0001
Revisionist initiator	5.0560** (0.128)	0.0145
Constant	−5.3448** (0.137)	
Baseline predicted probability of conflict		0.0029
Predicted probability of conflict when UD alliance with a major power to revisionist initiator		0.0198
Net change		0.0169
Predicted probability of conflict when CD alliance with a major power to revisionist initiator		0.0181
Net change		0.0152
Predicted probability of conflict when PD alliance to revisionist initiator		0.0178
Net change		0.0149
N	172196	172196
Log-Lik intercept only	−11477.2008	−11477.2008
Log-Lik full model	−5878.5889	−5878.5889

+$p < 0.10$; *$p < 0.05$; **$p < 0.01$

a revisionist initiator with a major power alliance commitments of both unconditional and conditional types of alliances increases the probability of conflict. The analysis in this model confirms that the power of a third-party defender has a significant impact on how much both unconditional and conditional deterrent alliance commitments embolden protégés.

Summary

This chapter presents evidence from observational alliance data that supports four central implications from my theory of moral hazard in international commitments. From the years between 1816 and 2000, revisionist states involved in ongoing disputes were much more likely to initiate militarized disputes when they received unconditional deterrent alliances than if they received no alliance at all. Similarly, moral hazard also results from conditional deterrent alliances, although the protégé is significantly more restrained in a conditional deterrent alliance than in an unconditional deterrent alliance. Additionally, during this time period, the emboldenment effect of unconditional and conditional deterrent commitments increased when the state extending the alliance was a major power. This effect is especially dramatic in the case of unconditional deterrence commitments held with major powers, wherein the effect of moral hazard rivals that of standard control variables that are known to be strongly associated with militarized disputes. Furthermore, as expected, probabilistic deterrent commitments do not embolden protégés to behave aggressively.

The results confirmed here are counter-intuitive for two reasons. First, we might not expect deterrent alliances, which are designed in most cases to safeguard the status quo, to cause the effect they were designed to avoid. However, as the theory predicts, unconditional and conditional deterrent alliances may open the door for reckless and aggressive behavior even though they are clearly designed to deter conflict. This suggests that moral hazard effects might be genuine – that both conditional and unconditional deterrent commitments from powerful third parties might embolden protégés in spite of the fact that obligations implied by such alliance agreements do not extend beyond providing military support to defend the status quo.

The theory laid out in Chapter 3 claims that to avoid its least preferred outcome of giving up the status quo, the third party must intervene to improve the protégé's chances of winning the war. However, the protégé knows that once the third party has entered the war, it may not be easy for the third party to limit the amount of its assistance. Therefore, to prevent the worst outcome of losing to the adversary, the third party may willingly give up a chance at its most preferred outcome. That is, in securing the primary objective of deterrence, the third party may decide to take the risk of emboldening the protégé. The empirical models examined in this chapter show that protégés will try to take advantage of some alliances, which is consistent with the theoretical story that they do so because they know third parties are often reluctant to abandon the alliance even when protégés are interested in expanding their gains beyond the status quo.

At this point, a caveat is in order. The analysis conducted in this chapter provides evidence of a relationship between the probability of winning a war (as signaled by certain alliance agreements) and the aggressiveness of protégés in initiating conflicts. Documenting this pattern by way of a broad-brush empirical approach is an important step. Although the patterns I find in the empirical estimations are consistent with the moral hazard argument in Chapter 3, one may worry that the empirical strategy misses important selection effects. Accordingly, in the next chapter, I turn to the insights from the formal analysis of alliance formation to provide a more nuanced explanation of effects that motivate states to design different types of alliance commitments. The equilibrium analysis in Chapter 5 gives us a better idea about the form of this kind of strategic behavior. Once the theory of alliance formation is developed, I then draw on that structure to uncover more subtle traces of the strategic incentives inducing alliance commitment design in the empirical analysis in Chapter 6.

5

A Theory of Commitment Design

As we have seen, guaranteed assistance from third-party defenders can create a moral hazard problem. In this chapter, I examine how third-party defenders design alliance contracts to deter aggression against an ally while mitigating the undesirable effects of moral hazard. The argument asserts that defenders select different commitment types depending on certain factors, such as countries' relative capabilities, their security and foreign policy goals, and the observability of their actions in war. One option for addressing moral hazard is to form an ambiguous or probabilistic commitment, which creates uncertainty about whether the defender will intervene on its ally's behalf. This uncertainty can balance the third party's competing objectives by tempering the disputants' reactions to the commitment. Ambiguity also has an additional advantage: it can induce policy settlements more to the third party's liking, because disputants that are unsure about whether the third party will intervene have incentives to make moderate demands in conflict bargaining.

The outline of the chapter is as follows. First, I will provide an intuitive explanation of the argument. Then I will illustrate the logic of the theory using three formal models. As in Chapter 3, conflict and war are incorporated into the theory using the standard bargaining model of conflict (Fearon 1995). Because the standard model has only two actors, the key distinction in the models provided here is the addition of a third-party defender that selects a type of commitment prior to conflict bargaining and then chooses a level of assistance to transfer to the protégé if bargaining fails and war occurs. The first model, which is presented in the fourth section, is a baseline model in which the third party forms a commitment with an ally in anticipation of an adversary initiating conflict bargaining. In this model, all the actions leading to war are observable to the third party. In the fifth section, I extend the baseline model to include the possibility that either the adversary or the protégé might initiate conflict bargaining. This extension of the analysis permits the examination of

A Theory of Commitment Design

truly conditional commitments, which are designed to activate if the disputants take certain actions specified in the alliance agreement.

In the third model, which is presented in the sixth section, I relax the assumption that actions are observable. This is a critical extension for both conceptual and practical reasons. The concept of moral hazard is often thought to apply to circumstances in which the agent's (in this case, the protégé's) actions are not perfectly observable (Rauchhaus 2005). Evaluating how third parties design their security commitments when they cannot observe the actions that disputants took to escalate to war limits the ability of the third party to include and enforce conditions in its commitment to become involved.

There is also a practical consideration when analyzing environments of hidden action: actions taken in the process of escalating to war are often truly difficult to observe. Clausewitz speaks of the "fog of war," referring to an inherent shroud of uncertainty prior to and during battle (Clausewitz 1989). This fog conceals information such as disputants' capabilities and intentions, but it can also obscure a clear view of their actions. Inaccurate intelligence, slow and broken communication, and close-quarter contact between disputants, as well as other complexities at the tactical level, can conceal actions and, from the perspective of third-party defenders, make it difficult to determine in real time which disputants took what actions. The possibility that actions may not be directly observable to a third-party defender inhibits it from adopting a conditional commitment, for it cannot ascribe blame and execute the prescribed response when it does not know the history of actions taken by each actor and, thus, how the war began. The third model, therefore, incorporates a simple extension designed to capture the problem of forming third-party security commitments when both disputants have hidden actions. In this situation, the third party chooses an *ex ante* commitment that is applied uniformly in war regardless of how or why war occurred. The chapter concludes with a section that summarizes the implications of the theory.

Moral Hazard and Incomplete Contracts

How can state leaders design alliance contracts to balance their goals of deterring an adversary and minimizing the effect of moral hazard on an ally? Let us first review the types of deterrence contracts leaders can write. In Chapter 2, a security commitment was defined as a promise by a third-party alliance member to deliver y if x occurs. The antecedent x, which constitutes the condition triggering the third party's obligation y, can either be specific, making the commitment conditional, or unspecific, in which case the third party's obligations hold unconditionally. The consequent y also can vary: the third party can promise complete support, a specific level of support, no support, or it can commit to support with some probability.

As explained in Chapter 2, historical alliance commitments in fact correspond to many of these design characteristics. Actual deterrent alliances can be classified as unconditional, conditional, and probabilistic. Of the commitments offering support, leaders may specify precise amounts of military assistance to be transferred or they may commit to transferring as much assistance as they are able or as required to accomplish the military objective. Alternatively, state leaders can form no commitment or explicitly commit not to intervene. An unconditional guarantee of full support provides the most deterrence, but it also exacerbates moral hazard. This is not a problem if the third party and protégé have identical preferences, because the third party would not worry about its commitment leading to undesirable aggression on the part of its ally. However, when their preferences diverge, then an unconditional commitment of full support can result in an outcome that makes the third party worse off, because the protégé may act more aggressively than desired. On the other hand, a promise to provide no support or to remain neutral does not carry moral hazard costs, but, of course, it does not add any deterrence benefits either. State leaders opt for this type of commitment when they care little about the security of the protégé and worry that any commitment will create incentives for the protégé to insist on a policy settlement that the third party does not like.

Commitments of full or no support are likely to occur when third parties care strongly about either deterrence or moral hazard, respectively, but not both. However, in many, if not most, cases, alliance members' preferences regarding the expected benefits of war and of different policy outcomes diverge enough that leaders weigh the trade-offs between deterrence and moral hazard when designing alliance contracts. For example, many protégés have revisionist aspirations in that they desire to make some gains at their adversary's expense. However, third parties often do not fully share these aspirations, preferring instead the status quo or some other more moderate result. In this case, the third party and protégé agree on the value of securing the protégé's defense, but disagree about how much of the disputed issue should be allocated to the protégé. The 2008 war between Russia and Georgia illustrates a similar situation. In spite of repeatedly stating its desire that Georgia's sovereignty be preserved, U.S. leaders did not share Georgia's desire to militarize and annex South Ossetia. It is possible, and perhaps even common, for third-party defenders to support the defense of an ally without sharing that ally's revisionist or expansionist aspirations.

The belief that states ally, at least in part, to restrain a potentially overly aggressive alliance partner has become commonplace in the study of alliances (Liska 1962; Schroeder 1976; Snyder 1997; Pressman 2008). Many scholars have observed that leaders often design the content of the alliance commitment specifically to restrain their allies. Snyder claims that the third party can respond to its fears that the protégé will respond too aggressively by reducing the strength of the commitment, loosening its terms, threatening to withhold support, or incorporating flexibility (Snyder 1984, 1997). Crawford echoes this point, asserting that leaders resort to ambiguity when they worry their allies will behave opportunistically by provoking conflict (Crawford 2003). Fearon says that states balance deterrence and moral hazard through partial threats or commitments (Fearon 1997). The study of alliances, however, has not yet produced a systematic analysis of how different types of commitments restrain allies while simultaneously deterring threats, nor has it pinned down the conditions under which different types of commitments are selected to maintain this balance. There are, in fact, three types of *ex ante* commitment that might be effective mechanisms when the third party is worried about both deterrence and moral hazard. These include a promise to deliver a specific amount of support if war occurs, a conditional commitment, and a probabilistic commitment. A fourth potential solution does not involve forming a commitment specifying what the third party will do if there is war but instead involves making a direct *ex ante* transfer of a specific lump-sum amount of military aid or support. I discuss each in turn.

The first commitment is a promise to deliver a specific amount of support if war occurs. Some military alliances, especially many written prior to the 1800s, spelled out in detail how many foot soldiers or how many horses alliance partners would transfer to one another in war. The advantage of such a commitment is that, if credible, the third party could promise to limit the level of support to an amount that would just offset the adversary's incentive to challenge the protégé and the protégé's incentive to provoke the adversary. There are some downsides to a contract that promises to transfer a precise level of military assistance in war. One difficulty is that alliance agreements often survive for years and sometimes decades, and, therefore, require some flexibility to adapt to the requirements of future crises, which often depend on unforeseeable circumstances. As a result, specific promises to deliver a precise amount of support apply only to circumstances known at the time the alliance is formed. Unsurprisingly, such alliances are often short-lived. Many early alliances that contained specific promises were designed to communicate what leaders could expect from one another in imminent crises, and the alliance terminated once the short-term objective had been met.

Another downside to precisely specifying the amount of support to transfer if there is war is that such a promise can unravel once war actually begins and the third party intervenes, because of the problem of time consistency discussed in Chapter 3. Once involved in the protégé's war with the adversary, the third party, which can furnish assistance that will influence the protégé's probability of winning, might have strong incentives to keep adding materiel to influence the outcome of war. When the third party feels pressures of mission creep to supply as much support as possible in war, the protégé is emboldened to push for more concessions in conflict bargaining with its adversary than it could expect to receive without third-party assistance. Thus, mission creep may induce the protégé to behave aggressively in crisis bargaining so as to receive larger-than-normal rent transfers from the adversary. This distortion increases with the third party's power: the more powerful the third party, the higher the protégé's expected payoff from fighting a war. This, in turn, increases the share of the disputed issue that the protégé expects to keep to prevent it from quitting the bargaining process and resorting to war. If the third party prefers a relatively modest policy outcome, then the protégé's aggression results in a "second-best" policy outcome for the third party, whereas the "first-best" would be for the disputants to agree to a settlement identical to the third party's ideal policy outcome and the worst outcome would be for the adversary to win at the protégé's expense.

Why might the third party be unable to make a credible commitment to a limited transfer that would induce the disputants to settle on a division equal to the third party's first-best outcome? In deterrence theory, leaders' threats to fully retaliate in the event of war are made credible through incurring hands-tying and sunk costs (Fearon 1997). Third parties typically suffer these costs when they fail to deliver or under-deliver their commitments. In the classic commitment problem in the deterrence literature, costs for reneging or under-delivery of a commitment include reputation loss or domestic audience backlash. However, under-delivery or failure to deliver on promises, not over-delivery, compromises credibility. As explained in Chapter 3, when the promise is to limit wartime involvement to a specific amount, it is difficult to imagine why a leader, who has already decided to intervene, would lose credibility for slightly over-delivering on its specified promise. If a third party pledges to give an ally 3,000 horses, would the third party really incur a reputational or domestic audience cost for delivering just one additional horse to the protégé? If over-delivery does not harm one's credibility, then mission creep pressures might cause a commitment of limited assistance to unravel, placing the third party in the position of intervening with unlimited transfers or reneging altogether by not intervening. As a result, third-party defenders often avoid making *ex ante* commitments to limit wartime transfers to a specified amount, even if they would like to use a threat of limited assistance to discourage the protégé from pushing too aggressively to gain concessions from the adversary.

A second possible type of commitment to balance deterrence and moral hazard is a conditional commitment. It is often convenient to make promises of assistance contingent on the adversary's initiation and/or the protégé's non-initiation of conflict. A conditional commitment may take one of two structures. The most common type is a straightforward conditional commitment, which stipulates that if war results from the adversary taking a specified action, then the third party will fully support the protégé. Therefore, the adversary's provocation is a sufficient condition to activate the third party's intervention, but the commitment also leaves open the possibility that the third party may or may not provide assistance if war breaks out because the protégé initiated the conflict. These commitments allow the third party to escape if the protégé becomes so aggressive that it turns violent. However, because the protégé knows it will get backing as long as it does not initiate hostilities, the commitment encourages it to push for large concessions in bargaining, which can be a disadvantage to the third party if its ideal policy settlement differs significantly from that of the protégé. Therefore, the third party may select such a commitment when it worries about the costs of moral hazard associated with the protégé initiating conflict, but is not so out of step with the protégé's preferences about the ideal bargaining settlement that it would feel that emboldening the protégé to drive a hard bargain would lead to an unacceptable policy outcome. A conditional commitment can be made credible in the same way the literature asserts that an unconditional commitment can be made credible – by incurring reputational or other costs for failing to deliver assistance when the specified condition obtains and war follows.

A special type of conditional commitment has a more restrictive structure. Pure conditional commitments obligate the third party if the adversary initiates the conflict and the protégé does not. The third party might, for example, promise to assist its ally only if an adversary attacks it, ruling out the possibility of providing assistance if the third party initiates hostilities. Ideal examples of pure conditional agreements that specify actual verifiable actions that both trigger intervention and nullify the commitment are rare in practice. Non-provocation agreements, however, are good approximations. As explained in Chapter 2, these commitments promise intervention if the adversary attacks and the protégé does not provoke. They do not perfectly correspond to the exact definition, because the threat not to intervene is conditional on the third party's subjective interpretation of what constitutes a provocation. This gives the third party a great deal of discretion to determine when to intervene, making the threat somewhat ambiguous. Another type of commitment that imperfectly resembles a pure conditional commitment is an active demilitarization or neutralization policy. Examples include Truman's neutralization of the Taiwan Strait at the outbreak of the Korean War in 1951, the UN demilitarization of the Eritrean border in 2000, and the demilitarized zone between North and South Korea in 1953. Policies such as these threaten to punish initiators by using force to resist aggression regardless of who the perpetrator is. They are dual deterrent threats rather than promises to support a protégé under one condition but not under another.

The third type of alliance mechanism that leaders can use for the purpose of balancing deterrence and moral hazard is a probabilistic commitment. Leaders can design contracts to stipulate that third parties might or might not intervene if there is war. In theory, this amounts to a promise that explicitly conditions the transfer of unlimited assistance on the realization of some automatic random process. For example, the third party might achieve its desired balance of deterrence and moral hazard if it can commit to intervening with a 25 percent chance. Therefore, as flippant as it might sound, the third party can achieve its desired balance by committing to defend its ally if an independent panel randomly selects two world leaders and objectively determines they are both taller than a third randomly selected leader. Credibility is achieved with a mechanism, such as delegating the randomization to another party or mechanism, in the same way we have traditionally thought that trip-wire and other commitments are made credible. If a leader promises to delegate the decision to a randomizing mechanism and then contravenes the decision of the device, then the leader would be required to pay the same kinds of *ex post* costs that would accrue if he or she violated any other kind of commitment (Fearon 1997; Smith 1995; Morrow 1994). Hence, if an unconditional commitment to intervene can be made credible, then so too can a commitment tied to a randomization device.

The thought of world leaders flipping coins and rolling dice to determine matters of war does not appeal to our sense of effective and humane leadership. In practice, leaders are less cavalier in the way they form probabilistic security commitments. Many actual probabilistic alliance agreements establish the risk of intervention by specifying terms in the agreement that condition intervention on processes beyond the third party's and protégé's control, the outcomes of which are not known with certainty at the time the agreement is formed. For example, leaders often defer to the decision of an external decision-making body, such as a country's legislature or a super-organization of states' leaders or representatives. The Collective Security Organization of the Commonwealth of Independent States, signed in 1993, subjects states' obligations to intervene to either the decision of "the Council of Heads or by the interested states taking into consideration their national legations." Almost all U.S. treaties stipulate that its decision to become involved in war depends on its "constitutional processes," which implies that the future opinion of Congress, which is not known at the time of the treaty signing, affects the final disposition of the U.S. decision to intervene. Delegation of some of the decision to Congress helps the credibility of the promise by removing the time-inconsistent decision of intervening probabilistically from the hands of the president. The uncertainty is created by the frequent turnover of elected officials in Congress, their many conflicting interests, and the relative murkiness of the bureaucratic process compared with the simple decision-making procedure of a lone actor.

In theory, probabilistic treaties can be effective devices for balancing deterrence and moral hazard, because random variables are relatively easy to fine-tune. When commitments precisely specifying the exact level of military transfer are vulnerable to mission creep, or when military transfers or the nature of war itself is coarse, randomization over the coarse alternatives may help smooth decisions. Additionally, compared with what a protégé expects to get from fighting a war with full support from the third-party defender, randomizing over discrete transfer options reduces the protégé's expected payoff from fighting a war. Therefore, if some random process can be manipulated in practice, then an incomplete contract that conditions actions on the realization of that random process can be fine-tuned to balance the third party's competing objectives while simultaneously tempering the protégé's expectations about what it will receive in war. Because both the protégé and adversary will expect modest returns from bargaining failure due to the third party's probabilistic intervention, both sides might agree to a more moderate settlement, thus yielding a more favorable payoff to the third party than what it expects to receive if it writes an enforceable conditional contract. Because moral hazard distortions increase with the divergence of preferences and the third party's power, more powerful third parties whose preferences on policy outcomes are more divergent from those of the protégé are more likely to benefit from probabilistic commitments.

However, although random variables may be easy to manipulate in theory, actually tying an *ex ante* security commitment to a precise randomization mechanism in an alliance treaty may be problematic in reality. The optimal randomization is highly sensitive to shifts in the preferences and relative capabilities of the third party, protégé, and adversary, as well as their costs of fighting, all of which may change during the life of an alliance agreement. An alliance treaty specifying the precise likelihood that the third party will intervene would have to give a schedule of probabilities for each targeted adversary of the alliance for each alliance member for the period during which the alliance is expected to be in force. Then the agreement would need to be renegotiated after every shift in relative capabilities and costs. This is an inefficient way to design a contract and explains why actual alliance agreements do not specify exact probabilities of intervention.

Instead, probabilistic commitments broadly establish uncertainty about intervention. This approach serves the demands of the security objective, because to mitigate incentives for moral hazard, the exact randomization need not be specified in the alliance agreement. The advantage of a probabilistic commitment is that it lowers the protégé's expected benefit of quitting bargaining to fight a war, inducing the protégé to accept more moderate bargaining settlements than it would with a guaranteed commitment of unlimited support. In this sense, any positive probability of intervention short of a guarantee bounds the bargaining settlement between what would be agreed to given no assistance and certain assistance. Therefore, for third parties that prefer more moderate settlements than their protégés, the uncertainty by itself, irrespective of the exact randomization, yields a settlement that improves over the settlement that would result from an unambiguous promise to intervene with unlimited support. This means that a probabilistic alliance commitment often serves as a beneficial framework that institutionalizes uncertainty into the security relationship between allies. With the commitment to uncertainty established in the framework of the alliance relationship, the third party may then be able to fine-tune policies to meet exigencies of particular circumstances over the lifetime of the alliance.

There is a possible fourth way to balance deterrence and moral hazard. Third parties may make *ex ante* lump-sum transfers, such as transferring military aid or giving or selling arms to other states. The upside to this approach is that it does not suffer the time-consistency problems that can plague some of the commitments we have discussed. It may be possible to transfer *ex ante* just enough to the protégé to deter both the protégé and adversary from making overly aggressive demands. By making such transfers, third parties pay sunk costs, causing them to incur the expense of the transfer whether or not there is a war. This approach can be more expensive than a conditional commitment, in which the third party pays the costs of assistance only if the bargaining fails *and* the condition specified in the agreement is triggered. It may also be more costly than a probabilistic commitment, in which military assistance is paid out only if bargaining fails and the probability of becoming involved obtains. In my theory, however, in both the cases of a conditional and probabilistic commitment, if the third party becomes involved, it transfers as much assistance as possible or as necessary to achieve the military objective. Hence, an *ex ante* lump-sum transfer may be better for the third party if the amount required to balance deterrence and moral hazard is very low compared with the amount it would provide in war with a probabilistic or conditional commitment after the probability of war and the probability that the third party would intervene are taken into consideration. On the other hand, if the amount required to deter challenges from the adversary is sufficiently high, then a conditional commitment or a probabilistic commitment will be a less expensive solution than the sunk cost.

In sum, third-party defenders often have incentives to devise mechanisms to mitigate moral hazard. Two possible solutions entail making an *ex ante* commitment to transfer an exact lump-sum amount of military assistance to the protégé. In one of these options, delivery of the assistance occurs if war breaks out. In the other, it is transferred prior to war breaking out. The first type of commitment is likely selected when leaders need speedy coordination of military plans when conflict is imminent or when a time-consistency problem of over-delivering support in war does not apply. The second mechanism – *ex ante* lump-sum transfers – are not state-contingent promises to deliver during war and are not typically formalized in alliance treaties. Such transfers likely occur when the cost of securing deterrence is not high relative to the costs of delivering on a probabilistic or conditional commitment.

The other two mechanisms – a conditional and a probabilistic commitment – are the most common types of mechanisms used in military alliances to deter adversaries and restrain allies. They may effectively balance deterrence and moral hazard even when the time-consistency problem of over-delivering assistance in war exists and *ex ante* transfers are costly. These commitments satisfy the time-consistency constraint because they are actually promises to deliver as much military support as possible or as necessary to the protégé, but only under some conditions or subject to some probability. In the next section, I discuss why leaders select probabilistic versus conditional commitments.

Conditional and Probabilistic Commitments

As the argument presented in Chapter 3 explains, when a protégé has expansionist goals and the third-party defender does not, then the third party might worry that an unconditional promise to defend the protégé could entice it to behave aggressively in crises. Under such circumstances, it might make sense to choose a conditional or probabilistic commitment rather than an unconditional promise to defend the protégé fully. To determine when a third party will select one type of commitment over another, I focus the argument on three factors that influence the design of a third-party security commitment: the relative preferences of the third party and the protégé; the relative strength or capabilities of the third party, protégé, and adversary; and the observability of the disputants' actions leading to war.

How do these factors affect the third party's choice of a commitment? First, consider the implications of any commitment. The responses of the adversary and protégé to a commitment may result in either a bargaining settlement or bargaining failure. Moral hazard is relevant for both outcomes, because a protégé covered by an alliance may behave so aggressively that it either gets a favorable settlement or causes a war. The degree to which it behaves aggressively in bargaining depends on how well it believes it will fare in a war with the adversary, which is directly linked to its own capabilities and how much assistance it expects to receive from the third party. The amount of support a protégé expects to receive is determined by how powerful the third party is and whether the security commitment constrains the protégé's ability to gain the full benefit of the third party's capabilities. The adversary's own behavior depends on the protégé's response to the commitment; it becomes more conciliatory as the protégé behaves more aggressively. The main implication for the third party is that the design of the commitment affects the actions of both the adversary and the protégé in crises, potentially deterring some challenges and either restraining or enabling bargaining demands and concessions. Thus, the type of security commitment the third party selects plays a critical role in shaping both war and bargaining outcomes. An unconditional commitment, for example, gives the protégé full access to the third party's capabilities regardless of how war occurs. Thus, when it is in possession of such a commitment, a protégé bargains as though its probability of winning a war is equivalent to the combined capabilities of it and the third party relative to the adversary.

Now, let us examine how the third party's preferences affect the type of security commitment it selects. Third parties have preferences over both war and policy outcomes. Because the design of the commitment affects both, divergence from the protégé on one or both dimensions may potentially influence what commitment the third party selects. A conditional commitment may effectively deter aggression initiated by the adversary, because the third party pledges full support if the adversary initiates a specified challenge. However, there is a subtle aspect to the way conditional commitments are designed that leads to a mixed effect on how well they restrain the protégé. To see this, consider the incentives of the protégé when the condition specified in the commitment does and does not obtain. Suppose the condition established in the commitment is an adversary's attack, so that the third party promises to intervene with full support if the adversary initiates conflict by attacking the protégé. If the attack never happens, then the protégé may not be able to infer anything from the commitment about what the third party will do if war breaks out. On the other hand, knowing that the third party will respond with full support if the adversary attacks encourages the protégé to bargain aggressively for concessions from the adversary in the amount of at least what it expects to receive if there is a war and the protégé receives full support from the third party. The result is a sizable bargaining transfer from the adversary to the protégé. Thus, conditional commitments are effective deterrents against specific challenges by the adversary and they might also restrain the protégé from initiating a war, but they can actually embolden the protégé to behave aggressively in bargaining to get a more favorable settlement.

The logic of this argument helps predict how the third party's preferences about security affect its choice of commitment type. Third parties favor conditional commitments over unconditional commitments when their preferences diverge modestly from the protégé's preferences. Conditioning intervention on the adversary's initiation of hostilities is especially useful when the third party values the protégé's security but worries that the protégé might pose a security risk if it receives an unconditional commitment. Leaving the protégé to judge for itself whether it will receive assistance if it initiates conflict, as a conditional commitment does, causes the protégé to be uncertain about the third party's response if it initiates a war against the adversary. Compared with an unconditional commitment, the protégé will be more reluctant to attack the adversary because it cannot expect as high a payoff in war. Thus, the conditional commitment deters the adversary's aggressive behavior without generating a moral hazard effect on the protégé's decision to initiate conflict. A pure conditional commitment goes even further to reduce the protégé's payoff for initiating a conflict. The impact of a pure conditional commitment on the adversary and the protégé is the same as in a standard conditional commitment. The difference is in the effect of the promise not to intervene if the protégé initiates the conflict. This pledge should deter the protégé from initiating conflict but should also embolden the adversary to bargain aggressively as long as it does not initiate the conflict. Thus, if the third party is sufficiently worried about the likelihood that either may initiate a conflict, then it will choose a pure conditional commitment.

Finally, for third parties that worry about the security implications of either disputant taking the initiative, a probabilistic commitment is an alternative to a pure conditional commitment. The uncertainty about how it will respond, regardless of who initiates, may induce caution by both the adversary and the protégé. What determines whether a probabilistic or pure conditional commitment is selected is the strength of the protégé compared with that of the adversary, for this determines whether choosing one party over the other has implications for the policy settlement. I discuss this more when I turn to the effect of countries' capabilities on the third party's choice of commitment type.

Now, let us turn to the effect of the third party's preferences regarding the policy settlement. Here, the question is, given that the protégé prefers to acquire total victory on the disputed issue, how divergence of the third party's preferences away from the protégé affects the design of the commitment? As just described, unconditional commitments fully distort the bargaining behavior of the protégé, inducing it to require an amount in bargaining at least equivalent to what it expects to receive by fighting a war with the unlimited support of the third party. Compared with all the other types of commitments, an unconditional commitment skews the policy settlement the furthest distance toward the protégé and away from the outcome that would obtain if there was no commitment at all. Conditional commitments have the next greatest impact on policy outcomes. They embolden the protégé to behave aggressively as long as it does not violate the condition specified in the agreement, leading to an extreme policy settlement modified somewhat by the inability of the protégé to gain an additional advantage by taking the initiative. The policy implication of a pure conditional commitment is a bit ambiguous, as this mechanism induces passive-aggressive behavior by both disputants. Neither side gains an advantage by initiating violent conflict, but both sides benefit from behaving aggressively if they are responding to bargaining demands. Finally, the type of commitment that leads to the most moderate policy settlement is a probabilistic commitment. Because the third party intervenes with some probability, the protégé does not benefit from war as much as it would if the commitment was any other type, and the adversary's expected war payoff is better if there was no commitment at all. Thus, the policy settlement induced by a probabilistic commitment lies somewhere between the outcome that would obtain if there was no expectation of third-party intervention in war and if there was a guaranteed intervention.

In summarizing these arguments, it is possible to state the main conclusions. With respect to differences in the third party's preferences for security, holding all else equal, we should expect the following implications to predict commitment type: (1) sharing the protégé's security concerns results in an unconditional commitment; (2) having some security concerns about the security risks posed by the protégé is likely to lead to a conditional commitment; and (3) worrying even more about the risks posed by the protégé initiating a conflict results in a pure conditional commitment or a probabilistic commitment. On the policy dimension, the degree to which there is a disparity in the preferences of the protégé and third party yields the following expectations about commitment design: (1) close similarities in preferences result in an unconditional commitment; (2) modest divergence leads to a conditional commitment or pure conditional commitment; and (3) more divergence results in a probabilistic commitment.

At the beginning of this section, I noted that three factors affect the selection of a commitment type. The second factor is the strength or capabilities of the actors. The capabilities of the protégé affect the likelihood that it can prevail in a bilateral war against the adversary. The third party's strength is the amount it improves the protégé's chances of winning if it transfers as much support to the protégé as it is capable of providing. The greater the amount of assistance transferred to the protégé, the larger the moral hazard distortion of the protégé's behavior in bargaining. Two moving parts affect the amount of transfer, one of which affects the upper bound and the other determines the lower bound. With respect to the upper bound, the third party will transfer as much as it can up to the minimum of its capacity constraint or what is required to guarantee victory. The lower bound is equal to the protégé's capabilities. Hence, the greater the gap between the capabilities of the third party and the protégé, the more aggressively the protégé will respond to any given commitment. If a weak protégé pairs with a powerful defender, then the result is a dramatic swing in the protégé's expected war payoff. This sizable shift in the value of the protégé's outside option emboldens it to require a significant expansion of its share of the disputed pie relative to what it could expect without any third-party support. If a settlement can be reached peacefully, then the policy outcome will be significantly more favorable toward the protégé.

The gap in the capabilities of the third party and protégé primarily has a moral hazard effect on the result of policy settlements, and the effectiveness of a commitment in managing this sort of distortion determines the likelihood it will be formed. By now it is clear how effective the different mechanisms are in resolving this problem. Probabilistic commitments are particularly well suited to minimize the incentives of the protégé to pursue an extreme policy settlement in bargaining. The uncertainty of a probabilistic commitment induces the protégé to be more accommodating in bargaining, resulting in a more moderate settlement. Thus, as the gap between the capabilities of the third party and protégé increases, the protégé selects a probabilistic commitment over other commitment options. This leads to two implications: holding all else equal, (1) increases in the capabilities of the third party increase the likelihood a probabilistic commitment will be selected; and (2) increases in the capabilities of the protégé relative to the adversary (the likelihood it will win fighting by itself) increase the likelihood a conditional or pure commitment will be chosen over probabilistic commitments.

Finally, the third factor affecting the choice of commitment is the observability of actions that the third party would otherwise use as conditions to justify its intervention. Often, disputants in a crisis may be able to take actions that are difficult to observe, especially for the third party. Many circumstances cause actions in crises and military campaigns to be hidden from third parties, including the location of states relative to each other, limitations of communication, the time of day, surveillance limitations, and even time lags for interpreting information when an immediate response is necessary. Observability is especially problematic if disputants are located in close proximity to one another or are embroiled in an ongoing dynamic dispute in which disputants have a long history of exchanging provocations. For example, in 2010, the *Cheonan*, a South Korean ship operated by the Republic of Korea Navy, sank on the South

A Theory of Commitment Design 103

Korean side of the line in the Yellow Sea dividing South and North Korean territory. It was not immediately clear whether North Korea was responsible for the ship's sinking, which would amount to an initiation of war. The close proximity of North and South Korean naval and other ships, the history of tensions between the two sides, and the shroud provided by the water created some uncertainty about the cause of the ship's sinking, as well as whether the sinking was provoked even if it was initiated by North Korea. Although South Korea and many of its allies, including the United States, claimed that North Korea sank the ship, North Korea and China denied that North Korea was responsible. In part because of the uncertainty, the United States and South Korea did not retaliate.

In fact, real-time identification of the parties responsible for initiating conflicts is often problematic. Determining responsibility for escalating violence in the Israeli–Palestinian conflict, for example, is notoriously difficult, because disputants invariably point to some previous provocative or hostile action by their opponent as the cause for their taking a subsequent hostile action. Likewise, in the crises in the 1950s between the Chinese Nationalists and Chinese Communists over several of China's offshore islands, it was not easy to form a commitment to identify and punish first-movers, because the situation was marked by ongoing skirmishes in areas of close proximity. President Eisenhower said of the problem, "As far as the Formosan question is concerned, I wish it were as simple as drawing a line and saying in effect, 'this far and no further,'" but, as Eisenhower further explained, "there were a thousand and one complicated factors that prevented an easy solution to the dilemma" (Dwight D. Eisenhower Confidential to Albert Coady Wedemeyer).

Conditional contracts are not enforceable if the parties and actions responsible for violating the conditions of the commitment cannot be identified by the time the third party is required to respond. Under such circumstances, leaders cannot design contracts conditional on actions related to the escalation of conflict. Ruling out conditional contracts significantly limits leaders' options. Most often, third-party defenders will choose probabilistic commitments, but they will occasionally resort instead to providing unlimited support to potential instigators of violence. The expectation of unlimited support creates incentives for protégés in a position to initiate conflict to do so. Alternatively, third-party defenders may consider the risks of moral hazard to be unacceptable and, therefore, will provide no assistance when they otherwise would if they could condition intervention on disputants' actions. Recognizing that the third party will not assist the protégé leads the adversary to initiate more aggressive bargaining demands, creating rents that flow from the protégé to the adversary. Consequently, when the third party is able to form only standard complete contracts, its inability to observe and contract on the actions leading to war generally causes it to form a probabilistic commitment; under some circumstances, however, hidden actions might instead lead to overcommitment and entrapment, or undercommitment and deterrence failure. The direction in which the third party leans depends on who it believes is most likely to be the initiator. The more it believes the initiator is likely to be the protégé, the more likely the third party will replace conditional commitments with probabilistic alternatives rather than opting for an unconditional commitment. On the other hand, if it believes that the adversary is more likely to be the initiator, then it will be more willing to give unconditional commitments.

To summarize, moral hazard may influence commitment design when allies do not see eye to eye on how much they value fighting wars and what they think the ideal settlement should be in a crisis between an adversary and an alliance partner. Under these conditions, either conditional or probabilistic commitments may be formed. Conditional commitments are most likely when third parties do not have quite as high a value for war as the protégé because they worry about the protégé initiating conflict. They also are more likely to emerge when the protégé is relatively strong compared with the adversary and thus does not require as much assistance from the third party. Compared with conditional commitments, probabilistic commitments occur when third parties are even less enthusiastic about war and have even more disparate preferences with respect to the settlement. A probabilistic commitment is especially likely when a protégé is weak and the third party is strong. Finally, when actions between disputants are unobservable, third parties are likely to select unconditional, probabilistic, or no commitments. When a commitment would be conditional under observable actions, it is most likely to be flexible when actions are not observable. However, because the potential loss of deterrence may be high when a probabilistic alternative replaces a conditional commitment, sometimes it is better for the third party to give an unconditional commitment when actions are unobservable.

In what follows, I begin the formal analysis of the third party's commitment decision in the shadow of a conflict plagued by problems of both deterrence and moral hazard. The next section introduces the models and explains the significance of their innovations in the context of the existing literature. I then present a baseline contracting model in which the adversary is the proposer in the bargaining stage and disputants do not have hidden actions. This model provides the basic intuition for the third party's commitment problem. The following sections consider extensions in which either disputant may initiate conflict bargaining and disputants have hidden actions.

A Formal Model of Alliance Commitment

Consider a model in which the third party chooses *ex ante* a type of contract that specifies actions to be taken if war occurs. There are four stages to the game. First, nature determines the private value of the war costs for the veto player in the bargaining game. Nature also determines whether the protégé or adversary is the proposer during bargaining. Second, the third party, C, writes a contract. The third stage is the bargaining phase, in which either the adversary,

A Theory of Commitment Design

A, or the protégé, B, is the proposer, and the other is the veto player. The proposer offers some settlement, and the veto player accepts or rejects. In the final stage, which occurs only if bargaining fails and war breaks out, C chooses some amount θ of military assistance to transfer to B.

The analysis begins with a baseline contracting model, in which A is the proposer and B the veto player, and C can observe the history leading to war. In the commitment stage, C chooses a probability $q \in [0, 1]$ with which it will make full transfers to B in war. The corner and interior options can be thought of as different types of commitments or alliance agreements. If $q = 0$, then C's commitment is not to intervene on B's behalf. If $0 < q < 1$, then C's commitment is a probabilistic alliance, which means C intervenes with some probability equal to q, and A and B, which both observe C's choice of q, are uncertain about whether transfers will be made. Finally, if $q = 1$, then C forms a complete contract that specifies it will automatically transfer support if there is war. However, this latter commitment is limited by the structure of the baseline game because C is obligated to deliver transfers only if A's offer has been rejected. Therefore, in the baseline model, if $q = 1$, then we will say that the third party makes a firm commitment. In Chapter 2, we saw that limiting commitments to a unique history of play in the basic extended deterrence and alliance models limited the scope of the theory to a particular type of commitment. For this reason, I consider extensions that allow the third party to provide assistance at multiple histories in the game. This modification permits the analysis of a range of conditional commitments.

The second model broadens the game to include the possibility that B initiates the conflict. This extension permits an examination of commitments that condition transfers on a particular initiator and those that are unconditional. Such a choice set reflects the possibility that when actions leading to war are observable, C can condition intervention on whichever player, A or B, initiates conflict bargaining. The result is a richer contracting space spanning commitment types more consistent with those observed in practice. These commitments include the following types of promises: unconditional commitments, which obligate C to defend B regardless of whether A or B initiates the conflict; conditional commitments, which stipulate that C will defend B if A initiates the conflict against B; pure conditional commitments, which obligate C to defend B if and only if A initiates conflict; and probabilistic commitments, which condition C's intervention on the realization of a random variable.

In the third model, the actions leading to war are unobservable to C. This inhibits C's ability to condition intervention on the history leading to war. Because it cannot extend a conditional commitment, C chooses some probability with which it will make unlimited transfers if war breaks out, regardless of which player initiated conflict.

The baseline contracting model builds on the model presented in Chapter 3 as well as existing extended deterrence and alliance models in the literature. As seen in Chapter 2, existing alliance models (Smith 1995; Morrow 1994) begin with a commitment stage in which the defender announces some *ex ante* commitment. Then, as in extended deterrence games, an adversary initiates a challenge, to which the protégé acquiesces or not. If it refuses to acquiesce, then war between the adversary and protégé breaks out, and the third-party defender can decide whether to intervene to assist the protégé. The third party's failure to intervene when it has promised to do so results in it incurring *ex post* costs for reneging on its commitment.

In constructing the models of this chapter, I choose to abstract away from signaling. Thus, the models here remain as close to the models of the previous chapter and extant work on crisis bargaining in international relations (e.g., Fearon 1995). In bargaining, the proposer does not have private information and the vetoer does. This means that when the protégé is the initiator, the adversary has an informational advantage and when the adversary is the initiator, the protégé has the informational advantage. (A richer model, in which both states possess private information about their own costs, might seem more natural, but this strategy imposes a high cost in terms of complexity and would be too disconnected from previous work.)

Additionally, all actions are observable in the baseline and second model. In the extension considered in the third model analyzed later, the third party is unable to observe the actions leading to war. Contracting under both the constraints of moral hazard and hidden actions when either the adversary or the protégé can initiate conflict may significantly affect the content of alliance commitments. Extending the model to capture these factors enables us to identify these effects.

To facilitate the analysis, I make the following assumptions. In Chapter 3, it was assumed that the third-party defender, C, is more powerful than the protégé, B. This assumption will be retained here. This gives:

Assumption 1. $1 > \mu > p$,

where μ denotes C's strength or the maximum transfer it is capable of providing and p represents the amount of military resources that B is capable of furnishing for itself. The assumption is not necessary for the results to obtain in equilibrium, but will be useful to illustrate the modeling intuition in some cases.

The next assumption is as follows:

Assumption 2. $1 - p - c_A > 0$ and $p - c_B > 0$.

These two inequalities imply that for both disputants, the expected payoff from war is positive. This assumption advances the analysis, as I am interested in understanding the role of military alliances in cases in which states may go to war.

The solution concept used in this game is perfect Bayesian equilibrium (PBE). As explained in Chapter 3, PBE is the natural equilibrium concept when there are no proper subgames because one or more players have private information.

A Theory of Commitment Design

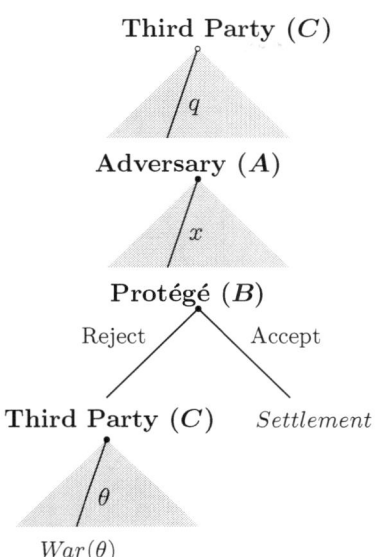

FIGURE 5.1. Sequence of moves in the baseline commitment design game.

In the baseline model as well as the extensions analyzed later, nature determines at the beginning of the game the war costs of the veto player, the player that responds to the proposal in bargaining by accepting or rejecting the offer. To arrive at a PBE in this game, it is necessary that players' moves are a best response at every information set given other players' strategies.

The Baseline Model of Commitment Design

The starting point for analyzing the third party's baseline commitment problem is an environment in which the adversary initiates conflict bargaining and the third party can fully observe all the actions leading to war. Figure 5.1 depicts the sequence of moves. First, the third party, C, chooses a type of commitment q. Once C has announced its commitment, the adversary A proposes some settlement $x \in [0, 1]$. The protégé, B, can accept, in which case the pie gets divided according to the agreement and the settlement payoffs are $(1 - x, x)$, where x is the amount allocated to B. Alternatively, B can reject the demand and fight a war against A. If B rejects A's offer, the third-party defender, C, chooses some transfer $\theta \in [0, 1]$ of military assistance to provide to its protégé, B.

As in the game with third-party intervention presented in Chapter 3, A's utility from a settlement is $U_A(x) = 1 - x$, and B receives $U_B(x) = x$. The outcome of war is settled by a lottery, in which B wins the entire pie with probability $p \in (0, 1)$. Players pay c_i to fight, where $i \in \{A, B\}$. Each disputant, A and B, receives different expected utilities from war depending on whether C makes an *ex post* transfer θ. War without C's intervention yields $EU_A(war) = 1 - p - c_A$ and $EU_B(war) = p - c_B$. War with third-party intervention results in $EU_A(war) = 1 - p - \theta - c_A$ and $EU_B(war) = p + \theta - c_B$. Because C's transfer depends on its choice of *ex ante* commitment q, player A's expected utility for war is

$$EU_A(war) = (q(1 - (p + \theta))) + (1 - q)(1 - p) - c_A.$$

B receives the following expected utility in war:

$$EU_B(war) = q(p + \theta) + (1 - q)(p) - c_B.$$

It is clear that B's war payoff increases and A's payoff decreases the higher the probability q that C intervenes in war. For example, if C chooses a firm commitment ($q = 1$), then B receives $p + \theta$, but if C chooses a probabilistic commitment ($0 < q < 1$), then its payoff is increased by θ with some probability q, but is unaffected with probability $1 - q$.

The risk of war in the model results from A's uncertainty about B's war costs, because in the baseline model B is the veto player. Players believe that B's war costs c_B are drawn from the uniform distribution on $[0, p]$, and these beliefs are common knowledge.

To arrive at a PBE in this game, it is convenient to solve players' decisions beginning at the final information set of the game, when C chooses θ given A and B bargaining strategies. C maximizes the following war utility:

$$EU_C(war) = \lambda(p + \theta - c_2) + (1 - \lambda)(-\theta).$$

As explained in Chapter 3, $\lambda \in [0, 1]$ is the weight C places on receiving the same war payoff as B. It measures how much C values B's security. For larger values of λ, C gets more utility from making larger transfers to B because C cares more that B wins. When λ is low, C's preferences diverge from B's, so C does not get as much utility from B's winning the war. C's utility with respect to θ is strictly increasing in θ if $\lambda \geq \frac{1}{2}$, but is decreasing if $\lambda < \frac{1}{2}$. Therefore, if C values B's war payoffs higher than its own disutility for paying the costs of helping B, then it will transfer as much military assistance to B as possible, or as necessary. This naturally gives rise to two possible cases: one in which the combined capabilities of C and B are sufficiently large to guarantee victory against A (that is, $\mu + p \geq 1$) and another in which those combined capabilities do not guarantee victory (that is, $\mu + p < 1$). If $\mu + p \geq 1$, then C may transfer assistance up to the point at which it is sufficient to prevail over A. However, C cannot transfer assistance beyond its own capacity constraint, μ. Therefore, the optimal amount of third-party transfer if C intervenes in a war between B and A is $\theta^* \in [0, \min\{1 - p, \mu\}]$. That is, C can choose any level of transfer, from no support to the minimum of either its total resource capacity μ or what is required to top off B's strength to guarantee victory. If $\lambda > \frac{1}{2}$, then C will

A Theory of Commitment Design

intervene and supply either $\theta^* = 1 - p$ or $\theta^* = \mu$. For the remainder of the analysis in this chapter, both cases will be considered.

Case 1: $\mu + p \geq 1$ and $\theta^* = 1 - p$.

Consider the bargaining game between A and B given that both players know that $\theta^* = 1 - p$ will be transferred to B if bargaining fails. The utility of war for B given θ^* is $U_B(war|\theta^* = 1 - p) = q + p - qp - c_B$, and A receives $U_A(war|\theta^* = 1 - p) = 1 - q - p + qp - c_A$. Player B accepts the offer from A if it is at least as great as what it can get by rejecting and going to war. Therefore, B rejects if $x_{AB} < q + p - qp - c_B$, where the subscripts AB denote the offer made in the baseline game in which A proposes to B. The probability of war is the probability that B rejects given it has private information about its war costs. In other words, the probability of war is the likelihood that c_B, which is uniformly distributed over $[0, p]$, is sufficiently low that A's offer does not offset B's expected benefit of war. Thus, the probability of war when A proposes to B in bargaining given θ^* is

$$\max\left\{0, \frac{q + p - qp - x_{AB}}{p}\right\}.$$

Now it is possible to consider A's decision problem as proposer in the bargaining game. It chooses x_{AB}, to maximize the following utility:

$$EU_A(x_{AB}|\theta^*) = \left(\frac{q + p - qp - x_{AB}}{p}\right)(1 - q - p + qp - c_A)$$
$$+ \left(\frac{qp - q + x_{AB}}{p}\right)(1 - x_{AB}).$$

Solving this maximization problem yields

$$x_{AB}^* = \frac{p + c_A}{2} + q(1 - p).$$

This expression corresponds to the amount B can expect to receive in bargaining when A is the proposer and when both parties know that the third party might intervene with $\theta = 1 - p$ if there is war. In contrast to the model of third-party intervention presented in Chapter 3, here B's share of the settlement is modified by q. Instead of taking full advantage of C's inability to limit θ, B can expect to gain only $q(1 - p)$, which implies that the amount it benefits depends on the probability that C intervenes.

The equilibrium probability of war given x_{AB}^* is

$$pr(W_{AB}) = \frac{p - c_A}{2p}.$$

The probability of war when C intervenes is the same as the model presented in Chapter 3 when C did not intervene. C's transfer emboldens B to behave aggressively in bargaining, which increases the expected risk of war for a given offer. In response to this increased risk, leader A lowers its demand to reduce the chance that B will reject.

Now, consider C's decision to choose a commitment type given that it knows how the disputants' expectation of its transfer of military assistance to B will affect bargaining. In choosing a commitment type q, C considers several factors. First, it takes into account the fact that its *ex post* transfer θ is made only in war and, as such, reflects only its wartime interests and not its *ex ante* peacetime interests. However, when C makes its commitment, bargaining has not yet occurred, and C has preferences over both the peaceful settlement and the outcome of war. Its preferences may diverge from the protégé's ideal settlement and war outcome.

Government C, therefore, chooses q to maximize its objective function:

$$EU_C\left(q|x^*_{AB}, \theta^*\right) = (1-\phi)\left(-\left(x^*_{AB}-\delta\right)^2\right) \\ + \phi\left((q)\left(\lambda U_B^{W|\theta^*} + (1-\lambda)(-\theta)\right) + (1-q)\left(\lambda U_B^{W|\sim\theta^*}\right)\right),$$

where ϕ is the probability of war, $1-\phi$ is the probability of an agreement, $U_B^{W|\theta}$ is B's utility from war given it receives the transfer θ^*, $U_B^{W|\sim\theta}$ is B's utility from war given it receives no transfer, and x^*_{AB} is the optimal settlement offered to B in bargaining when A is the proposer. As before, the parameter λ reflects the degree to which C shares B's preferences in war. The new parameter $\delta \in [0, 1]$ represents C's ideal bargaining settlement. If $\delta = 1$, then C shares B's preference for a settlement in which B completely wins the disputed issue or receives the entire disputed territory. As δ decreases, C's preferred settlement is more moderate than B's ideal outcome. To think about it in terms often used in the international relations vernacular, if there is some intermediate status quo division of a disputed territory and $\delta = 1$, then both B and C would be considered revisionist. Alternatively, if $\delta < 1$ and it is approximately equivalent to the status quo division, then B is revisionist and C is a status quo power.

Having defined δ, the term $-(x^*_{AB}-\delta)^2$ is now easy to interpret. It is a squared loss function that represents C's loss in utility the more the bargaining settlement differs from its own ideal policy settlement. With both λ and δ, the model captures C's ideal settlement and war preferences relative to B. The higher the value of δ, the more aligned B and C are on their preferred outcome regarding the division of the disputed issue with A. Higher values of λ can be interpreted to mean that C is more willing to fight for B in war, which is to say that the defense or security of B is important to C.

How should C's objective function be interpreted? It states that with some probability $1-\phi$, the disputants settle their crisis without going to war. If so, C's utility depends on how much the policy settlement x^*_{AB} differs from C's ideal settlement δ. However, with probability ϕ, bargaining fails and war results. If there is war, then C's payoff depends on the probability q that it intervenes. If war breaks out and $q = 1$, then C receives B's war payoffs weighted by λ

A Theory of Commitment Design

minus its costs of transferring θ weighted by $1 - \lambda$. If λ is high, then C receives very close to B's war utility and suffers a small disutility for transferring θ. However, if λ is low, then C mostly feels the costs from transferring θ^*. On the other hand, C will not make any transfer if $q = 0$. In this case, C receives the payoff B gets if it fights alone without any assistance from C. This payoff, too, is weighted by λ, and thus depends on how much C values A's security.

Substituting $\theta^* = 1 - p$ and $x^*_{AB} = \frac{p+c_A}{2} + q(1 - p)$ into C's objective function and solving to find the optimal q^* gives

$$q^* = \frac{(2\lambda - 1)(p - c_A) + (2\delta - (p + c_A))(p + c_A)}{2(p + c_A)(1 - p)}.$$

By assumption, $1 > p + c_A$. Therefore, if $p > c_A$, then it can be seen that q^* is increasing in λ and δ. That is, C's choice of deterrence commitment depends on the divergence of B and C's preferences over war and settlement. C's commitment tends to grow firmer as its preferences converge on B's preferences, both with respect to their utilities from war and for the bargaining settlement. However, as their preferences diverge, C is more likely to choose a probabilistic commitment or no commitment. The type of commitment also depends on p, although interpreting the effect is complicated by the fact that the mechanism of commitment depends both on p, which is a measure of relative power or capability, and the size of the third party's capabilities. In this case, in which C is sufficiently powerful to be decisive in a war, then the moral hazard distortion is most dramatic for low values of p. Consequently, the stronger the third party and the weaker the protégé, the less firm the third party's commitment will be. Therefore, strong third parties with relatively weak protégés tend to form probabilistic commitments, especially if their preferences are not identical.

From inspection of q^*, we see that a sufficient condition for the commitment level to be nontrivial is that $p > c_A$. This condition and assumption 2 are jointly satisfied when the relative powers of the disputants are not too dissimilar. Throughout the remainder of the analysis, I assume this condition and focus on interior solutions. In general, if the condition fails, q^* might be equal to 0, and the comparative statics might be weak. More generally, in expressing equilibrium values, it would be less ambiguous to say that the probability of commitment is given by the formula $\max\{0, \min\{q^*, 1\}\}$. Throughout, I avoid being explicit about these floors and ceilings for ease of readability.

Figure 5.2 depicts the effect of C's preferences on its choice of commitment type, as defined by q^*, for fixed values of B's and C's military capabilities and A's war costs. In this illustration, $p = 0.2$ and $c_A = 0.1$. Based on these values, the protégé is weak and unlikely to win a war against the adversary, but unlimited assistance from the third-party defender dramatically increases the protégé's probability of winning. In the figure, δ, C's ideal settlement, is organized along the x-axis, and λ, C's value of the war outcome, along the y-axis.

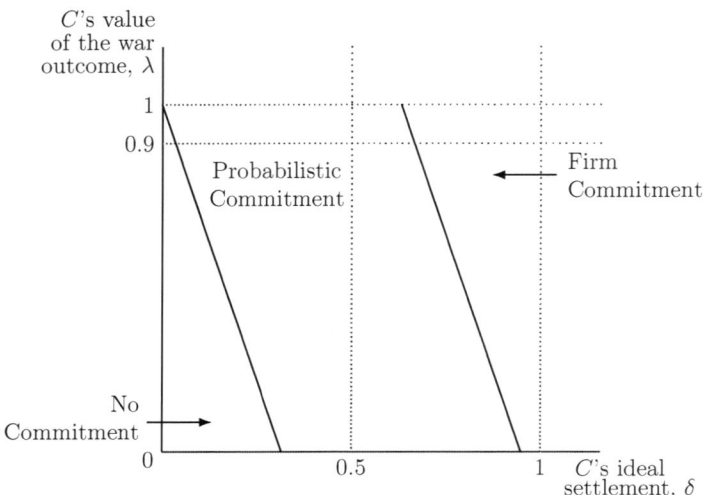

FIGURE 5.2. Third-party preferences and commitment choice, q^*, when $\theta = 1 - p$.

The "No Commitment" region on the left side is the set of all values λ and δ for which C is not willing to extend any commitment of support. In these cases, $q^* = 0$. The "Firm Commitment" region on the right is the area in which $q^* = 1$ when C will provide unlimited assistance. The diagonal region through the middle of the figure depicts the "Probabilistic Commitment" region. It corresponds to the values of λ and δ for which $q \in (0, 1)$, which is the probability that C will intervene.

The firmness of the commitment is increasing in both δ and λ, indicating that the choice of the commitment type, q, depends on C's preferences for war and settlement outcomes. As δ decreases, meaning that C is not as revisionist as B, then C is more likely to extend a probabilistic commitment than a firm commitment. Similarly, high values of λ correlate with firmer commitments. As C's interest in defending B decreases, it is more likely to shift from a firm commitment to a probabilistic commitment.

The relative responsiveness of the choice of commitment type, q, to shifts in δ versus λ corresponds to $-(\frac{p+c_A}{p-c_A})$, which is the slope of the parallel diagonal lines in the figure. As p increases, the probabilistic commitment region shrinks, implying that probabilistic commitments depend crucially on the power of the allies. Stronger protégés do better than weaker protégés in both war and bargaining. Compared with weak protégés, they also do not stand to gain as much from receiving large military transfers. As a result, a third party whose optimal commitment is probabilistic when the protégé is weak might receive the same utility from switching its commitment to no commitment or firm commitment when the protégé is strong, because a stronger protégé is more

A Theory of Commitment Design

likely to win a war and, therefore, will receive a greater share of the pie in bargaining.

C's choice of commitment type also depends on c_A. The choice is more responsive to changes in δ than λ as c_A increases, because shifts in c_A have a direct impact on the bargaining settlement, whereas they have less of an impact on B and C's war payoff – and only then because A is uncertain about B's war costs and, therefore, makes demands based on its own war costs relative to its probability of winning. Consequently, there are many cases in which C's choice of the type of alliance commitment is unaffected by λ, but it always depends on δ.

Figure 5.2 also shows how a third party that is very concerned about deterrence might nevertheless choose a probabilistic commitment because it prefers a moderate settlement outcome. Suppose, for example, $\lambda = 0.90$ and $\delta = 0.50$. In this case, B's security is a very high priority for C, but C prefers a moderate settlement and does not share B's revisionist policy goals. As can be seen in the figure, C would choose a probabilistic commitment in this case, because it can deter A with a probabilistic threat of intervening with unlimited support while simultaneously inducing B to make concessions in prewar bargaining such that C will be made better off with a less extreme policy settlement that is more to its liking. If, alternatively, C chooses a firm commitment, then A would be deterred, but B would behave aggressively in bargaining, resulting in a policy settlement closer to B's ideal division and further from C's more moderate ideal outcome.

Case 2: $\mu + p < 1$ and $\theta^* = \mu$.

In case 1, we saw that commitments are more likely to be probabilistic than firm as λ and δ decrease. Let us check to see whether the same conditions hold under case 2, where $\theta^* = \mu$. The logic of the analysis parallels that of case 1.

Because $\theta^* = \mu$, the utilities of war for B and A are as follows:

$$U_B(war|\theta^* = \mu) = p + q\mu - c_B,$$

and

$$U_A(war|\theta^* = \mu) = 1 - p - q\mu - c_A.$$

A chooses x_{AB} to solve the following program:

$$EU_A(x_{AB}|\theta^*) = \left(\frac{p + q\mu - x_{AB}}{p}\right)(1 - p - q\mu - c_A)$$
$$+ \left(\frac{x_{AB} - q\mu}{p}\right)(1 - x_{AB}).$$

Solving this maximization problem yields the following offer made by A to B:

$$x^*_{AB} = \frac{p + c_A}{2} + q(\mu).$$

It is evident that B expects its share of a peaceful settlement to increase by an amount that depends on C's capabilities, μ, and the likelihood that C intervenes, q. The greater C's capabilities and the more likely it is to intervene, the more B expects to receive in a bargaining settlement with A.

It is now possible to solve for C's choice of commitment type. Because the probability of war does not depend on how much C transfers to B, the solution to C's optimal choice of q is

$$q^* = \frac{(2\lambda - 1)(p - c_A) + (2\delta - (p + c_A))(p + c_A)}{2\mu(p + c_A)}.$$

As in case 1, q^* is increasing in λ and δ. The key difference between cases 1 and 2 with respect to the comparative statics on λ and δ is that there is a larger range of values of these parameters for which C will form a firm commitment in case 2. This distinction derives from the fact that the third party in case 2 is not decisive in conflict, and ambiguity about its intervention further reduces allies' expected payoffs from war. Thus, for some range of the third party's preferences in which it would make a probabilistic commitment in case 1, instead it will choose to eliminate that ambiguity and opt for a firm commitment in case 2.

Because in case 2 C is not decisive in war, the effect of C's capabilities, μ, becomes relevant. It is clear that q^* is decreasing in μ, which may be interpreted to mean that commitments are not likely to be firm when C is powerful. This effect may be dramatic if the difference in allies' capabilities is large, implying that commitments are more likely to be probabilistic than firm when the relative strength of B is low and C's capabilities are high.

These two results – that commitments are more likely to be probabilistic when C's preferences for war and the settlement diverge from B and when C's capabilities are significantly greater than B's – highlight the impact of moral hazard on commitment design. Third parties are reluctant to form firm commitments when their protégés have incentives to take advantage of the commitment to extract benefits in crisis bargaining, and the incentive to behave aggressively is especially pronounced when the protégé is relatively weak and the third party is relatively strong. Under these circumstances, third parties prefer probabilistic to firm commitments.

The effects of allies' capabilities on commitment type can be illustrated with an example. Figure 5.3 represents C's choice of commitment type when the values of both p and μ vary, but the other parameters are fixed at $\delta = 0.55$, $\delta = 0.9$, and $c_A = 0.1$. These values represent a scenario in which the third party cares a great deal about the protégé's security but prefers a more moderate division of the pie in bargaining – albeit one that still slightly favors the protégé. In the figure, C's power, μ, lies along the x-axis, and B's power, p, lies along the y-axis. The downward-sloping diagonal from (0, 1) to (1, 0) represents the upward boundary of the figure as denoted by the constraints implied by the

A Theory of Commitment Design

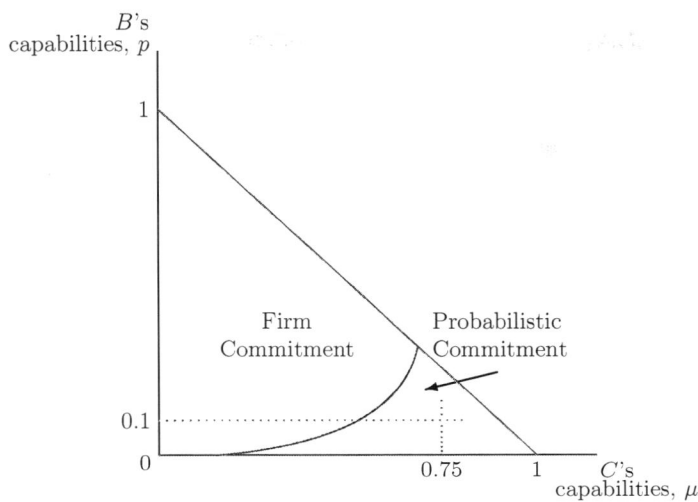

FIGURE 5.3. Allies' capabilities and commitment choice, q^*, when $\theta = \mu$.

conditions of case 2, in that the only relevant outcomes in the parameter space are those for which $1 > p + \mu$.

The region to the left of the upward sloping curve beneath the diagonal corresponds to the values of allies' capabilities for which C prefers to extend a firm commitment to B. The area to the right and below the curve represents the region for which C prefers to select a probabilistic commitment. The figure illustrates that C tends to prefer probabilistic commitments when it is powerful relative to B. For relatively low values of μ, C will prefer to make a firm commitment. For sufficiently low μ, this decision does not depend on p. As μ increases, C is more likely to select a probabilistic commitment. Inspecting the figure, it is clear that for low values of both p and μ, where the combined strength of the allies does not put the odds of victory in the favor of the alliance, C's commitment will be firm to increase the probability of defeat as much as possible. However, as C's own capabilities increase (to, say, $\mu = 0.75$), and B remains weak (for example, $p = 0.10$), then C worries about moral hazard and switches to a probabilistic commitment.

Model of Conditional and Unconditional Commitment

The model analyzed in the previous section includes the innovation that third-party defenders may design probabilistic commitments to allies. However, it is still restrictive because it confines the choice of commitment type to a subset of those actually formed in practice. In particular, the model applies only to promises of intervention in wars that result from an adversary making an unacceptable demand of the protégé. Only three possible commitment types can be analyzed and compared in the game form: the third party can form no alliance commitment; it can select a probabilistic commitment; or it can commit firmly to provide unlimited transfers if the adversary initiates conflict bargaining.

Missing from the analysis are unconditional commitments – alliances in which the third party promises to intervene regardless of which disputant initiated conflict. The model also lacks a more fleshed-out concept of conditional commitment, in which the third party pledges to intervene if the adversary initiates conflict but not necessarily if the protégé is the initiator. Without a fuller menu of commitment options that includes these additional types of alliance promises, it is not possible to draw conclusions across a broad range of commitments observed in practice. This requires an extension to the model that allows the third party to choose a commitment that obligates it to intervene with unlimited military support regardless of which disputant initiates conflict. In this section, I extend the analysis to allow either disputant, A or B, to act as proposer in the crisis bargaining stage – thus, either the protégé or adversary may initiate conflict by making a proposal to the other. I then include a richer contracting space, which permits the third party also to condition intervention on who initiates a crisis. The results will identify the factors that cause the third party to switch among no commitment, probabilistic commitment, unconditional commitment, conditional commitment, and pure conditional commitment.

To specify the contracting environment, let C choose an alliance $Z = \{q, r\}$, where q is the probability it will intervene if A is the proposer and r is the probability it intervenes if B is the proposer. We have already solved for C's optimal q^*. Therefore, the remaining task is to solve for r^* if B is the proposer, and then identify the conditions that lead the third party to choose between no commitment (0, 0), unconditional commitment (1, 1), conditional commitment ($q = 1$ and $r < 1$), pure conditional commitment (1, 0), and probabilistic commitment ($q \in (0, 1)$ and $r < 1$).

The analysis for C's choice of q was completed in the baseline model given earlier. Now, consider a model in which C chooses a type of commitment r, after which B proposes some settlement $x_{BA} \in [0, 1]$. If A accepts B's demand, the pie gets divided according to the agreement and settlement payoffs are $(x_{BA}, 1 - x_{BA})$, where x_{BA} is the amount allocated to B. If A rejects, war breaks out between A and B and, as in the baseline model, C chooses some transfer $\theta \in [0, 1]$ of military assistance to provide to its protégé, B. Regardless of which side proposes, risk always results from the proposer's uncertainty about the veto player's war costs. Therefore, when the protégé proposes, A's war costs are drawn from the uniform distribution on $[0, 1 - p]$. Without some risk of war, the concept of military alliance becomes significantly less meaningful. For analyzing the question of alliance design, however, it is not critically important to differentiate the sources of uncertainty that can increase the risk of war, so this is a convenient way to introduce uncertainty and the risk of war into the model.

A Theory of Commitment Design

A's utility from a settlement is $U_A(x_{BA}) = 1 - x_{BA}$, and B receives $U_B(x_{BA}) = x_{BA}$. The war lottery is unchanged from the previous model, except that payoffs are awarded depending on the probability r that C intervenes. In the final stage of the game, C transfers $\theta^* = min\{1 - p, \mu\}$ if $\lambda \geq \frac{1}{2}$, but transfers nothing if $\lambda < \frac{1}{2}$. Let us consider both cases in which C transfers assistance.

Case 1: $\mu + p \geq 1$ and $\theta^* = 1 - p$.

When C's optimal transfer of assistance is $\theta^* = 1 - p$, then the war payoffs for the disputants are as follows:

$$U_B(war|\theta, r) = r + p - rp - c_B$$
$$U_A(war|\theta, r) = 1 - r - p + rp - c_A.$$

When B is the proposer in bargaining, its take of the pie reflects the moral hazard distortion and its advantage from initiating the conflict process. Player B will demand from A an amount no greater than what it expects to receive in war. A rejects if $1 - x_{BA} < 1 - r - p + rp - c_A$. In other words, A rejects if its portion of the proposed settlement is less than its war payoff. Because B is uncertain about A's war costs, the probability of war corresponds to the likelihood that B will demand an amount greater than A's war payoff. Thus, the probability of war given that B proposes to A is

$$pr(W_{BA}) = \frac{rp - r - p + x_{BA}}{1 - p}.$$

B demands x_{BA} to maximize the following utility:

$$EU_B(x_{BA}|\theta) = \left(\frac{rp - r - p + x_{BA}}{1 - p}\right)(r + p - rp - c_B)$$
$$+ \left(\frac{1 - rp + r - x_{BA}}{1 - p}\right)(x_{BA}).$$

B expects to receive its war payoff, $U_B(war|\theta, r)$, with probability $pr(W_{BA})$ and its bargaining payoff x_{BA} with the probability that there will be a settlement and not a war, $1 - pr(W_{BA})$. Solving this maximization problem yields

$$x_{BA}^* = \frac{1 + p - c_B}{2} + r(1 - p).$$

The equilibrium probability of war that corresponds to this demand is

$$pr(W_{BA}) = \frac{1 - p - c_B}{2(1 - p)}.$$

This probability of war is equal to the probability of war if C does not intervene. C's transfer of assistance makes B more aggressive, which increases the risk of conflict, but A accepts a less favorable division to reduce these risks.

The rents captured by B due to moral hazard are equal to $r(1 - p)$. If $q = r$, this amount is the same as when A is the proposer. The advantage to B of being the proposer is equivalent to $\frac{1-c_A-c_B}{2}$, which implies that there are gains from initiating conflict when $1 > c_B + c_A$. Therefore, when C forms a commitment for a potential conflict that might occur as a result of its protégé, B, initiating conflict bargaining, it must account for distortions resulting from both moral hazard and B's first-mover advantage.

Now, it is possible to solve for C's optimal commitment, r^*, given $x_{BA}^* = \frac{1+p-c_B}{2} + r(1-p)$ and $\theta^* = 1 - p$. C chooses r to maximize the following objective function:

$$EU_C(r|x_{BA}^*, \theta^*) = (1-\phi)\left(-\left(x_{BA}^* - \delta\right)^2\right)$$
$$+ \phi\left((r)\left(\lambda U_B^{W|\theta^*} + (1-\lambda)(-\theta)\right) + (1-r)\left(\lambda U_B^{W|\sim\theta^*}\right)\right).$$

This is the same utility function for C when it chooses q^*, except that the values of the variables represent the game in which B is the proposer. Substituting these values into the function and solving C's maximization program gives

$$r^* = \frac{2\lambda(1-(p+c_B)) + 2\delta(1-p+c_B) + (p-c_B)^2 + (p+c_B) - 2}{2(1-p)(1-p+c_B)}.$$

Because $1 > p$, r^* is increasing in δ. That is, C is more likely to commit to providing assistance when its ideal settlement is close to B's preference. The effect of λ on r^* is also increasing if $1 - p > c_B$. The positive relationship between these factors and r^* is the same as when C chooses q^*, but the magnitude of the effects, which depends on p, is different. For high values of p, increases in δ and λ have a larger positive effect on q^* than r^*, but when p is low, positive shifts in δ and λ lead to a relatively larger increase in r^*. The key to this difference is the adversary's bargaining advantage when it is the proposer. Powerful third-party defenders that are revisionist (high δ) or very supportive of the protégé in war (high λ) are more likely to give firm support to protégés when the adversary's proposal power results in the protégé receiving a smaller share of the pie.

A sufficient condition for $r^* > 0$ is that $1 - p > c_B$. This condition and assumption 2 may be interpreted as saying that B's costs of fighting are intermediate. If the condition fails, r^* might equal 0, in which case the comparative statics are weak.

Combining the results from the foregoing analyses of q^* and r^*, it is now possible to inspect the content of the full contract $Z = \{q, r\}$. Figure 5.4 depicts the effect of C's preferences (both δ and λ) on its choice of commitment, $Z = \{q, r\}$, based on the formal conditions for fixed values of B's and C's military capabilities and A's war costs. In this illustration, $p = 0.2$ and $c_A = 0.1$, which are the same values as in Figure 5.2. The small triangle in the top right corner is the "Unconditional Commitment" region. In this region, C commits to the transfer of unlimited military assistance to its protégé regardless of which disputant initiates conflict. As δ and λ decrease, C's commitment changes as it crosses into the "Conditional Commitment" region. In this space, C promises to provide automatic unlimited assistance if A initiates conflict. The "Probabilistic

A Theory of Commitment Design

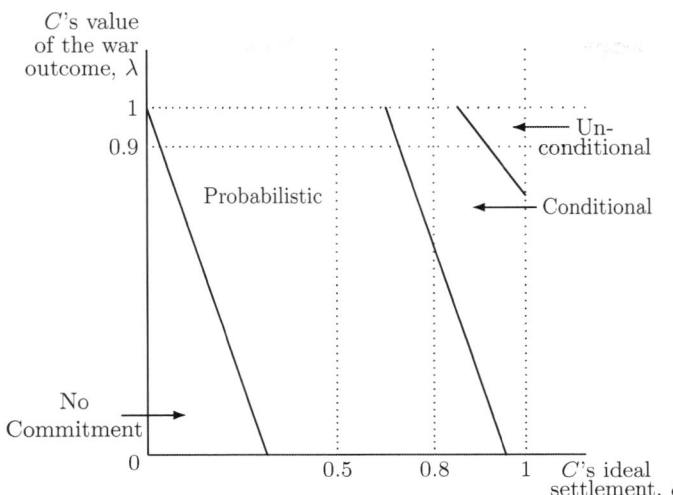

FIGURE 5.4. Third-party preferences and commitment choice, $Z = \{q, r\}$, when $\theta^* = 1 - p$.

Commitment" region exists for intermediate values λ and δ. Finally, the triangle in the bottom left-hand corner is the set of all values λ and δ for which C is not willing to extend any commitment of support, regardless of who initiates. In these cases, $q^* = r^* = 0$.

Unconditional commitments are most likely when δ and λ are large. As δ decreases, then C prefers conditional commitments to unconditional commitments. For middling values of δ, probabilistic commitment is preferred to both conditional and unconditional commitments even if λ is high. The reason is that the third party can use uncertainty about whether it will intervene to induce bargaining outcomes closer to C's ideal settlement. Consider, for example, a third party that is very concerned about B's security ($\lambda = 0.90$) but prefers a moderate bargaining settlement ($\delta = 0.50$). As can be seen in the figure, C would choose a probabilistic commitment in this case, because it can deter A with a probabilistic threat of intervening with unlimited support while simultaneously inducing B to make concessions in prewar bargaining such that C will be made better off with a less extreme policy settlement that is more to its liking.

If C's preference for the bargaining settlement begins to converge on B's ideal settlement (say, $\delta = 0.8$), then the optimal commitment changes to a conditional commitment. As λ decreases, C will continue to choose a conditional commitment for a greater range of λ (compared with changes along the δ dimension), because changes along the λ dimension represent shifts in C's preferences for B's security. For low values of δ and λ, C will not intervene.

The protégé's relative capabilities, p, also have an effect on the type of the contract that the third party selects. The analysis of the baseline contracting model predicted that powerful third parties were especially reluctant to extend firm commitments to weak protégés, which stand to benefit the most from exploiting the commitment of an unlimited transfer of military assistance. The effect in this case, when the protégé can initiate conflict bargaining, is similar, even though it may use both its first-mover advantage and moral hazard to distribute rents to itself. In general, third parties that are decisive in war are more likely to form probabilistic commitments or to condition intervention on the protégé being attacked.

An example illustrates the logic. Suppose, as we did in the illustration depicted in Figure 5.3, that the third party has tepid enthusiasm for supporting the protégé's policy goal, so $\delta = 0.55$, but its support for the protégé's security is strong at $\lambda = 0.9$. Also assume that $c_A = c_B = 0.1$. In this example, the third party is likely to give a probabilistic commitment to a relatively weak protégé, which would stand to benefit a great deal from a transfer of $\theta = 1 - p$. As the protégé's capabilities increase relative to those of the adversary, the distortion of moral hazard is less of a concern if the adversary initiates, but there is still concern if the protégé can initiate. Therefore, for relatively high values of p, the third party chooses a conditional commitment, and, for high values, it chooses a pure conditional commitment. The choice of a pure conditional commitment for powerful protégés is motivated by the third party's desire to make it clear that it is unwilling to provide assistance if the protégé initiates the conflict.

In sum, when C's intervention is decisive, lower values of p tend to predict probabilistic commitments. As p increases, C can generally do better by switching to a conditional commitment, and, for higher levels of p, the optimal commitment is a pure conditional commitment. This general pattern holds for varying levels of λ and δ. As either or both values of C's preferences increase, then the likelihood of observing a conditional commitment versus a probabilistic commitment increases, because the downsides of moral hazard to C are not as severe when C and B's preferences converge.

Case 2: $\mu + p < 1$ and $\theta^* = \mu$.

The results for case 2 are similar to those of case 1, so it is possible to walk through the analysis quickly. When $\theta^* = \mu$, the utilities of war for B and A are as follows:

$$U_B(war|\theta^* = \mu) = p + r\mu - c_B,$$

and

$$U_A(war|\theta^* = \mu) = 1 - p - r\mu - c_A.$$

A Theory of Commitment Design

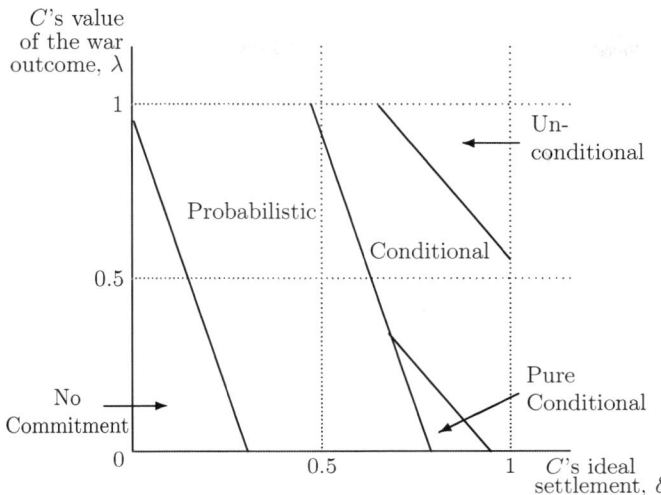

FIGURE 5.5. Third-party preferences and commitment choice, $Z = \{q, r\}$, when $\theta^* = \mu$.

A chooses x_{BA} to solve the following program:

$$EU_A(x_{BA}|\theta^*) = \left(\frac{p + r\mu - x_{BA}}{1 - p}\right)(1 - p - r\mu - c_A)$$
$$+ \left(\frac{x_{BA} - r\mu}{1 - p}\right)(1 - x_{BA}).$$

Solving this maximization problem yields the following offer made by B to A:

$$x^*_{BA} = \frac{1 + p - c_B}{2} + r(\mu).$$

It is evident that B expects its share of a peaceful settlement to increase by an amount that depends on C's capabilities, μ, and the commitment type, r. The greater C's capabilities and the more likely it is to intervene, the more B expects to receive in a bargaining settlement with A.

Solving now for C's choice of commitment type, the solution is

$$r^* = \frac{2\lambda(1 - (p + c_B)) + 2\delta(1 - p + c_B) + (p - c_B)^2 + (p + c_B) - 2}{2\mu(1 - p + c_B)}.$$

As in case 1, r^* is increasing λ and δ. An example is depicted in Figure 5.5. The values of fixed parameters are the same as in Figure 5.4 ($p = 0.2$ and $c_B = 0.1$), but now the value of C's capabilities is relevant. In this illustration, C's capabilities $\mu = 0.5$, so together B and C have a 0.70 chance of defeating A if there is a war in which C joins B against A. There are five distinct regions in the figure, representing different types of commitments C can select. Unconditional commitments are in the top right corner for large values of both λ and δ. As λ

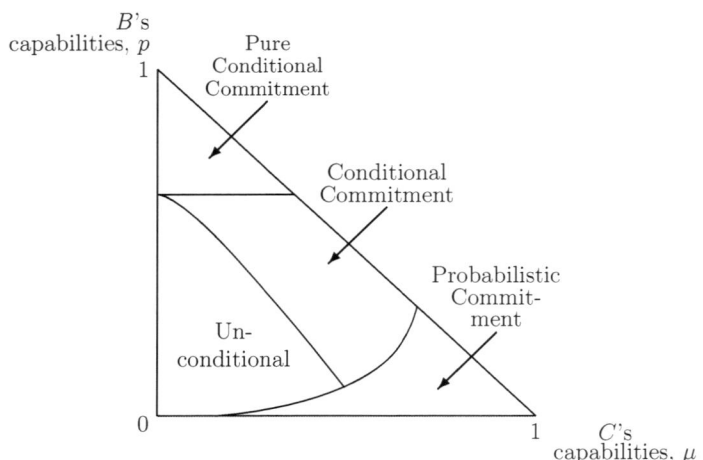

FIGURE 5.6. Allies' capabilities and commitment choice, $Z = \{q, r\}$, when $\theta^* = \mu$.

and δ decrease, C's optimal commitment changes to a conditional commitment, because C wants to offset the moral hazard effect by stipulating that it is obligated to defend B only if A initiates the conflict.

For very low values of λ and high values of δ, C prefers to form a pure conditional commitment. This is a special case in which, without a commitment, C would not intervene at all, because $\lambda < \frac{1}{2}$. The advantage of such a commitment is that it induces B to bargain aggressively toward a settlement that is actually favorable to C, as the value of δ is large. However, if B can initiate conflict, the distortion of moral hazard introduces risks that B's demands would be too aggressive, leading to a settlement too extreme for C or a war that C clearly prefers to avoid.

Figure 5.5 further shows that probabilistic commitments are favored over both unconditional and conditional commitments as λ, and especially δ, decrease. For example, if C and B are not closely aligned on either security or policy goals (say, $\lambda = 0.55$ and $\delta = 0.55$), then C worries much more about the distortion due to moral hazard. Accordingly, it opts for a probabilistic commitment, as the uncertainty of C's intervention induces moderate bargaining behavior by both B and A.

The effect of the protégé's strength, p, is more complicated, because the levels of p and μ are relevant both to the overall probability of the alliance prevailing in war and to the moral hazard effect on B in crisis bargaining.

Figure 5.6 plots the values of μ against p using fixed values of δ, λ, c_A, and c_B. In this example, $\delta = 0.9$, $\lambda = 0.55$, and $c_A = c_B = 0.1$. These values illustrate an example in which C cares a great deal about the security of B but prefers a moderate settlement that only just favors B. C's power, μ, lies along the x-axis, and B's power, p, along the y-axis. The downward-sloping

A Theory of Commitment Design

diagonal line bounds the figure to those values of μ and p that correspond to the parameter values, implied by the conditions defining case 2, in which $1 > p + \mu$.

In this illustration, unconditional commitments occur for low values of p and μ. Because the combined strength of C and B is not sufficient to guarantee victory in war, then there is an incentive to add an unconditional commitment to their relationship when both their capabilities are low. This type of guarantee, depicted in the bottom left corner of Figure 5.6, removes any ambiguity about C's willingness to intervene and gives C and B the best chance of winning a conflict given their low combined strength relative to A.

Government C is much more likely to opt for a conditional or probabilistic commitment as μ increases. The reason is C's anticipation that B will have an incentive to take advantage of C's capabilities for its own benefit in bargaining. Although both C and B welcome increases in their strength to improve their chances of winning against A, dramatic disparities in capabilities between the allies exacerbate the risk of moral hazard. Thus, in this example, probabilistic commitments are much more likely to be selected than any other type of commitment for large values of μ and small values of p.

As can be seen in Figure 5.6, pure conditional commitments occupy the region in the top left corner. In this instance, the protégé, B, is more powerful than the third party, C. Although we assumed at the outset that $\mu > p$, relaxing this assumption would result in the formation of a pure conditional commitment for large values of μ and small values of p. The explanation stems from the fact that C's relative contribution to the fight is so small that randomizing over an unlimited contribution and no contribution would not induce enough moderation on the part of B to have a significant effect on the resultant bargaining settlement. Moreover, in contrast to the small contribution B might offer in a fight, it may actually worry more about B's behavior if it may act as the initiator in a crisis. Therefore, C may best control the risk of moral hazard by making a pure conditional commitment. On the other hand, if we hold fast to the assumption that the third party is more powerful than the protégé, then we may concentrate on the region in the figure below (and to the right) of the imaginary diagonal line running upward from the origin to (0.5, 0.5). This region shows that increases in the disparity between allies' capabilities results in a switch from an unconditional to conditional commitment and then to a probabilistic commitment.

When actions leading to war are observable and, therefore, it is possible to make a contract conditional on the history of play, we see that there are some general implications for the formation of alliance commitments. If the third party is not revisionist or prefers a more moderate settlement but the security of the protégé is still important, then the likelihood of the third party selecting a probabilistic commitment is high. Additionally, powerful third parties with weak protégés are the most likely to form probabilistic commitments. If the relative power disparity between the third party and the protégé is less dramatic, then the third party will choose a conditional commitment. Less powerful third parties worry about deterrence more. Consequently, they are willing to trade off the risks of moral hazard, which are less severe with a relatively powerful protégé, to gain the deterrence advantage of a clear conditional commitment. This inclination for conditional commitment is especially pronounced as the third party's preferences for security and policy outcome shift toward the protégé's preferences. Finally, unconditional commitments are reserved for weak protégés and weak, revisionist third parties.

Extension to Unobservable Actions

Suppose C cannot observe which actor – the adversary or the protégé – initiates conflict leading to war. I consider an extension of the previous model that assigns a random recognition rule $\beta \in [0, 1]$ to determine which disputant is the proposer. Country C does not observe crisis bargaining between A and B, but sees only whether there is a bargaining settlement or war. If war occurs, C believes that A initiated with probability β. At the beginning of the game, C chooses a commitment type s to be realized in war, regardless of the path leading there. Because the history of actions at war is unobservable to C, it cannot enforce a conditional or pure conditional type of commitment. Therefore, C either makes a firm commitment, $s^* = 1$; a probabilistic commitment, $0 < s^* < 1$; or no commitment, $s^* = 0$. Because conditional commitments are not effective mechanisms when the disputants have hidden actions, the key question to address in this section is whether C will select a probabilistic, firm, or no commitment for the parameter values for which it is optimal to form conditional types of commitment when actions are observable.

C's objective function to solve for s^* is

$$EU_C(s) = \beta \left(EU_C(q|x^*_{AB}, \theta^*) \right) + (1 - \beta) \left(EU_C(r|x^*_{BA}, \theta^*) \right),$$

where $EU_C(q|x^*_{AB}, \theta^*)$ is C's payoff for forming a commitment when A initiates crisis bargaining, and $EU_C(r|x^*_{BA}, \theta^*)$ is C's utility for making a commitment when B initiates. Both these utilities are evaluated in the preceding sections. To find C's optimal choice of s^*, substitute s for q and r and then maximize C's objective function with respect to s.

By inspection, it is clear that s^* bears resemblance to the solutions r^* and q^*, and this similarity is consistent regardless of whether $\theta^* = 1 - p$ or $\theta^* = \mu$. The numerator in s^* is the difference between the weighted numerators in r^* and q^*. Likewise, the denominator is the difference between the weighted denominators in r^* and q^*. Therefore, s^* can be simplified. Let the numerator of $r^* = r_n$ and the denominator of $r^* = r_d$. In addition, let the numerator of $q^* = q_n$ and the denominator of $q^* = q_d$. The solution for s^* can then be

A Theory of Commitment Design

simplified to the following:

$$s^* = \frac{\frac{\beta}{p}(q_n)}{\frac{\beta}{p}(q_d) - \frac{(1-\beta)}{(1-p)}(r_d)} - \frac{\frac{(1-\beta)}{(1-p)}(r_n)}{\frac{\beta}{p}(q_d) - \frac{(1-\beta)}{(1-p)}(r_d)}.$$

It is clear that if $q^* \geq r^*$, then $q^* \geq s^* \geq r^*$. This implies that if a commitment is unconditional when actions are observable, $Z = (1, 1)$, then it is firm when actions are unobservable ($s = 1$). Also, if it is optimal to form no commitment when actions are observable, $Z = (0, 0)$, then C will also select no commitment when actions are observable, $s = 0$.

Less obvious is what type of commitment is chosen when C would select a conditional, pure conditional, or probabilistic commitment under conditions of observable actions. In general, when actions are unobservable, then C will make no commitment in many instances when it would make probabilistic commitments with observable actions. Additionally, it will form either probabilistic or firm commitments when observable actions would otherwise make it possible to design conditional commitments. How much more willing C is to go with the no commitment or probabilistic commitment options rather than choose a firm commitment depends on who C believes is at fault for initiating the conflict, β, but it also depends to some extent on the relative power, p, of B. Of course, it makes sense that whether s^* is closer to q^* or r^* depends on β. The more C believes A is likely to initiate a crisis and, therefore, the closer s^* is to q^*, the more C will go with a firm commitment when it would otherwise form a conditional type of commitment. On the other hand, if B is more likely to initiate the crisis, then C will try to counter its fear of B's aggressiveness by selecting a probabilistic commitment. However, p also matters. For example, for low values of p, commitments that would be conditional under observable actions are more likely to be ambiguous rather than unconditional under unobservable actions. This makes sense, as C is worried about moral hazard for small partners. Thus, this implication is consistent with the more general inferences that obtain throughout the analysis that increases in p lead to conditional types of commitment, whereas decreases increase the likelihood that the commitment will be probabilistic.

Figure 5.7 represents the intuition guiding the selection of commitments in an environment of hidden actions. This figure shows C's selection of commitments given variation in values of λ and δ. We can compare the optimal commitment, s^*, when actions are unobservable to the choice of commitment, $Z = (q^*, r^*)$, when they are observable. Therefore, the figure is identical to Figure 5.5, with the exception that I have overlaid, with the gray shaded area, the range of parameters for which C will select a probabilistic commitment, $0 > s > 1$, under conditions of unobservable actions and when $\theta = \mu$. The commitment regions under observable actions, which are identical in position to Figure 5.5, are marked by thin dotted lines. Laying the commitments made under unobservable actions over those made under observable actions allows

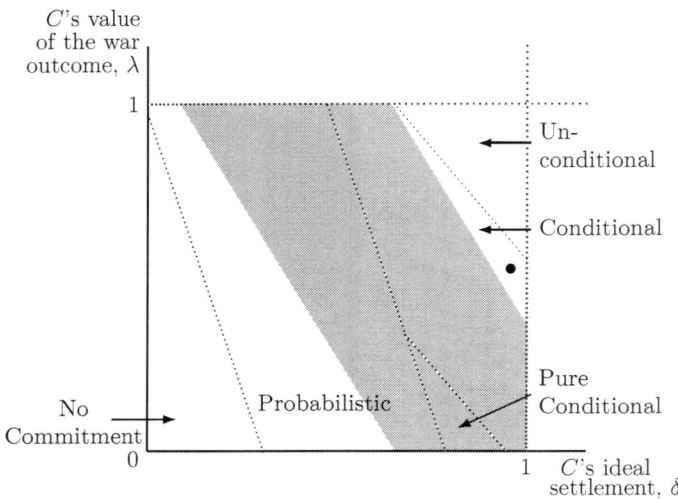

FIGURE 5.7. Comparing commitments when actions are observable and unobservable.

us to compare the effect of hidden actions on the choice of commitment type for the same parameters. The labels of commitment types in the figure refer to the types of commitment that correspond to the observable commitment environment. The gray shaded region refers to probabilistic commitments under unobservable actions. Everything to the right of the shaded region denotes unconditional commitments under unobservability, and everything to the left of the shaded region represents the no commitment region under unobservability. For the point indicated on the figure, C would select a conditional commitment if the disputants' actions were observable. This is because C's preferences on the policy settlement are close to B, and, therefore, it has little to fear from a conditional commitment as long as it can condition intervention on an attack by A on B. However, if actions are unobservable, then C would choose an unconditional commitment for the parameter values denoted by the point. This is because when disputants have hidden actions, the third party has a choice between choosing a probabilistic commitment, unconditional commitment, or no commitment. If it chooses a probabilistic commitment, then its expected payoff from the settlement will be lower than committing unconditionally because it does not know who the initiator is. If it happens to be A, then a probabilistic commitment yields too little deterrence of A's challenges.

What can be inferred about the impact of unobservability on C's choice of commitment? If C chooses an unconditional commitment, $s \geq 1$, when hostilities are unobservable, then when actions are observable the commitment is at least a pure conditional commitment $\{1, 0\}$. Depending on β, it could also be a conditional or unconditional alliance. If the commitment is probabilistic, $s \in (0, 1)$, when actions are unobservable, then the commitment will be

A Theory of Commitment Design

probabilistic, conditional, or unconditional if actions are observable. Furthermore, if alliances are probabilistic when actions are observable, then they will be probabilistic or there will be no commitment when actions are unobservable. Therefore, unobservability has the effect of increasing the likelihood of probabilistic and unconditional commitments, as C substitutes these types of commitments for the conditional commitments that it cannot make.

Implications

In conclusion, we can combine what we know from the analysis of q^*, r^*, and s^* to make some inferences about the design of an alliance contract when either A or B may initiate conflict. I will draw some general implications, which hold under both cases 1 and 2 in the preceding analysis, for C to choose different types of commitments, $Z = (q^*, r^*)$ and s^*.

1. C is more likely to choose a $(1, 1)$ unconditional commitment than any other type of commitment as λ increases, δ increases, and μ decreases.
2. C is more likely to choose a $(q = 1$ and $r < 1)$ conditional commitment than a $(1, 1)$ unconditional commitment when λ decreases, δ decreases, μ increases, and p increases.
3. C is more likely to choose a $(1, 0)$ pure conditional commitment than a $(1, 1)$ unconditional commitment and a $(q = 1$ and $r < 1)$ conditional commitment when λ decreases, δ decreases, and p increases.
4. C is more likely to choose a $(q \in (0, 1)$ and $r < 1)$ probabilistic commitment than a $(1, 1)$ unconditional, $(q = 1$ and $r < 1)$ conditional, and $(1, 0)$ pure conditional commitment when λ decreases, δ decreases, μ increases, and p decreases.
5. C is more likely to choose a $0 < s^* < 1$ probabilistic commitment or a $s^* = 1$ unconditional commitment than a $(q = 1$ and $r < 1)$ conditional and $(1, 0)$ pure conditional commitment when actions are unobservable.

6

Testing the Implications for Alliance Design

My theory of commitment design presented in Chapter 5 demonstrates that two types of mechanisms – conditional commitment and probabilistic commitment – can be effective instruments for balancing the demands for deterrence against the effects of moral hazard on conflict. Probabilistic commitments have the added advantage of minimizing moral hazard distortions on the expected bargaining settlement. The question addressed in this chapter is whether these mechanisms – which satisfy the third party's maximization problem in the theory – are actually implemented in practice for the same purposes they are designed to accomplish according to the theory. In this chapter, I test various effects derived from the theory in Chapter 5.

The theory produces a number of testable predictions that apply to military alliances. In this chapter, I analyze the following four implications: (1) incongruent policy preferences between alliance members increase the likelihood that alliances will be probabilistic; (2) sizable disparities in capabilities between weak protégés and powerful third-party defenders increase the chances that states will form probabilistic commitments; (3) more powerful protégés are more likely to receive conditional types of commitments; and (4) the presence of unobservable actions tends to favor probabilistic alliances and unconditional commitments over conditional alternatives.

Each of these implications makes a statement about how specific factors will affect the choice of commitment when that commitment is compared with other commitments. In this chapter, I first summarize the explanation for the theoretical implications and generate hypotheses of the expected effects. I then adapt these hypotheses to the structure of the available data by creating variables that can serve as proxies for some of the explanatory factors derived from the theory. I test the effects in two datasets of deterrent alliances: a dataset of alliance agreements generated from the typology in Chapter 2 and a dyadic dataset used in Chapter 4.

Foreign Policy Preferences

The first implication states that the preferences of the third party make a difference in how the commitment is designed. Not only do preferences regarding security matter, but so, too, do the third party's preferences for policy or how the dispute gets resolved if war can be avoided. Incongruent policy preferences increase the likelihood the third party will form a probabilistic alliance relative to any other kind of deterrent alliance. The theory explains how commitments that promise full support, such as unconditional and conditional agreements, may result in extreme policy outcomes, whereas probabilistic commitments induce moderate policy settlements more closely aligned with the third parties' preferences.

The explanation for these effects given in the theory highlights the impact of moral hazard on policy outcomes as well as conflict. Third-party defenders whose preferences for foreign policies diverge from those of the protégé are more likely to be sensitive to the distortions in policy outcomes that result from moral hazard. Committing to the protégé expands the bargaining clout of the protégé by increasing the probability that it will win a war, which the third party can then leverage to achieve a bargaining settlement more consistent with its own policy preferences. The more assistance the protégé expects to receive from the third party, the more a full commitment distorts the policy settlement. This is not a problem if the third party has similar policy preferences to those of the protégé, but the more the third party's ideal policy outcome diverges from that of the protégé, the more an unconditional deterrent alliance will shift policy outcomes away from the third party. On the other hand, as the preferences of the third party and protégé converge, then commitments guaranteeing transfers are more likely to result in policy outcomes that both alliance members find beneficial. Consequently, the third party's optimal choice of alliance mechanism is directly related to how similar its policy preferences are to those of the protégé. The more divergent these preferences, the less likely it is that the third party will form unconditional deterrent alliances.

In these circumstances, what type of commitment best serves the interests of the third party? Conditional commitments may have a similar distortionary effect to unconditional commitments. Although conditional commitments stipulate that intervention depends on some action such as the adversary attacking, the protégé expects full support from the third party if there is a war. Thus, its expected payoff from war is the same as it is with an unconditional commitment. The difference is that with a conditional commitment, the protégé is not guaranteed to receive its expected war payoff if it attacks first. It nevertheless has an incentive to bargain aggressively to extract an offer equal to what it can get if the adversary attacks, there is a war, and the third party delivers on its promise to provide full support. If the third party cannot limit its transfers in war, then both a conditional and an unconditional deterrent alliance will result in extreme bargaining settlements. On the other hand, abandoning the protégé leads to a policy outcome at the other extreme. Thus, committing fully and abandoning the protégé result in different but extreme outcomes that, for third parties with moderate policy tastes, are far from ideal.

In contrast, a probabilistic commitment mechanism may induce a more moderate policy settlement in bargaining. To see why, recall that probabilistic alliances create uncertainty about the third party's likelihood of intervening with unlimited assistance. The uncertainty about the likelihood of receiving assistance from the third party causes the protégé to shoulder some risk because it cannot know whether it will receive assistance. If there is war, the protégé will get the higher expected benefit from receiving the third party's support. However, there is also a chance that the third party will not support it, in which case its expected payoff is considerably lower. Knowing that if there is a war it only has a chance to receive the extreme outcome it favors but may end up instead getting an extremely unfavorable outcome reduces the protégé's expected payoffs in war. As a result, the protégé will bargain less aggressively, holding out only for an amount roughly equal to its lower expected war payoff. A probabilistic commitment, therefore, restrains the protégé from pushing aggressively for an extreme bargaining outcome.

Similarly, probabilistic commitments also curb the adversary's behavior. Compared with a situation in which the third party chooses to abandon the protégé, the adversary cannot demand too much if the third party gives a probabilistic commitment because the protégé may decide it is worth the risk to gamble on the chance the third party might intervene in a war. Hence, to reach a bargaining settlement that is short of war, the disputants have an incentive to respond to probabilistic commitments by finding some intermediate division of the pie. As the theory demonstrates, not only does this produce a policy outcome that is closer to the third party's ideal point, but, in theory, the third party can also actually bring about its ideal bargaining outcome by setting the probability that it intervenes at a level that just produces an expected payoff of war equal to the third party's preferred division of the pie. Such clever manipulation would induce the third party's ideal settlement.

The implication for the empirical relationship between the third party's policy preferences and the choice of commitment is that the closer the third party's and protégé's preferences are, the more likely that they will choose an unconditional deterrent alliance. The more divergent these preferences are, the more likely that the third party will choose a probabilistic alliance over any other type of alliance. This gives the first hypothesis:

H1. As *preference incongruence* between the alliance partners with the most divergent policy preferences increases, the type of the alliance commitment is more likely to be *probabilistic* than *unconditional, conditional,* or *pure conditional.*

Testing the Implications for Alliance Design

To test this hypothesis, I use *s-score* to proxy for the preference incongruence measure. S-scores approximate the similarity of alliance members' foreign policy interests (Signorino and Ritter 1999). To obtain a measure of preference incongruence, I invert the score. For bilateral alliances, I take the preference incongruence between the two prospective alliance partners in the year the alliance is signed. Because some alliances are multilateral, I measure s-scores for all possible pairings of alliance members and use the most incongruent pairing as the representative score for the alliance. The hypothesis predicts that preference incongruence should be positively associated with probabilistic commitments when those commitments are compared with any other kind of deterrent alliance. In the analysis that follows, I estimate this relationship in the agreement data where s-scores can be measured for prospective alliance partners at the time the alliance was formed. The results of this estimation are presented in Tables 6.1 and 6.2.

Capabilities of the Third Party

The second implication analyzed in this chapter asserts that the effect of the third party's capabilities affects the design of the alliance agreement. It is clear by now that a third party's preferences over policies affect its choice of commitment type; the less the third party shares the protégé's policy preferences, the more likely it will be to extend a probabilistic commitment. As explained in Chapter 5, choosing a probabilistic commitment also depends on how powerful the third party is relative to the protégé. Because weak third-party defenders do not have a lot to offer, their impact on the protégé's war payoff is relatively small. Strong third parties, though, may make a dramatic impact on bargaining, especially if they cannot limit the amount of their support once they are involved in a war. The benefit to the protégé is most stark if the protégé is relatively weak. A strong protégé may need only a modest contribution to accomplish its war objectives. In this circumstance, even if a third party possesses overwhelming strength, it will be required to supply only the small amount necessary to cover the gap between the capabilities of the protégé and those of the adversary. We may conclude, then, that the distortion of moral hazard is greatest when the difference between the capabilities of the third party and protégé is large. If third-party intervention is guaranteed, then the greater the difference in alliance partners' capabilities, the more the policy settlement will differ from what it would have been without the third party's assistance. If the third party's ideal position is somewhere between those extremes, then an unconditional or conditional commitment will result in a less than ideal settlement. As we have seen already, the third party can induce moderation on the part of the protégé by choosing a probabilistic commitment. Thus, the greater the difference in capabilities between the third party and protégé, the more likely the resulting commitment will be probabilistic. It is possible to state the second hypothesis:

H2. If an alliance has a major power and at least one revisionist minor power, the alliance agreement will more likely be a *probabilistic* commitment than an *unconditional*, *conditional*, or *pure conditional* commitment.

This relationship is nuanced in the theory, and the subtleties need to be addressed in the specification of the model. First, in the theory, the capability of the third party is a measure of how much the third party's full contribution might help the protégé. The wider the gap between the third party and protégé, the more likely it is that the alliance is probabilistic. Second, if the allies have similar preferences, then the disparity in capabilities should have no effect, regardless of how wide the gap may be. Thus, to test the hypothesized effect, it is important to establish both disparities in power and preference among alliance partners. This is possible using the agreement data. I first create an indicator variable called *major-minor alliance* that flags all alliances containing a major power and at least one minor power. This variable identifies alliances with stark power disparities. Then I create another variable, called *revisionist minor power*, that indicates whether an alliance has a revisionist minor power. To generate this variable, I use the same measure of revisionism that I used in Chapter 4.

The variable of interest for the hypothesis test lies at the intersection of these two variables, for we want to know whether prospective alliances containing a major power and a revisionist minor power at the time the alliance was formed were more likely to be probabilistic. To create this variable, which is called *major-revisionist minor*, I code as 1 all alliances that are both a *major-minor alliance* and have a *revisionist minor power*. Then, I recode the other two variables as 0 if the *revisionist minor power* variable is equal to 1. This generates three mutually exclusive categories, making it possible to evaluate separately the effects of prospective alliances in which (1) there are disparities in power between signatories but the less powerful allies are not revisionist, (2) at least one revisionist minor power is present but there is no power disparity that comes with having a major ally present, and (3) there are disparities in power and there is at least one revisionist weaker power. The last category should have a positive effect on the likelihood that the alliance is probabilistic. I analyze this hypothesis in the agreement data, and the results are presented in Tables 6.1 and 6.2.

Capabilities of the Protégé

The third hypothesis claims that the protégé's power has an effect on the form of a security commitment. We just described how sizable disparities in alliance partners' capabilities predict probabilistic commitments. As the protégé's capabilities increase, this gap narrows, minimizing the moral hazard distortion. From the third party's perspective, it is more willing to give a

Testing the Implications for Alliance Design 133

guaranteed security commitment if so doing does not embolden the protégé to insist on a policy outcome that the third party finds unattractive. This holds true even if the third party's preferences for policy and security diverge somewhat from those of the protégé. If a protégé does not require much support because it is relatively strong compared with the adversary, then offering guaranteed security boosts deterrence without imposing unacceptable harm to the policy interests of the third party. However, there will still be some moral hazard distortion for even small amounts of divergence in alliance partners' preferences, especially because unrestrained protégés may gain an additional benefit by initiating the conflict. This type of moral hazard can be minimized by imposing conditions on intervention. We now have the third hypothesis:

H3. As the *protégé's capability* increases, the alliance it holds is more likely to be *conditional* or *pure conditional* than either *unconditional* or *probabilistic*.

Generating the variable for *protégé's capability* is accomplished by calculating the strength of the prospective initiator in a dyad relative to the target. This involves computing the proportion of the prospective initiator's capabilities to the combined capabilities of both the initiator and target in the dyad. Thus, I estimate the hypothesized effect in the directed dyad data and present the results in Tables 6.3 and 6.4.

Contiguity and Hidden Actions

Finally, the type of alliance depends on whether actions leading to war are observable. The theory shows that, under some conditions, third parties prefer to create alliances that specify conditions under which their treaty obligations become active. However, even under these circumstances, conditional alliance contracts are impossible to enforce when the actions that serve as the conditions are unobservable to the third party. When actions are not observable, probabilistic and unconditional commitments are more likely to emerge than any conditional or pure conditional types of alliance commitments.

Several factors might limit the third party's ability to observe destabilizing actions in crises. These are discussed in greater detail in Chapter 7, in which a version of this hypothesis is tested qualitatively. In this chapter, I use a measure of contiguity as a proxy for observability, because it is easier to observe provocations between states whose borders are far away from each other. Intuition suggests that it is more difficult to observe and punish provocations the closer disputants are to one another.

To measure contiguity, I create an ordinal categorical variable that increases in value the closer dyad states' borders are to one another. The variable is coded 0 if the disputants (dyad states) are farther than 400 miles away from each other, 1 if they are between 150 and 400 miles from each other, 2 if that distance is 25 to 150 miles, 3 if it is 13 to 24 miles, 4 if it is 1 to 12 miles, and 5 if states are directly contiguous by land. One possible objection is that the most significant loss of observability should occur at the border and a better measure is an indicator for direct land contiguity. However, advances in naval and air force technology over the past century make it possible for disputants to clash with one another if they are within sea or air range of each other. The 2010 sinking of the *Cheonan*, a South Korean naval ship, underscores this point. Although North Korea, which is widely believed to have carried out the attack on the *Cheonan*, shares a land border with South Korea, the incident took place at sea, where it was difficult to verify at the time what caused the sinking and whether North Korea was responsible. For robustness, I conduct the analysis using both measures of contiguity; the results are even stronger using the contiguity dummy variable. Nevertheless, I report the weaker effects from the ordinal variable, as I believe it better approximates a concept of increasing shifts in unobservability of destabilizing actions.

I estimate the effect of contiguity on the choice of alliances in the directed dyad data, as the agreement data do not account for the distance between all the alliance members and all the targets of the alliance. The results are presented in Tables 6.3 and 6.4.

Research Design and Data

I test these four hypotheses using two datasets. The first is the directed dyad-year alliance dataset introduced in Chapter 4. The second is an agreement dataset, in which the unit of analysis is the alliance agreement in the year that it was formed. The agreement data differ from the directed dyad-year design, in which the unit of analysis is a dyad year, because dyad years extend data on alliances beyond the year of the alliance formation. Both approaches have strengths and weaknesses. The agreement data make it possible to look inside the alliance commitment and to analyze the effect of key determinants on leaders' decisions to form the alliance. On the other hand, the dyad data have the advantage of large numbers of observations and available covariates, as well as the ability to investigate the effects in the years after the alliance was formed.

A key distinction between the dyad-year and agreement datasets is that by using data on directed dyads, one can draw inferences about the likelihood that a state will hold a given commitment in any given dyad year. The downside is that in the analysis of directed dyads, an observed relationship reveals only the likelihood that a dyad state *receives* or *holds* an alliance. As a result, there are limits to using dyad-year data to make causal inferences about the third party's strategic decision to *form* a commitment. Another shortcoming of using directed dyads is that institutional inertia may make it difficult over time to change a commitment to meet new demands – old alliances may not reflect new realities because of the costs associated with changing the alliance.

Testing the Implications for Alliance Design

The agreement data also have limitations. First, there are constraints on what variables may be imported into this framework. Many alliances are multilateral, making it problematic to disentangle characteristics associated with particular alliance members and to identify purposive strategic effects. Another problem is that there are relatively few alliances in the data, and the key explanatory variables are measured only in the year each alliance is formed.

Given the data imperfections present in each type of analysis, I report the results from both approaches. Each approach makes it possible to test different relationships derived from the theory. To the extent that consistent effects emerge across both types of designs, we may gain confidence that the results are not due to the shortcomings particular to each approach and that the effects instead provide support for the relationships in question.

I estimate two multinomial logit models to test the hypothesized comparisons. Hypotheses 1 and 2 are tested using the agreement data, and hypotheses 3 and 4 are analyzed with the dyadic data. The dependent variable for both models is a nominal outcome variable ordered by the types of alliances examined in the theory. Thus, the variable includes categories for *unconditional* deterrent commitment, *conditional* deterrent commitment, *pure conditional* deterrent commitment, *probabilistic* deterrent commitment, and *no commitment*. In the agreement data, the no commitment category contains neutrality pacts, and, in the dyad dataset, it contains either dyads in which the initiator holds a neutrality pact or no alliance at all. To isolate the effect of specific commitment mechanisms, each commitment category is mutually exclusive of other commitment types, even though it is possible for a dyad initiator to have more than one type of commitment targeting the dyad target, and some agreements contain more than one type of provision. The theory does not draw inferences about which commitments trump when more than one is in play. Therefore, the categories contain only agreements that have one clear provision that corresponds with one of the commitment categories in the typology.

In the agreement data, I include some control variables, as there are other possible explanations for the selection of types of commitments. The first is the *multilateral* variable, which is an indicator variable that identifies alliances that have more than two signatories. It is plausible that divergence of preferences among many signatories makes agreement on provisions difficult. This raises the contracting costs, and may thus increase the likelihood that signatories will write an ambiguous alliance agreement. Because alliances with ambiguous language are coded as *probabilistic* commitments, *multilateral* alliances may be more likely to lead to *probabilistic* commitments.

Another control variable is *start year*, which simply indicates the year in which the alliance was formed. Benson (2011), for example, shows that most alliances traditionally regarded as defensive pacts were signed after the onset of World War II, and the temporal pattern for these signings depends on the type of commitment included in the agreement. Temporal factors may lead to these

TABLE 6.1. *Multinomial Logit Estimate of the Likelihood an Agreement Is a Given Type (Agreement Data, 1816–2000)*

	(1) Probabilistic vs. Unconditional	(2) Probabilistic vs. Conditional	(3) Probabilistic vs. Pure Conditional
Preference incongruence	2.625** (1.013)	3.103** (0.753)	2.592* (1.242)
Major-revisionist minor	2.767* (1.199)	1.604* (0.777)	0.586 (1.029)
Multilateral	1.818* (0.743)	1.300* (0.619)	1.922+ (1.000)
Start year	0.005 (0.008)	0.003 (0.007)	0.018* (0.008)
Major-minor agreement	0.736 (0.662)	1.050+ (0.606)	1.564+ (0.008)
Revisionist minor power	−1.336 (1.143)	−2.166* (1.070)	−1.436 (1.572)
Constant	−12.299 (15.800)	−8.305 (14.631)	−34.731* (15.089)
N	279		
Log-Lik intercept only	−387.126		
Log-Lik full model	−338.746		
Likelihood ratio	96.759**		
McFadden's pseudo R^2	0.125		
AIC	2.629		
BIC	38.390		

Standard errors in parentheses.
$+p < 0.10$; $*p < 0.05$; $**p < 0.01$

waves of agreement signings. If types of commitments are trendy for reasons not explicated in the theory, it is important to control for them in the models. Hence, the models using the agreement data include both *multilateral* and *start year* control variables.

Empirical Analysis

I now analyze the first model, which estimates the logistic effect of *preference incongruence* and *major-revisionist minor* on the type of commitment. Table 6.1 presents three comparisons of categories of the dependent variable: *probabilistic* versus *unconditional*, *probabilistic* versus *conditional*, and *probabilistic* versus *pure conditional*. For all three comparisons, *preference incongruence* is positively associated with *probabilistic commitments*. This effect is statistically significant at the $p < 0.01$ level when *probabilistic commitments* are compared with *unconditional* and *conditional* commitments, and it is significant at the $p < 0.05$ level when they are compared with *pure conditional commitments*. The coefficients in all three cases are relatively large. As can be seen from the display of the substantive effects in Table 6.2, the impact of *preference incongruence* on the likelihood that a *probabilistic commitment* will be formed is striking. Increasing *preference incongruence* one positive standard deviation from the mean changes the predicted probability that an alliance agreement is *probabilistic* from 0.0330 to 0.1060, which is an impressive 221 percent change. The result is especially stark when we consider that

TABLE 6.2. *Substantive Effects of Changes in Predictors on the Predicted Probability That an Agreement Is a Given Type (Agreement Data, 1816–2000)*

	No Deterrent Commitment	Probabilistic	Pure Conditional	Conditional	Unconditional
Preference incongruence					
At mean	0.4987	0.0330	0.0306	0.2944	0.1433
+1 s.d.	0.7602	0.1060	0.0189	0.0313	0.0837
Difference	0.2615	0.0729	−0.0117	−0.2631	−0.0595
% change	0.5243	2.2092	−0.3828	−0.8937	−0.4156
Major-revisionist minor					
No	0.4987	0.0330	0.0306	0.2944	0.1433
Yes	0.3615	0.1783	0.0919	0.3198	0.0486
Difference	−0.1373	0.1453	0.0613	0.0253	−0.0946
% change	−0.2752	4.3995	2.0044	0.0861	−0.6606
Multilateral					
No	0.4987	0.0330	0.0306	0.2944	0.1433
Yes	0.0801	0.2154	0.0292	0.5237	0.1517
Difference	−0.4187	0.1824	−0.0014	0.2292	0.0084
% change	−0.8395	5.5243	−0.0453	0.7786	0.0587
Start year					
At mean	0.4987	0.0330	0.0306	0.2944	0.1433
+1 s.d.	0.4999	0.0331	0.0301	0.2942	0.1428
Difference	0.0012	0.0001	−0.0005	−0.0003	−0.0005
% change	0.0023	0.0018	−0.0157	−0.0009	−0.0034
Major-minor agreement					
No	0.4987	0.0330	0.0306	0.2944	0.1433
Yes	0.2818	0.1124	0.0218	0.3505	0.2335
Difference	−0.2169	0.0793	−0.0088	0.0561	0.0902
% change	−0.4349	2.4033	−0.2879	0.1906	0.6297
Revisionist minor power					
No	0.4987	0.0330	0.0306	0.2944	0.1433
Yes	0.4450	0.0056	0.0218	0.4353	0.0924
Difference	−0.0537	−0.0274	−0.0088	0.1408	−0.0509
% change	−0.1077	−0.8306	−0.2876	0.4783	−0.3554

Predicted probabilities are estimated by increasing continuous covariates one s.d. and dummy variables from 0 to 1 while holding dummy variables at 0 and all other variables at their mean. The difference is calculated by subtracting the changed predicted probability from the baseline predicted probability.

the impact of a positive shift in *preference incongruence* reduces the likelihood of all the other types of deterrent commitments. For example, increasing *preference congruence* by one standard deviation decreases the probability of an *unconditional commitment* from 0.1433 to 0.0837. The results from model 1 provide strong evidence in support of hypothesis 1, leading to the conclusion that in the alliance agreements formed between 1816 and 2000, prospective allies that had widely divergent foreign policy preferences were more likely to form probabilistic deterrent commitments than all the other types of deterrent commitments.

The second finding in the model lends support to hypothesis 2. The results are presented in Table 6.1. *Major-revisionist minor* is positively associated with *probabilistic commitments* in every comparison. The effect is statistically significant in two of those cases – when *positive commitments* are compared with *unconditional* and *conditional commitments*. We see the largest effect of any covariate in the comparison of *probabilistic* versus *unconditional*. The coefficient is 2.767, and it is statistically significant at the $p < 0.05$ level. The substantive interpretation of this estimate, as shown in Table 6.2, is that when an alliance forms, the probability that the agreement will be *probabilistic* is 0.1783 when a major power joins with at least one revisionist minor power, compared with 0.0330 if the power configuration within the alliance is structured any other way. This amounts to a 440 percent change in the predicted probability. When contrasted with the 66 percent decrease in the predicted probability of an *unconditional commitment*, it is evident that large disparities in capabilities between major and revisionist minor power allies strongly predict that the alliance will be *probabilistic* when compared with *unconditional commitments*.

The model also confirms that *major-revisionist minor* has a positive and significant effect on *probabilistic* versus *conditional*. In the case of *probabilistic* versus *pure conditional*, the effect is not statistically significant, probably because differences may be subtler between neighboring categories. Additionally, there are relatively few *probabilistic* and *pure conditional commitments*, which may weaken the effects when they are compared with one another. Overall, the findings for all three comparisons support hypothesis 2.

The control variables in model 1 are also related to the design of security commitments. *Multilateral* alliances are more likely to be probabilistic than any other type of alliance, and there is also a positive relationship between *start year* and the comparison between *probabilistic* and *pure conditional commitments*, implying that, over time, signatories are more likely to adopt *probabilistic* versus *pure conditional commitments*. Removing these control variables from the model does not significantly alter the substantive findings for the variables of interest.

Turning to model 2, which analyzes the presence of commitments in the dyadic data, we see that in every comparison *protégé's capabilities* is more likely to result in either *conditional* or *pure conditional commitments*. The coefficient estimates are reported in Table 6.3. In all four cases, *protégé's*

TABLE 6.3. *Multinomial Logit Estimate of the Likelihood That a Prospective Dyad Initiator Possesses a Given Type of Alliance Commitment (Directed Dyad Data, 1816–2000)*

	(1) Conditional vs. Probabilistic	(2) Conditional vs. Unconditional	(3) Pure Conditional vs. Probabilistic	(4) Pure Conditional vs. Unconditional
Protégé's capabilities	2.031** (0.147)	1.930** (0.376)	2.943** (0.207)	2.841** (0.404)
Contiguity	−0.171** (0.026)	−0.187** (0.046)	−0.283** (0.044)	−0.299** (0.059)
Constant	1.661** (0.095)	3.463** (0.189)	−1.574** (0.152)	0.228** (0.225)
N	145059			
Log-Lik intercept only	−136709.641			
Log-Lik full model	−133435.037			
Likelihood ratio	6549.207**			
McFadden's pseudo R^2	0.024			
AIC	1.840			
BIC	−6454.127			

Standard errors in parentheses.
$+p < 0.10$; $*p < 0.05$; $**p < 0.01$

capabilities is statistically significant at the $p < 0.01$ level, implying that increases in the protégé's strength result in conditional types of commitments (including *pure conditional commitments*) rather than *probabilistic* or *unconditional commitments*. The largest effects are on the selection of *pure conditional commitments*. As shown in Table 6.4, the predicted probability that a prospective initiator in a directed dyad possesses a *pure conditional commitment* is 0.0184 when *protégé's capabilities* is set to its mean value, and it changes to 0.0437 if *protégé's capabilities* increases by one standard deviation. Interpreting this effect, a positive shift in the protégé's strength relative to the adversary increases the change in the predicted probability that the protégé possesses a *pure conditional commitment* by 138 percent.

The model also predicts that stronger protégés are more likely to possess *conditional commitments*. As *protégé's capabilities* increases, the predicted probability that a protégé possesses a *conditional commitment* increases from 0.3610 to 0.5284, which is a 46 percent change. Consistent with hypothesis 3, the model confirms that increases in the relative capabilities of the protégé decrease the chance that the protégé will possess either a *probabilistic* or *unconditional commitment* and increase the likelihood that the protégé will receive either a *conditional* or *pure conditional* type.

TABLE 6.4. *Substantive Effects of Changes in Predictors on the Predicted Probability That a Prospective Dyad Initiator Possesses a Given Type of Alliance Agreement (Directed Dyad Data, 1816–2000)*

	No Deterrent Commitment	Probabilistic	Pure Conditional	Conditional	Unconditional
Protégé's capabilities					
At mean	0.5798	0.0347	0.0184	0.3610	0.0061
+1 s.d.	0.4506	−0.0198	0.0437	0.5284	−0.0029
Difference	−0.1292	−0.0545	0.0253	0.1674	−0.0090
% change	−0.2228	−1.5706	1.3750	0.4637	−1.4754
Contiguity					
At mean	0.5798	0.0347	0.0184	0.3610	0.0061
+1 s.d.	0.5801	0.0402	0.0161	0.3564	0.0072
Difference	0.0003	0.0055	−0.0023	−0.0046	0.0011
% change	0.0005	0.1585	−0.1250	−0.0127	0.1803

Predicted probabilities are estimated by increasing continuous covariates one s.d. and dummy variables from 0 to 1 while holding dummy variables at 0 and all other variables at their mean. The difference is calculated by subtracting the changed predicted probability from the baseline predicted probability.

Now, let us examine the evidence for hypothesis 4, which, if confirmed, corroborates the theoretical expectation that the design of alliance agreements depends on the observability of the actions between alliance members and their prospective disputants. To test the hypothesized relationship, I analyze the impact of ordinal increases in contiguity on the likelihood that the prospective dyad initiator, which in the data proxies for the alliance protégé, possesses a *probabilistic commitment*. From the results of the model presented in Table 6.3, it is clear that *contiguity* is positively associated with *probabilistic* and *unconditional commitments* in all the comparisons. Both *conditional* and *unconditional commitments* are less likely to obtain when the prospective disputants in the dyad are in close geographic proximity, presumably because hostilities between geographically proximate states are more difficult to observe and, thus, to include as conditions in a commitment. As expected, then, *conditional* and *pure conditional commitments* do not stack up so well when there is not much distance between the potential disputants. Substantively, increasing *contiguity* by one ordinal category increases the predicted probability of a *probabilistic commitment* from 0.0347 to 0.0402, which corresponds to a 16 percent increase. And, the predicted probability of *unconditional* changes by 18 percent, from 0.0061 to 0.0072. The effect on *pure conditional* and *conditional commitments* is negative. Although the substantive effects are not as dramatic as the relationships tested in the other three hypotheses, they nevertheless supply support for hypothesis 4. A variable that more directly measures

Testing the Implications for Alliance Design

the observability of disputants' actions might yield stronger results. I take this matter up in a qualitative test of comparative case studies in Chapter 7.

Summary

In this chapter, I analyze four main implications derived from my theory of commitment design. First, incongruence of policy preferences between the third party and the protégé increases the likelihood that the third party will form a probabilistic alliance over any other kind of deterrent alliance, because uncertainty about whether the third party will intervene induces moderate policy settlements. Second, when major powers sign alliances with revisionist minor powers, then third parties also prefer probabilistic to other types of commitments. The reason is that significant gaps in capabilities between alliance partners exacerbate moral hazard. Third, the greater the protégé's capabilities relative to its adversary, the more likely a third party will form a conditional or pure conditional commitment versus either a probabilistic or unconditional commitment. Reducing the size of the required contribution from the third party minimizes the moral hazard distortion on policy settlements, making conditional commitments more suitable mechanisms for restraining the protégé's incentive to initiate crises. Fourth, a third party whose protégé is located in close geographic proximity to the adversary is unlikely to choose conditional types of commitments, because the conditions cannot be enforced. Instead, it will form probabilistic or unconditional commitments.

The results of the analysis confirm that, in practice, leaders' decisions to choose particular commitment mechanisms depend on the hypothesized factors, including the third party's policy preferences, the amount of contribution made by the third party, the protégé's capabilities relative to the adversary, and the observability of the disputants' actions leading to war. In general, unconditional deterrent commitments are rarely positively associated with any of these factors. In the analysis, they are negatively correlated with the first three factors, because the risks and associated costs of moral hazard are too high for the third party to justify an unconditional commitment. The preferred mechanisms for dealing with moral hazard in these cases are either probabilistic commitments, pure conditional commitments, or conditional deterrent commitments. The conditional and pure conditional commitments tend to be selected when conflicts can be observed and the distortion to policy does not dominate the third party's decision to commit. The last of the four factors does positively correlate with unconditional commitments. Unobservable actions can lead to probabilistic or unconditional commitments; the selection of unconditional commitments in these circumstances is somewhat counter-intuitive, as hidden actions may exacerbate moral hazard. Nevertheless, third parties will select such commitments when conditioning on actions is not possible and going with a probabilistic commitment does not do enough to deter the aggressiveness of the adversary.

7

Deterrent Commitments in East Asia

This chapter presents a comparative historical analysis of cases of U.S. commitment making in East Asia during the 1950s. The purpose of the analysis is to examine one of the main causal mechanisms in the theory that explains why leaders might select probabilistic deterrence commitments rather than conditional commitment alternatives when trying to balance extended deterrence with ally restraint. The analysis demonstrates that when disputants can take actions in a crisis to initiate or escalate conflict and those actions are hidden from third-party defenders, then a third party intending to ally with one of the disputants will prefer to extend a probabilistic deterrence commitment to its prospective ally. On the other hand, when the disputants' actions are clearly observable to the third party, then, all else being equal, the third party will design a commitment conditional on the disputants' actions leading to war. The particular cases presented here were selected because they have several features in common, making it possible to hold some factors constant while comparing the observability of disputants' actions and the third party's choice of commitment type across all cases.

The examination of this historical evidence complements the quantitative tests in Chapters 4 and 6 in several ways. The first contribution of the case studies considered here is that they show the application of the theory to security commitments beyond formal military alliances. In this chapter, I compare Truman's 1950 policy to neutralize the Taiwan Strait, which was not announced as part of a formal military alliance, with three formal military alliances signed by the United States in East Asia between 1950 and 1954. On September 8, 1951, the United States and Japan signed a formal military alliance. The United States and the Republic of Korea (ROK) entered into a mutual defense treaty on October 1, 1953. Then, just a few months later, on December 2, 1954, the United States signed another defensive treaty with the Republic of China (ROC) government on Taiwan.

Deterrent Commitments in East Asia

By contrast, the commitments in the observational data analyzed in Chapters 4 and 6 include only formal military alliances. However, the theoretical implications for commitment design are also relevant for extended deterrence commitments not formalized in military treaties. Confirming that the causal processes described in the theory of commitments influenced U.S. leaders' selection of both military alliance agreements and formal extended deterrence commitments shows the breadth of the theory's application.

Second, studying the historical cases provides an opportunity to examine directly the connection between the variables of interest and the design of the commitment: Do the variables matter to real decision makers? Under what conditions? Statistical tests permit us to estimate these relationships, but the inferences depend on the accuracy of the measurements of the key variables. However, some of the variables that were included in the empirical models in Chapters 4 and 6 are difficult to measure quantitatively; thus, I employed proxies that substitute for the real variables of interest. As such, they are "next best" approximations. For instance, to show the effect of hidden actions on commitment design, I used contiguity as a proxy for hidden action, because it becomes increasingly difficult for third parties to observe the sequence of hostilities in a dispute as the distance between disputants shortens. To be satisfied that the third party's inability to observe hostilities does, in fact, influence its choice of commitment, it is instructive to see how decision makers considered this factor in a historical context.

Third, a close reading of the historical record also highlights subtleties missed in the quantitative analysis, resulting in a rich and more nuanced accounting of these relationships. Categorizing data requires adopting coding rules, which are necessarily coarse, and glossing over some of the historical details. For example, the terminology of one of the alliance agreements in this chapter – the United States–ROK alliance – meets the definition of a probabilistic commitment in the coding scheme used in Chapters 4 and 6. However, the actual commitment has the force of a conditional commitment because supplementary treaty materials, not used for classifying and coding the agreements themselves, create expectations on the part of the signatories that the U.S. defensive obligations are indeed conditional on an external attack. Such historical detail justifies going beyond the quantitative analysis to gain additional perspective on how decision makers weigh different factors and ultimately design their security commitments.

A fourth benefit of the historical analysis presented here is that these four commitments share many characteristics with one another, differing mainly in one dimension. This enables us to isolate the effect of a single variable on the design of the commitments and thereby assess whether the causal mechanisms described by the theory correspond to leaders' actual decision making. Each of the four cases here involves the same third-party defender – the United States – and the same network of adversaries – the tripartite alliance of the Soviet Union, the People's Republic of China, and the Democratic People's Republic of Korea. In each case, the United States' primary objective in forming the commitment was to deter this adversary from challenging a protégé. Furthermore, each of the protégés was relatively weak and revisionist, causing the United States to be concerned about the security implications of moral hazard. What varies, then, is the observability of disputants' actions leading to war.

These shared characteristics facilitate the historical analysis. The similarities imply that there is not much variation in relative capabilities or in preferences, which are the other variables in the theory that affect the content of the commitment. In each of the four cases, the considerable disparities in power and preferences between the United States and its protégés indicate that countering the downsides of moral hazard should be a top priority. Therefore, the other independent variables in the theory can be held constant to isolate the effect of hidden actions when restraining the protégé is a main concern.

Other potentially confounding factors are also common across the cases. For example, the four commitments were formed during approximately the same time period, thus reducing the impact of time-variant influences. Moreover, the protégés shared geostrategic commonalities insofar as they were located in the same international neighborhood and, as either islands or peninsulas, had similar security needs. These commonalities across cases make it possible to focus on comparisons of the key variables in question: the observability of the disputants' actions leading to war and the type of commitment selected by the United States.

The chapter proceeds as follows: In the first section, I explain the hypothesis being tested in the analysis of the cases. The second section presents a comparison of the content of the four different deterrent commitments, showing how they vary from one another. In the next three sections, I examine each of the three conditional deterrent commitments in turn, explaining the factors that influenced the type of commitment that the United States offered in each case. The next step is to show how the unobservability of destabilizing moves in the Taiwan Strait led the United States to choose a probabilistic defensive commitment with Taiwan. The trend was the opposite in South Korea, where the establishment of the demilitarized zone improved the observability of destabilizing moves and led to a decrease in the probabilistic nature of the U.S. commitment to defend South Korea. The concluding section contains a summary of the main results.

Hidden Actions and Commitment Design

In this chapter, I test the following implication from the theory developed in Chapter 5: when the policy preferences of the third party and the protégé diverge (because the protégé is revisionist) and the third party is significantly stronger than the protégé, then the third-party defender will prefer to form a conditional deterrent commitment when the actions leading to war are observable, but the third party will prefer forming a probabilistic commitment when actions are not observable. This hypothesis, which is summarized in Table 7.1,

TABLE 7.1. *Effect of Hidden Actions on Commitment Type*

	Actions Leading to War	
	Observable	Unobservable
The optimal commitment given that the protégé is revisionist (and the U.S. is not) and there is a large disparity in capabilities between the U.S. and the protégé	Conditional	Probabilistic

is tested by analyzing the relationship between the differences in the degree of observability of the disputants' actions in crises and different types of U.S. security commitments. Because many confounding factors can be held constant across the cases, it is possible to evaluate the effects of the treatment condition (the observability of conflict initiation) on the variable of interest (the U.S. choice of commitment type). Because a conditional commitment stipulates that the defender's defensive obligation depends on whether the adversary initiated a hostile action, this type of commitment is not useful when disputants can take hidden actions. In these circumstances, the third party will select a probabilistic commitment to both deter the adversary and restrain the protégé.

An important step in the argument is to show that moral hazard influenced the United States to avoid unconditional commitments in all four cases. Showing that, in each case, the third party and the protégé held divergent preferences enables me to hold a key variable constant to isolate the effect of differences in the observability of disputants' actions. That is, according to the theory, when the third party is worried primarily about the danger of moral hazard, it will trade off some deterrence benefits of an unconditional commitment and instead form either conditional or probabilistic commitments. Given that these conditions obtained in all four cases, the central question is why the United States chose conditional commitments in three of the cases and a probabilistic commitment in one case. Table 7.2 provides a succinct breakdown of the distribution of cases over these two possible categories of commitment design.

TABLE 7.2. *Cases*

Actions Leading to War	
Observable	Unobservable
1951 US–Japan	1954 US–ROC
1950 US–ROC	
1953 US–ROK	

In this chapter, I argue that the difference in the content of commitments is explained mainly by the observability of disputants' actions.[1]

The key result confirmed in this chapter is that the difficulty of observing destabilizing actions by adversaries in the Taiwan Strait caused the U.S. leadership to introduce more ambiguity into its commitment with the ROC than with its other allies. Although the U.S. leadership worried about the downsides of moral hazard from extending defense commitments to both Chiang Kaishek and Syngman Rhee, the first president of South Korea, the commitments made to each differed in important respects. In the case of the ROC, the United States shifted its policy from conditional deterrence to probabilistic deterrence once it became difficult to observe initiations of conflict over the territories disputed by the ROC and China. This shift occurred when the United States moved its line of defense from the Taiwan Strait to a string of small islands located along China's mainland coast. With the ROK, the U.S. commitment was considerably less ambiguous than that with the ROC. Considering only the text of the agreement itself, the formal United States–ROK alliance is technically a probabilistic commitment, but supplementary treaty language supplied during the Senate ratification hearing and the armistice agreement conditioned any military assistance on an external attack and violation of the defensive line established along the demilitarized zone. This makes the form of the U.S. commitment clearly conditional.

Content of the Commitments

After the Japanese surrendered in 1945, the Allied Powers, led by the United States, administered Japan until September 8, 1951, when the San Francisco Treaty formally ended the Allied occupation. At the same time that the San Francisco Treaty was signed, the United States and Japan entered into a security alliance in which the United States committed

> to contribute to the maintenance of international peace and security in the Far East and to the security of Japan against armed attack from without, including assistance given at the express request of the Japanese Government to put down large-scale internal riots and disturbances in Japan, caused through instigation or intervention by an outside power or powers (Security Treaty Between the United States and Japan, Article I).

The alliance formally committed the United States to defend Japan, and the pledge to defend Japan from external aggression caused "through instigation or

---

[1] There also may have been subtle differences across these alliances related to the magnitudes of differences between the allies' relative preferences or their capabilities, and these differences may have contributed to the choice of probabilistic versus conditional commitments. In Chapter 8, I explore the possibility that disparities between allies' preferences and capabilities affect two current policies: the policy of the United States toward Taiwan and China, and China's formal military alliance with North Korea. However, in this chapter I focus mostly on the effect of unobservable actions on the 1950s alliances formed by the United States in East Asia.

intervention by an outside power" conditioned this defense on an adversary's challenge. Its structure, therefore, is a standard conditional deterrent alliance: if a foreign power initiated a challenge against Japan, the United States would defend it.

Unlike the United States–Japan agreement, the formal language of the mutual defense treaty between the United States and the Republic of Korea, signed on October 1, 1953, spelled out a probabilistic commitment. Article III of the alliance includes language that permits the possibility for the United States to avoid its commitment to defend Korea by tying the decision to intervene to "constitutional processes," but the exact criteria for ensuring the U.S. defense are never defined. The alliance states:

Each Party recognizes that an armed attack in the Pacific area on either of the Parties in territories now under their respective administrative control, or hereafter recognized by one of the Parties as lawfully brought under the administrative control of the other, would be dangerous to its own peace and safety and declares that it would act to meet the common danger in accordance with its constitutional processes (Mutual Defense Treaty Between the United States and the Republic of Korea, Article III).

Most of the language in Article III is standard in U.S. bilateral security agreements. The key ambiguous phrase is the one that delegates ultimate decision-making power to "constitutional processes." Uncertainty about how internal politics will affect future decisions creates a random quality to the commitment mechanism. The condition for activating this agreement can be seen in the terminology that obligates the United States to respond only in circumstances of an armed attack on territories under lawful "administrative control" of one of the signatories. Therefore, the terminology of the agreement gives the commitment the following structure: if any adversary attacks South Korea's sovereign territory, then the United States *may*, depending on domestic political factors (i.e., "constitutional processes"), defend South Korea.

During the ratification hearing for this alliance, the Senate Foreign Relations Committee added the following explanation for Article III to the treaty. The added treaty note was presented to and approved by the Republic of Korea:

It is the understanding of the United States that neither party is obligated, under Article III of the above Treaty, to come to the aid of the other except in case of an external armed attack against such party; nor shall anything in the present Treaty be construed as requiring the United States to give assistance to Korea *except in the event of an armed attack against territory* which has been recognized by the United States as lawfully brought under the administrative control of the Republic of Korea (Understanding of the United States; emphasis added).

This addition at once clarified both the commitment condition and the subsequent U.S. defensive obligation in the formal treaty. There was concern in the U.S. government that the unspecific language in the treaty regarding the defensive obligation might be interpreted by Syngman Rhee to cover the entire

Korean peninsula, as he perceived that the "administrative control" of the territory was under dispute. The additional language specifically ruled out any U.S. obligation to defend South Korea "*except* in the event of an *armed attack* against territory which has been *recognized* by the United States" (emphasis added). This statement conditioned U.S. intervention to an external attack on ROK sovereign territory, as legally recognized by the United States. Although the United States was obligated to defend the ROK if there was an attack against the ROK, the United States was not necessarily obligated by the terms of the treaty or ratification language to aid South Korea if South Korea initiated conflict. This statement, therefore, clarified the ambiguous language in the formal treaty. The conditionality of the United States–ROK treaty is affirmed by the armistice agreement ending the Korean War, which clarifies the territories under the lawful "administrative control" of the two Koreas. Thus, there is no ambiguity about the U.S. promise to the ROK: if there is an attack against any territory of the ROK delineated by the armistice agreement, then the United States will act to defend the ROK control over that territory. This commitment made by the United States to the ROK, which derives from treaty and multiple policy statements, is rather closer to a conditional than a probabilistic deterrent commitment.

Truman's decision to neutralize the Taiwan Strait in 1950 is another example of a conditional defensive commitment.[2] When war broke out in Korea in June 1950, the U.S. administration's plans to disentangle itself completely from the Chinese Nationalists were put on hold (Chang 1990, 60–62). Almost immediately, Secretary of State Dean Acheson, who only days earlier had been prepared to accept the inevitable fall of Taiwan, now advised Truman to interpose the Seventh Fleet in the Taiwan Strait to prevent the conflict in Korea from spreading to the Taiwan Strait (Christensen 1996, 134). On June 27, Truman made this decision official in a public announcement:

The attack upon Korea makes it plain beyond all doubt that communism has passed beyond the use of subversion to conquer independent nations and will now use armed invasion and war. It has defied the orders of the Security Council of the United Nations issued to preserve international peace and security. In these circumstances the occupation of Formosa [Taiwan] by Communist forces would be a direct threat to the security of the Pacific area and to United States forces performing their lawful and necessary functions in that area.

Accordingly I have ordered the Seventh Fleet *to prevent any attack on Formosa*. As a corollary of this action I am calling upon the Chinese Government on Formosa *to cease all air and sea operations against the Mainland*. The Seventh Fleet will see that this is done. The determination of the future status of Formosa must await the restoration of security in the Pacific, a peace settlement with Japan, or consideration by the

---

[2] Some of the following discussion related to the U.S. policy toward China during the Korean War and the first Taiwan Strait crisis draws on Benson (2006 101–148).

Deterrent Commitments in East Asia

United Nations (Finkelstein 1993, 333; Statement by the President, June 27, 1950; emphasis added).

The language in Truman's policy statement is clear. The Seventh Fleet was tasked with the responsibility of defending Taiwan from the PRC *and* preventing ROC operations against the mainland. This meets the definition of a pure conditional commitment defined in the theory in Chapter 5, because the United States effectively committed to defend Taiwan (the island of Formosa) if and only if the Chinese Communists initiated conflict. The commitment is a threat to punish whichever side disrupts the status quo.

In sum, the United States–Japan, United States–ROK, and Truman's neutralization commitments were similar in the sense that U.S. intervention was made conditional on some event that would trigger the U.S. defense obligation; in no instance did the United States promise to provide military support no matter the circumstances. Consequently, all three commitments belong to the class of conditional deterrent commitments. However, within that class, each commitment differed in important ways. Of the three, the United States–Japan agreement makes the strongest commitment to the defense of Japan, as the United States assumes responsibility for Japan's security and the condition for providing security is broader than that of the other two agreements. This latter point is clear from the language specifying the condition; it requires the United States to provide assistance in the case of any kind of "instigation" in addition to "intervention by an outside power."

At the other end of the category of conditional commitments lies the pure conditional commitment of the U.S. neutralization policy in the Taiwan Strait. Compared with the other two, the U.S. obligations to the ROC were the weakest, as the commitment clearly implied that the United States would not assist the ROC if it initiated conflict against the Chinese Communists. In fact, the United States even threatened to use the Seventh Fleet to deter hostilities initiated by the ROC. The United States–ROK commitment lay in between the other two. It is weaker than the United States–Japan commitment, because the United States is obligated to defend the ROK only in the event of "armed attack against territory which has been recognized by the United States as lawfully brought under the administrative control of the Republic of Korea." Not just any instigation or provocation by an outside power is sufficient to activate the U.S. obligations to provide military support; it takes an "armed attack" to trigger the defense obligation. On the other hand, the commitment does not impose as many conditions on defense as a pure conditional commitment, because the United States stops just short of declaring it will support South Korea *only if* it is attacked. Nevertheless, the United States brushes up against the edge of this boundary in taking the additional and uncharacteristic step of making it extremely clear that its obligations end if South Korea initiates conflict. The variation of the strength of these three commitments within the category of conditional commitment is depicted in Table 7.3.

TABLE 7.3. *Categorizing the Cases by Type*

		Observable	Unobservable
Conditional deterrent	Intervene if targeted adversary instigates any disturbance.	1951 US–Japan	
	Intervene if targeted adversary attacks.	1953 US–ROK	
Pure conditional deterrent	Intervene if and only if targeted adversary attacks.	1950 US–ROC	
Probabilistic deterrent	Maybe intervene.		1954 US–ROC

The fourth commitment to be evaluated in this chapter is the mutual defense treaty between the United States and the Republic of China, signed December 2, 1954. Article V states:

Each Party recognizes that an armed attack in the West Pacific Area directed against the territories of either of the Parties would be dangerous to its own peace and safety and declares that it would act to meet the common danger in accordance with its constitutional processes.

The commitment appears similar to the agreement with South Korea, but there are three key differences. First, the Eisenhower administration did not specify the legality of territorial administration as a condition for intervention. In fact, the next article of the agreement with the ROC limits automatic defense obligations to a few specific territories, such as Taiwan itself and the Pescadores, but deliberately leaves open the option for U.S. involvement "to such other territories as may be determined by mutual agreement" (Article VI).

Second, in a secret exchange of treaty notes with the ROC government, the United States weakened the commitment by emphasizing that military intervention would not be triggered automatically and would always be at the discretion of the United States. Secretary of State John Foster Dulles insisted to George K. C. Yeh, minister of foreign affairs for the Republic of China, that any use of force in the region by either side "will be a matter of joint agreement," meaning that even defense of Taiwan and the Pescadores was not automatic (Exchange of Notes, December 12, 1954). Knowing that the United States would use its discretion to determine whether to intervene even for Taiwan and the Pescadores would have caused the Nationalist government to view these secret treaty notes as enhancing the ambiguity of the alliance.

Third, both the ROC and ROK alliances included the ambiguous language about defensive obligations depending on "constitutional processes." However, as we have seen, the ambiguity about U.S. obligations to the ROK was clarified in the ratification process. This did not occur in the ROC case. Therefore, in contrast to the United States–ROK agreement, which clearly stipulated that the United States would defend if there was an external attack on sovereign South Korean territory, the United States–ROC agreement committed the United States to *maybe* defend, depending on the U.S. constitutional processes. Moreover, the contract did not specify any clear condition under which the agreement would be activated. Thus, the neutralization commitment that the United States made in 1950 to defend the ROC, which was unambiguously a pure conditional commitment, shifted in 1954 to a probabilistic deterrent commitment.

In sum, in the space of four years' time, the United States made four alliances in East Asia. The basic U.S. assurances to the ROC in 1950, Japan in 1951, and the ROK in 1953 were all conditional deterrent commitments obligating the United States to defend each protégé *if it was attacked*. To be sure, there were some subtle differences. The asymmetrical United States–Japan agreement was designed to deter threats while simultaneously preventing Japan from renewing aggression. The asymmetrical conditional commitment to the ROC in 1950 promised to defend Taiwan if and only if the ROC did not initiate conflict. In addition, whereas the formal alliance with the ROK is probabilistic, the actual United States commitment derived in conjunction with the supporting policy statements is a conditional deterrent commitment to defend South Korea if it is attacked. The probabilistic deterrent commitment to the ROC in 1954 is the most dissimilar to the other three. It provided for the possibility that the United States might intervene regardless of how a war involving the ROC occurs. The following sections will discuss what factors caused the United States to choose the type of commitment in each case.

Deterrence and Control in Postwar Japan

It is not surprising that the United States would avoid making an open-ended military commitment to Japan in 1951, as the United States had fresh memories of Japan as an aggressor and an adversary in the bitter fighting of World War II. At the time the alliance was formed, the United States and its allies occupied Japan, which, as a vanquished and occupied power, did not have the capability of pursing an aggressive revisionist agenda even if it had such preferences. The primary goal of the Allied occupation was to eliminate Japan's incentives and facility for future belligerence. The occupational government held war tribunals for Japan's military leaders and purged militarists from government ranks in hopes of eliminating aggressive players and establishing a pacifistic culture. In addition, concerns about poverty and starvation in postwar Japan focused people's concerns about governance on reconstruction rather than militarism.

The occupying government also imposed structural changes to prevent renewed aggression. It disarmed Japan's military, banned rearmament in

Japan's postwar constitution, and dismantled some of Japan's industry. It stationed thousands of troops on the Japanese islands, many of whom remained based in Japan after the formal end of Allied occupation in 1952. Restraining renewed Japanese aggression was clearly a primary goal of the Allies in 1951 when the United States extended a conditional deterrent commitment to Japan. In this vein, the U.S. commitment was designed not only to deter would-be threats to Japan but also to restrain Japan from reverting to revisionism and aggression. The alliance was asymmetric, extending U.S. defense to Japan but not the other way around. In addition, the alliance granted the United States ongoing rights to base and station troops in Japan, and it made the United States the sole guarantor of security from both external and domestic threats. These measures were aimed at controlling Japan, ensuring that it could not challenge the United States or its allies.

The example of the U.S. commitment to Japan is a useful baseline case because a conditional deterrent commitment is optimal for a third party that (1) wants to deter threats to its protégé, but (2) has some concern that the protégé may take revisionist actions at some point, and (3) has no concern about its ability to observe and prevent the protégé's aggressive actions. Because of the alliance and the postwar occupation, which involved thousands of U.S. troops on the ground in Japan, the United States was able to directly observe and control Japan's military actions. Consequently, because observability was not a concern, U.S. leaders chose to form a standard conditional deterrent commitment.

Revisionism in the ROC and Neutralizing the Taiwan Strait

In 1937, Chiang Kaishek's incumbent Chinese Nationalists (Guomindang, GMD) and the challenger Chinese Communist Party (CCP) led by Mao Zedong formed a united front to fight against the Japanese invasion of China. This tenuous alliance was vulnerable, because both sides sought opportunities to make gains at the expense of the other. Officials in the U.S. government learned during World War II that Chiang was looking for an opportunity to draw the United States into a broader conflict on the side of the Nationalists against the Chinese Communists. Chiang's opportunism, such as ordering Nationalist supporters in Burma and on the mainland to undertake raids against the People's Liberation Army (PLA), remained a constant factor in U.S. strategic decision making in East Asia for years to come (Cha 2009a, 169–173). Dean Acheson, U.S. Secretary of State in the Truman administration, believed as late as 1958 that Chiang's intentions remained "to embroil the United States with his enemies, the [Chinese] Communists" (Acheson 1958).

After World War II ended, the United States turned its focus to China's civil war between the CCP and GMD. Within months of the end of World War II, President Truman dispatched General George C. Marshall on a diplomatic mission to negotiate a unified government between the CCP and the

GMD. Although the United States was decidedly anti-Communist, it was also exhausted from fighting and hoped that the leaders of the two sides would come to an agreement that ended hostilities. However, Marshall grew frustrated with Chiang's overconfidence in the level of U.S. commitment to his cause, which made Chiang resistant to compromise with Mao. On October 5, 1946, Marshall recommended his own recall to "dispel the confident belief of government generals that they [the Nationalists] can drag along the United States while carrying out their campaign of force" (U.S. Department of State, *U.S. Relations with China*, 192).

Between 1946 and 1949, the GMD and CCP waged civil war. The CCP won the war and established the People's Republic of China (PRC) in 1949. After losing the mainland to the CCP and fleeing to Taiwan, Chiang resolved to reclaim mainland China. Unable to achieve this objective by himself, Chiang understood that his success depended on involving the United States on his side. His strategy consisted of two parts. First, he sought to secure the survivability of his retreating regime, which entailed shoring up Nationalist morale after its demoralizing loss of the mainland and building his military capacity and Taiwan's economy with U.S. support. Second, he aimed to tighten ties between his regime and the United States, with an eye toward drawing the United States into a conflict with the PRC (Accinelli 1996, 4–5).

Throughout this time, Chiang's aggressive effort to induce U.S. support of his goal to prevail over the Chinese Communists and consolidate his power over China had a direct impact on the evolution of the U.S. commitment to the Nationalists and its foreign policy strategy for China. During the winter of 1947–48, the Truman administration began to distance itself from Chiang. To be sure, efforts to avoid committing to Chiang and his Nationalists encountered much resistance among domestic groups in the United States. Powerful pro-Nationalist forces in Congress, the military, and the media put up a fight, clamoring for the U.S. government to extend greater support to the GMD. Facing pressure from these groups to aid the Nationalists but fearing that Chiang's efforts to draw the United States into war might succeed if the United States did provide military assistance, the administration's policy under Secretary of State Marshall drifted. The United States neither extricated itself from the conflict nor fully committed to it. The United States reduced its military presence in mainland China, its direct cooperation with Chiang, and the amount of financial aid to the Nationalists, although it continued to extend periodic and limited transfers. It is important to note that this is not equivalent to choosing deliberately to extend partial transfers to the protégé, which would contradict the argument about coarse intervention decisions in Chapter 3. Rather, the United States at the time was working toward distancing itself from the GMD, and the key decision makers had all but given up on helping Chiang to win the civil war. The U.S. transfers, which had been ongoing since 1941, continued mostly to placate domestic pressures while the administration worked to separate itself from the ROC (Christensen 1996, 58–61).

Thus, in spite of providing some basic assistance to the Nationalists, the Truman administration was not wholeheartedly committed to them. Behind the thin veneer of U.S. aid, Marshall believed that there was little to no possibility of the Nationalists and Communists reconciling their differences. Moreover, he believed that the Nationalists were unlikely to prevail in a civil war. He calculated that to reduce the Chinese Communists to a negligible factor in China, "it would be necessary for the United States to underwrite the Chinese [Nationalist] Government's military effort, on a wide and probably constantly increasing scale, as well as the Chinese economy" (May 1975, 81). He estimated that such an effort would require the United States to be "prepared virtually to take over the Chinese Government and administer its economic, military and governmental affairs," a cost that Marshall believed the "American people would never knowingly accept" (May 1975, 81).

Once it was clear that the Nationalists were doomed to lose the civil war, the Truman administration did not again give serious consideration to the possibility that more aid would turn the tide in China. Indeed, as Thomas Christensen (1996, 64–66) points out, aid continued to be granted not as a serious investment in Nationalist leadership, but rather as a concession to appease domestic pressures. Not enough to tip the war in Chiang's favor but enough to keep him fighting, the trickle of U.S. financial assistance likely did nothing more than merely prolong the civil war.

Dean Acheson, who succeeded Marshall as secretary of state in 1949, despised Chiang's regime and his persistent efforts to embroil the United States in China's civil war (Accinelli 1996, 5). After the Nationalists retreated to Taiwan and the PRC was established on October 1, 1949, Truman and Acheson resolved to abandon Chiang altogether. The administration resigned itself to the complete collapse and subjugation of the Nationalists and Taiwan to the PRC, and, in early 1950, began to prepare Congress for Taiwan's fall. On January 5, 1950, Truman publicly announced that the United States would not become involved in any further dispute between the Nationalists and Communists. Dean Acheson reaffirmed Truman's statement and ruled out any support, including direct aid, to the Nationalists (Truman, January 5, 1950). The administration also notified the British that the United States had no intention of defending Taiwan (Cohen 1980, 30).

In the months that followed its abandonment of the Nationalists, the United States expected the PRC to attack and try to overtake Taiwan. Then in June, war broke out in Korea, and U.S. policy changed immediately. The Truman administration's plans to disentangle itself from the Nationalists were put on hold as the United States moved to signal its intention to defend Taiwan to prevent the conflict in Korea from spreading to the Taiwan Strait. Truman administration officials feared that without a firebreak, the limited conflict in Korea could become a widespread regional conflict with the possibility of PRC and, worse yet, Soviet involvement and expansion (Christensen 1996, 133–137).

However, the administration believed that Chiang remained committed to his goal of reclaiming the mainland. The administration worried that Chiang's ambition would lead him to incite a crisis with the PRC purposely to expand the scope of the conflict, betting that the United States would now come to his defense to prevent a Communist win. Consequently, Acheson, who only days earlier had been prepared to accept the inevitable fall of Taiwan, now advised Truman to interpose the Seventh Fleet in the Taiwan Strait to prevent the conflict in Korea from spreading there. Acheson's reasoning for the move was specific: The Seventh Fleet would "prevent an attack on Formosa from the mainland" and "[a]t the same time, operations from Formosa against the mainland should be prevented" (Finkelstein 1993, 332; Memorandum of Conversation, June 25, 1950). Acheson adamantly opposed allowing Chiang an opportunity to exploit the U.S. military presence to open up an offensive against the PRC (Cohen 1980, 43). Thus, although defending Taiwan against Communist occupation was certainly a primary objective of the neutralization strategy, no less important to the Truman administration was the simultaneous restraining of Chiang from manipulating the situation to draw the United States back into the Chinese civil war.

Revisionist ROK and Conditional Commitments

The Truman administration held similar concerns about the territorial ambitions and opportunistic motives of Syngman Rhee – who was elected the first president of South Korea on July 20, 1948 – as they did about Chiang Kaishek. Following the conclusion of World War II and the fall of Japan, the Korean peninsula was occupied and administered by the Soviet Union in the north and the United States in the south. They were tasked with reestablishing the Korean state, but this plan quickly evaporated as the Soviets began arming Communist factions in the north. The U.S. leadership, which was in the process of distancing itself from Chiang's Chinese Nationalists at the time, was also fearful that Rhee's desire to unite the Korean peninsula at any cost would drag the United States into war. In no uncertain terms, the United States began to withdraw its support from South Korea. It decided against extending military or economic aid to South Korea or intervening unilaterally in the event North and South Korea came to blows (Donovan 1982, 95; Schnabel and Watson 1979, 23, 25–27). As evidence of the U.S. desire to disengage, it began withdrawing the American troops that had been stationed in Korea since the end of World War II. This policy was described by Acheson, who, in his famous January 12, 1950 National Press Club speech, confirmed that the United States had redrawn the U.S. defense perimeter to exclude both Korea and Taiwan. General Douglas MacArthur, too, noted in his memoirs the wisdom of these changes: "Anyone who commits the American army on the mainland of Asia ought to have his head examined" (MacArthur 1964, 322; Baldwin 1954, 771). Thus, it was well known in the higher ranks of the U.S. government and military that the

United States was in the process of withdrawing politically and militarily from both Taiwan and Korea.

Thus, on the eve of the Korean War, the U.S. government had effectively abandoned both Taiwan and South Korea, largely as a result of the widespread perception that Chiang and Rhee would exploit firm U.S. commitments by dragging the United States into military contests over disputed territories. In a cable to Acheson, U.S. Ambassador to Korea John Muccio explained his concerns about Rhee's unification ambitions and his reasons for resisting Rhee's requests for support: "We were in a very difficult position, a very subtle position, because if we gave Rhee and his cohorts what they wanted, they could have started to move north the same as the North started to move south. And the onus would have been on us" (Ambassador Muccio to Butterworth, November 1, 1949; quoted in Cha 2009a, note 33).

North Korean troops invaded South Korea on the morning of June 25, 1950; the start of this war changed the U.S. policy toward Korea just as it changed the U.S. attitude toward the Taiwan Strait. After the United States entered the Korean War on the ROK's behalf, Rhee became even bolder in demanding U.S. support, especially near the end as armistice negotiations progressed (Cha 2009a, 173–179). Worried that a peace agreement ending the Korean War would fail to unite the peninsula, Rhee deliberately sought to undermine the armistice talks and angle for a mutual security pact with the United States instead (Schnabel and Watson 1979, 987). He threatened to act unilaterally to provoke North Korea while simultaneously pushing the United States for a firm commitment formalized in a mutual defense treaty, increased economic aid, and abandonment of armistice efforts. Rhee also threatened not to withdraw his forces from the proposed demilitarized zone. U.S. General Mark Clark, who represented the United Nations in armistice talks as the commander of UN forces, grumbled that Rhee posed the "biggest trouble" between South Korea and the North Korean Communists (Cha 2009a, 175; Park 1975, 97). The United States found that threatening to withdraw the United Nations Command was the most effective tool for restraining Rhee's aggressive opportunism (Kim 2001, 90–91, 141). Recognizing the effectiveness of such threats proved useful when designing the conditions that later appeared in the mutual defense treaty.

In January 1953, Dwight D. Eisenhower became president of the United States, promising to end the war in Korea. His administration agreed to enter into a mutual defense treaty with South Korea in exchange for Rhee's cooperation on the armistice agreement. Rhee accepted this exchange but made sure that this agreement contained certain concessions in addition to the defense treaty, including increased U.S. economic and military aid (Schnabel and Watson 1979, 1018–1019). Once the armistice was signed, however, U.S. officials immediately maneuvered to establish conditions on the U.S. commitment to defend South Korea. Walter S. Robertson, U.S. Assistant Secretary of State for Far Eastern Affairs, explained to the Joint Chiefs of Staff that he established

Deterrent Commitments in East Asia

some boundaries in his treaty discussions with Rhee: "I repeatedly explained to Rhee that even if President Eisenhower desired to he could not bind the U.S. to reopen hostilities. This would require action by the Congress. I also repeatedly told Rhee that we would have to preserve complete liberty of action as to what we did if the political conference should not succeed" (*Foreign Relations of the United States*, 1952–1954, XV, 1455).

The State Department framed the dual deterrence goals of the mutual defense treaty as follows: "Deterring future Communist aggression and preventing any attempts to achieve reunification by force were Washington's twin objectives in 'bestowing' a mutual defense treaty on South Korea. The joint communiqué asserted that there would be no unilateral South Korean action during the forthcoming political conference" (*U.S. Department of State Bulletin* XXIX, August 17, 1953, 203–204). In a message to the Senate, Eisenhower confirmed the dual aims of the treaty: to deter aggression by warning both North and South Korea that the United States would not tolerate any attempts to settle remaining problems by force while restraining the Chinese Nationalists (Dwight D. Eisenhower to U.S. Senate, January 11, 1954; *New York Times*, January 13, 1954; Chang-Il 1993).

On October 1, 1953, the United States and the ROK signed the mutual defense treaty; although the formal treaty language is ambiguous, the commitment clearly pinned U.S. defensive obligations on the condition that conflict be initiated by external forces that attacked territories recognized by the United States as under the sovereign control of the ROK. If, instead, conflict arose as a result of ROK initiation, the United States would not lend its support. The content of the agreement was shaped by U.S. motivations to deter potential aggression directed at South Korea while restraining South Korea from taking aggressive actions toward another state.

From Conditional to Probabilistic Deterrence

The previous sections established that the United States extended conditional deterrent commitments to the ROC in 1950, Japan in 1951, and the ROK in 1953. Why was the probabilistic U.S. commitment to the ROC in 1954 different? In particular, why did the type of U.S. deterrent commitment to the ROC change from a conditional neutralization strategy in 1950 to a probabilistic mutual defense treaty in 1954? The argument presented here is that the United States adopted a probabilistic commitment in reaction to a shift in the contest between Chiang and the Chinese Communists that resulted in circumstances that made it difficult for the United States to observe the initiator of hostile actions between the Chinese Communists and the Chinese Nationalists. Moral hazard was a primary U.S. concern in both 1950 and 1954, as Chiang continued to harbor his aspiration of involving the United States to assist his forces in retaking mainland China throughout this time period. However, in 1954 the line of defense shifted from the Taiwan Strait, which is a focal and defensible position, to a long string of islands along China's mainland coast, which meant that the disputants were now in close contact and exchanging hostilities regularly. This complicated the U.S. ability to draw and enforce a clear defense line, which was necessary for the United States to commit to defending Taiwan on the condition that the Chinese Communists initiated hostilities by violating the line.

In this section, I describe how Truman's conditional commitment in 1950 followed from the clear defense line in the Taiwan Strait that made it possible to observe initiations of conflict. Then I explain how Eisenhower's move to deneutralize the Taiwan Strait was interpreted by Chiang as a strengthening of the U.S. commitment. Chiang responded aggressively by reinforcing his position in the offshore islands. I show how this move reduced the observability of actions leading to war and led the Eisenhower administration to form a probabilistic commitment with the Nationalists, replacing the previous conditional commitment.

When the Nationalists retreated to Taiwan, they retained control of several small island groupings, including Quemoy and the Dachens, which lay within just a few miles of China's mainland coast. However, the Nationalist position on the islands was weak, and in the months leading up to Truman's neutralization order, several of them fell to the Communist People's Liberation Army (PLA). It was generally believed at the time that the Nationalists were not strong enough to retain the remaining offshore islands and that these islands, too, would fall to the PLA. When Truman issued his order to neutralize the Taiwan Strait in 1950, he noticeably excluded these Nationalist-held offshore islands from the scope of the U.S. defensive commitment. In fact, Secretary of Defense Louis Johnson told the Joint Chiefs of Staff that the order should exclude the offshore islands (Li 1990, 47). Thus, the United States knowingly abandoned those territories that were located just a few miles off of China's coast and concentrated on preserving Nationalist control of Taiwan, which was a much more defensible territory.

The primary reason that Taiwan is relatively easy to defend is because of the large expanse of water that separates it from any substantial land mass. Because military provocations directed at or from Taiwan can be verified without difficulty, a third-party ally committed to its defense can effectively identify and punish infringements. Schelling describes the Taiwan Strait as a prominent natural dividing line for limiting war:

The Formosan Straits made it possible to stabilize a line between the Communist and National government forces of China, not solely because water favored the defender and inhibited attack, but because an island is an integral unit and water is a conspicuous boundary. The sacrifice of any part of the island would have made the resulting line unstable; the retention of any part of the mainland would have been similarly unstable. Except at the water's edge, all movement is a matter of degree; an attack across water is a declaration that the "agreement" has been terminated (Schelling 1960, 76).

Schelling's claim that the Taiwan Strait is a focal defense line applies to provocative military actions originating from either side of the strait. It is conspicuous, easy to patrol, and unsusceptible to imperceptible initiations of conflict. Separated by a geographical feature such as the Taiwan Strait, the two opponents are less likely to engage in frequent instigations and fence-pushing tactics such as posturing, probing, hassling, and skirmishes that might lead to the escalation of conflict between closely situated foes. To provoke and escalate conflict between Taiwan and mainland China, the initiator must first project power across the water to the other's territory. Thus, the strait delimits the set of moves that can be considered provocative and makes a conditional threat such as Truman's neutralization strategy effective.

In early 1953, the Eisenhower administration decided to abandon neutralization by removing the Seventh Fleet from the Taiwan Strait, a decision that reflected the level of enmity between the United States and Communist China during the war in Korea. Eisenhower announced in his February 2, 1953, State of the Union address that the Seventh Fleet would no longer be required to "shield Communist China" from the Nationalists. Eisenhower justified the new policy by claiming that the United States had "no obligation to protect a nation fighting us in Korea." Dulles and Eisenhower interpreted stalemated armistice talks with the Chinese and massive Chinese reinforcements in and around Korea as a signal that the PRC did not have intentions to end the war (Zhang 1992, 119–120). They also worried about possible Chinese intervention in Indochina. Eisenhower and Dulles felt that the United States could better bring about a speedy conclusion to the Korean War and deter Communist aggression elsewhere by threatening to extend and broaden the conflict with the use of Nationalist troops and nuclear weapons (Accinelli 1996, 115).

After the Seventh Fleet was removed, the U.S. commitment to the Chinese Nationalists strengthened. By November 6, 1953, Eisenhower and the National Security Council had put a new Taiwan policy in place. The new policy directive, NSC 146/2, established several objectives for U.S. policy: (1) Taiwan should be kept independent and noncommunist as an "essential element in the U.S. Far East defense position"; (2) aid should be supplied to Taiwan for the purpose of building its military, economy, and political infrastructure, and improving its international profile; and (3) Taiwan should be used as a base of operations against the mainland to prevent the buildup of Communist forces elsewhere.[3] To accomplish these goals, the United States began transferring substantial financial and military resources, as well as psychological support, to Chiang's Nationalists.

As expected, the Nationalists responded to the strengthened U.S. commitment by stepping up their aggression toward the Chinese Communists on the offshore islands. They carried out an offensive assault on Dongshan,

---

[3] For a discussion of NSC 146/2, see Accinelli 1996, 134–135; Garver 1997, 115–116; and Zhang 1992, 201–202.

hit-and-run raids on the mainland, and maritime interdictions off China's coast. Chiang also amassed troops on some of the islands, ostensibly to firm up the defense of those islands but also to prepare for an eventual assault on the mainland. Accounts reported over 50,000 Nationalist soldiers stationed on Quemoy alone (Chang 1988, 99) with more deployed to other island groupings as far north as the Dachens (Accinelli 1996, 124).

The Nationalists' concentration on the offshore islands moved the defense line from the Taiwan Strait to China's mainland coast, putting Nationalist and Communist troops in direct contact with each other. Chiang chose to relocate a significant percentage of his troops to the offshore islands with the express purpose of entrapping the United States. *New York Times* columnist C. L. Sulzberger (1955; quoted in Sigal 1970) described Chiang's plan for heavily reinforcing the garrisons on Quemoy and Matsu as follows: "Should they be attacked, he would like to develop the biggest possible battle. Thus, by stirring our emotions, he could ensure our full support. Only by general Asian war can Chiang now hope to return to the mainland." If loss of the islands meant also losing much of the Nationalist force in battle, then defending the islands was in fact integral to defending Taiwan, because a drastically reduced Nationalist military would prove insufficient to protect Taiwan from the PLA. Thus, according to Chiang's calculation, perhaps the United States would feel more compelled to protect the islands if the survival of the Nationalist regime and defense of Taiwan depended on it. Chiang's strategy of "creating an artificially manufactured tie" between the offshore islands and the defense of Taiwan was reminiscent of his 1945 move to entrap the United States in China's civil war by advancing his troops into Manchuria and forcing the United States to choose between supporting the Nationalists or risking the loss of all of China (Tsou 1959, 1078–1079). Chiang adopted this strategy of entrapment on the offshore islands in 1953, and he continued it well into the second Quemoy crisis in 1958 (Lewis 1962, 14; Tsou 1959, 1075; Sigal 1970), in spite of Eisenhower's attempts to discourage him from continually amassing troops on the islands because it might provoke a conflict (Eisenhower 1963, 466).

Having tied both the psychological and military survival of the Nationalists to the preservation of their control of the offshore islands, Chiang helped to blur what was previously a clear defense line in the Taiwan Strait. Reinstating Truman's neutralization line without Chiang's cooperation would be equivalent to unilaterally abandoning the islands, which would jeopardize a significant percentage of the Nationalist military force and devastate the Nationalists' dreams of reclaiming the mainland, both of which were believed to be necessary for the survival of the Nationalists on Taiwan. Once the battleground moved from the Taiwan Strait to the offshore islands, drawing a line in the sand and specifying that whoever crossed the line first was the initiator of the crisis became considerably more difficult.

The difficulty establishing a clear defense line stemmed from several factors in addition to the linkage between the security of the offshore islands and the Nationalists' morale and Taiwan's defense. In the first place, the line now stretched along a significant distance, from the Dachens in the north to Quemoy in the south, which meant there was more area to monitor: the longer the line, the more potential flashpoints that could trigger a conflict. Additionally, the islands were located only a few miles off of China's coast. The close proximity created an incentive for the disputants to engage in low-level harassments and skirmishes such as sinking of fishing boats, harassing trade, and limited shelling campaigns on the islands. Moreover, the status quo was dynamic. Soldiers, fishermen, and farmers from both sides clashed frequently in the areas surrounding the islands. Foreign Service Officer and China expert O. Edmund Clubb described the situation as one of rapid movement with civil war still ablaze (Clubb 1959, 530). With both sides already exchanging blows, an attempt to identify the first mover would lead to an infinite regress of blame. Even if the status quo could, in theory, be frozen, it would still be costly, and perhaps even impossible, for the United States to identify who initiated the small skirmishes that would inevitably break out again.

There was another complicating factor: the offshore islands had always belonged to the mainland. By drawing a transparent defense line around those little islands, the United States would be denying the government of mainland China territory that historically belonged to it. By contrast, the international status of Taiwan's sovereignty at the time was more flexible. Eisenhower felt that the United States would be justified in defending the offshore islands only if a Communist attack on those islands was a prelude to an attack on Taiwan. But how could the U.S. military differentiate such an attack from an attack that had as its only objective the occupation of the offshore islands and nothing more?

Former British Prime Minister Winston Churchill understood the difficulty of defending the offshore islands and urged Eisenhower to push the line of defense back to the natural defense line in the Taiwan Strait (Boyle 1990, 192–195). This logic of establishing natural and focal defense lines was not lost on Eisenhower, a military general who had led U.S. troops in World War II. After all, he, like Schelling, recognized that the waistline on the Korean peninsula was the most natural position to establish a defensible demilitarized zone to end the Korean War (Zhang 1992, 124). Surely he also realized that establishing and sustaining a line of defense were much less complicated from the Taiwan Strait than from the offshore islands. However, Eisenhower seemed to accept that the survival of Taiwan was tied to the defense of the offshore islands both because of the Nationalist troops stationed there and because of the Nationalists' psychological tie to the islands.

Mao's response to the Nationalists' aggression on the offshore islands was to escalate the conflict. In 1954, three offshore island groups – the Quemoys, Matsus, and Dachens – still lay in the hands of the Nationalists. On September 3, 1954, the PRC began heavily shelling the Quemoy islands. The shelling campaign lasted intermittently for the next several months. Eisenhower provided the following description of the islands:

> The nineteen rocky, treeless Matsus, covering twelve square miles, blocked the port of Foochow on the Chinese mainland, just ten miles away, while the Quemoys, covering sixty square miles of land which supported several thousand farmers and fisherman, blocked the port Amoy, only two miles away. Thus the two contending forces in China were face to face across a few thousand yards of water (Eisenhower 1963, 461).

The Dachens were located approximately 200 miles farther north, also only a few miles away from the Chinese mainland.

Although Eisenhower, who strongly favored protecting the island of Taiwan, did not believe that the Nationalist occupation of the offshore islands was necessary for the military defense of Taiwan, he did believe that preserving the morale of the Nationalists was necessary (Rushkoff 1981, 469–473). Many Nationalists believed that the loss of the islands to the Communists would have "bad, possibly disastrous, psychological effects" on the Chinese Nationalists (Rushkoff 1981, 463). Because the Nationalists regarded the offshore islands as "stepping stones" to reacquire the mainland (Eisenhower 1963, 470), they would likely have perceived any attempt on the part of the United States to abandon these offshore islands as an attempt to appease the Communists and a severe blow to the Nationalists, mainland aspirations. The Eisenhower administration worried that abandoning the offshore islands would forever dash the hopes of the Nationalist promise to reclaim the mainland and, therefore, would undermine the legitimacy of the Nationalist government to rule China, perhaps exposing Taiwan to the possibility of Communist expansion. Whether a psychological Communist revolution of Taiwan was actually a reasonable fear, Eisenhower nevertheless wrote to Churchill, "The morale of the Chinese Nationalists is important to us, so for the moment, and under existing conditions, we feel they must have certain assurances with respect to the offshore islands" (Rushkoff 1981, 463).

Although the Eisenhower administration worried that loss of the offshore islands could lead to the loss of Taiwan, it was also sensitive to the fact that defending the islands could mean becoming involved in another war. Three of the four members of the Joint Chiefs of Staff advised Eisenhower to authorize Chiang to bomb the mainland in response to the Communist shelling of Quemoy and, if the Communists attacked Quemoy with ground troops, to permit U.S. forces to help defend the island. This approach, however, would have essentially extended to Chiang a blank check guaranteeing the use of U.S. military might to engage PRC troops on the mainland. The dissenting Chief of Staff, General Ridgway, argued that such an action would lead to full-scale war. Eisenhower agreed: "We're not talking now about a limited, brush-fire war. We're talking about going to the threshold of World War III. If we attack China, we're not going to impose limits on our military actions, as in Korea. Moreover, if we get into a general war, the logical enemy will be

Russia and China, and we'll have to strike there" (Eisenhower 1963, 463–464). Eisenhower's concern echoes the discussion about the third party's coarse warfighting incentives described in Chapters 3 and 5; once involved, it would be difficult for the U.S. to limit its support.

Eisenhower believed that he faced a "horrible dilemma" between "appeasement and global war" (Eisenhower 1963, 463, 483). His solution was a policy that Secretary of State Dulles later described as "deterrence by uncertainty" (Chang and Di 1993, 1511). The foremost objectives of this strategy were (1) to discourage a Communist attack on the offshore islands by fostering the belief that U.S. defense of the islands was a distinct possibility while (2) convincing Chiang that he could not take for granted that the United States would become embroiled in a confrontation with the PRC on his behalf. The ambiguity of the probabilistic commitment was established in the framework of a mutual defense agreement with Taiwan and then later reinforced through such measures as the Formosa Resolution, which was a joint congressional resolution allowing Eisenhower to commit troops to defend the offshore islands.

Eisenhower sent Dulles to Taiwan in September 1954 to conduct talks with Chiang that would explore the possibility of forming a mutual defense treaty with the Nationalist government. Dulles knew that Chiang had long sought such an agreement, and he worried that forming the commitment now would enable Chiang to drag the United States into a dangerous military conflict with China (Dulles 1972, 151–152). Reluctant to allow the United States to become actively committed to the Nationalists, Dulles returned to Washington to craft a treaty that would deter the PRC without emboldening the ROC. On December 2, 1954, the United States and Taiwan agreed to a mutual defense treaty. Superficially, it appeared that Chiang had obtained his long sought-after prize – but the treaty actually restrained rather than enabled him. Although the treaty explicitly confirmed the United States commitment to the defense of Taiwan, the language in the treaty, insisted on by Eisenhower and Dulles, intentionally extended this commitment only to "such other territories as may be determined by mutual agreement" (Exchange of Notes, December 10, 1954). In other words, the offshore islands were *not* explicitly included under the umbrella of U.S. defense, but the possibility remained that they could be. Dulles intentionally wanted to "fuzz up" the treaty language to maintain "doubt in the minds of the Communists as to how the U.S. would react to an attack on the offshore islands" (Zhang 1992, 21). Additionally, tying its promise to "constitutional processes" created additional uncertainty about whether the United States would, in fact, intervene. Although the Communists had no way of knowing whether further PRC military action aimed at the offshore islands would provoke a U.S. response, the Nationalists also were not provided any guarantee that the United States would come to their aid should they intentionally try to provoke the Communists.

In addition to fuzzing up the formal language of the treaty, Dulles and Yeh exchanged treaty notes, which the administration and the Nationalists agreed to keep secret (Eisenhower 1963, 466). Intended to rein in opportunistic behavior on Chiang's part, the treaty notes stipulated that any "use of force" from any area controlled by Chiang "will be a matter of joint agreement." The notes also established that the Nationalists would not resort to force for any reason other than self-defense (Dulles 1972, 152). The understanding that the United States would have to sanction any Nationalist military action against the PRC combined with the uncertainty about whether the treaty extended to the offshore islands meant that the new United States–ROC mutual defense treaty did not provide the assurance that Chiang longed for and made it difficult for him to use it to expand the conflict with the Communists.

Dulles commented that the treaty negotiations had been difficult, but the final agreement "stakes out unqualifiedly our interests in Formosa and the Pescadores and does so on a basis which will not enable the Chinese Nationalists to involve us in a war with Communist China" (Garver 1997, 114). The ambiguous language of the treaty served two purposes: (1) to send a message to the Communists indicating an explicit U.S. commitment to defend Taiwan and an ambiguous U.S. commitment to the offshore islands, and (2) to restrain Chiang from making provocative military actions. Because the treaty notes were secret, the only signal that the PRC received was the tougher deterrence language in the treaty itself, which may or may not have extended to the offshore islands. The Chinese Communists did not know that the United States had taken the additional step of preempting a unilateral offensive move by Chiang or that the ROC was bound by the secret treaty notes to confer with the United States before antagonizing the PRC. Following the signing of the treaty, Chiang pushed Eisenhower to expand the treaty to include the offshore islands. Eisenhower denied the request (Eisenhower 1963, 466).

Why a Probabilistic Commitment?

Several of Eisenhower's closest advisors felt uneasy about the probabilistic commitment because they worried that it might not be strong enough to deter China and that the uncertainty could inadvertently cause conflict. As a result, they encouraged the president to adopt a policy that provided more certainty about U.S. intentions (Chang and Di 1993, 1511). Scholars, too, have criticized Eisenhower's strategy. Both George and Smoke (1974) and Schelling (1960) argue that this shift in policy in the 1954–1955 Quemoy crisis was not optimal. Schelling specifically objected to the ambiguity in the new probabilistic policy, arguing that the discretion permitted in the new commitment undermined the credibility of the U.S. threat to defend Taiwan. In his discussion of the Quemoy crisis, he emphasized the importance of visibility and transparency to the credibility of commitments: "Any loopholes the threatening party leaves himself, if they are visible to the threatened party, weaken the visible commitment and hence reduce the credibility of the threat. (An example may be the ambiguous treatment of Quemoy in the Formosa Resolution and Treaty)" (Schelling 1960,

40). According to Schelling, given that the United States wanted to deter China from attacking the offshore islands, its commitment to defend should have been firm and transparent.

However, the type of commitment proposed by Schelling ran the risk of emboldening the Nationalists to provoke the PRC, which was a real danger given Chiang's revisionism and the unobservability of destabilizing moves between the offshore islands and the mainland. According to John Lewis Gaddis, "Determined not to yield further territory to the People's Republic, and yet convinced of Chiang's error in seeking to hold military positions not critical to the defense of Taiwan, the Eisenhower administration found itself once again, as in Korea, attempting simultaneously to deter action by an adversary and to minimize the risk of American involvement at the hands of an ally" (Gaddis 1987, 133). The Eisenhower administration did fear that distancing itself from Taiwan or even refusing to respond to the shelling campaign of Quemoy would embolden China. This was an outcome it wholeheartedly wished to avoid; a loss in the Taiwan Strait would add humiliation and loss of credibility to setbacks already suffered in Indochina and Korea. On the other hand, committing the United States to the defense of the offshore islands meant committing to an offensive forward position that too easily could draw the United States into war. Defending the islands from a sustained attack would require the United States to retaliate against mainland targets. Further escalation against China would likely involve the Soviet Union and possibly the use of nuclear weapons (Eisenhower 1963, 463–465). Emboldening Chiang, then, was not a simple nuisance; it risked unleashing nuclear war.

If the United States was this concerned about the possible outcome of emboldening Chiang, why did it elect to form a probabilistic commitment instead of a conditional deterrent commitment, as in Japan or South Korea? Why did it not return to Truman's neutralization strategy?

The answer lies in the difficulty of drawing a clear defense line and conditioning a commitment on the non-violation of that line. After Chiang linked the defense of the offshore islands with the survivability of Nationalist Taiwan, three major factors made specifying a first provocative move all but impossible. First, the close proximity of the islands to the mainland and the length of the line increased chances for skirmishes while decreasing the ability of the third-party defender to monitor the exchanges and punish the perpetrator accordingly. Second, the frequent skirmishes meant that the status quo was dynamic – it was not possible to identify a first mover because finger-pointing would regress almost indefinitely, with each new skirmish attributable to a previous hostile action by the other side. Third, it was difficult to distinguish a Communist attack that had as its objective a further attack on Taiwan from a limited attack to harass the Nationalist forces on the offshore islands. Because of the difficulty in specifying and punishing a first mover, drawing a line in the sand was not so easily done. Eisenhower provided the strongest justification for his choice of a probabilistic commitment with the ROC when he lamented in a private letter, "As far as the Formosan question is concerned, I wish it were as simple as drawing a line and saying in effect, 'this far and no further.' I assure you that there are a thousand and one complicated factors that prevent such an easy solution" (Eisenhower 1996). Eisenhower would likely have preferred a conditional deterrence had such a strategy been available. However, because he seemed to believe that Taiwan's survival was linked to the defense of at least some of the offshore islands and the position of the islands prevented him from drawing a clear line, he concluded that neutralizing the Taiwan Strait was no longer possible. Consequently, strategic ambiguity in the form of the probabilistic commitment described above became the next-best alternative.

Comparing the ROC with the ROK

As the preceding history described, the commitment in Taiwan was probabilistic, whereas the commitment in South Korea was conditional deterrent. To attribute this difference to the degree of observability of hostile actions in the two cases, it must be shown that it was easier to observe initiations of conflict across the defense line in South Korea than across the defense line along the islands just off the shore of mainland China. Indeed, the particular geography of the two regions affected observability in important ways. One of the main points of the armistice agreement that ended the fighting in the Korean War was to set up a clear line of demarcation between North and South (Korean War Armistice Agreement, Paragraph 1). As mentioned earlier, Eisenhower believed that the waist of Korea was a natural defense line because it shortened the border between the two sides and therefore reduced the number of potential flashpoints for conflict. The U.S. leadership also wanted to widen the defense line by establishing a demilitarized zone that spanned the width of the peninsula approximately 160 miles across, which would make it harder for one side to initiate a hostility without the action being observed by others. The language of the armistice agreement reads: "A military demarcation line shall be fixed and both sides shall withdraw two (2) kilometers from this line so as to establish a demilitarized zone between the opposing forces. A demilitarized zone shall be established as a buffer zone to prevent the occurrence of incidents which might lead to a resumption of hostilities" (Paragraph 1, Korean War Armistice Agreement). Then, Paragraph 6 states: "Neither side shall execute any hostile act within, from, or against the demilitarized zone." By shortening and widening the line and then neutralizing the space in between, violations of the demilitarized zone become significantly more observable.

By contrast, the defensive line along the offshore islands was not so easily shortened and widened. Eisenhower managed at least to convince Chiang to evacuate and abandon the Dachen island grouping. Nevertheless, there was approximately 150 miles of open water between the remaining islands of Quemoy and Matsu, both of which were within just a few of miles of China's mainland but over 100 miles from Taiwan. Because of the close proximity of the offshore islands to the mainland and the significant distance both between the two island groupings and between the islands and Taiwan, monitoring hostilities between the Nationalists and the Communists on and around Quemoy and Matsu was problematic for the United States. Additionally, ongoing skirmishes between the Nationalists and Communists in the vicinity of the islands further complicated an effort to freeze and defend the status quo.

The matter of the defensibility of Quemoy and Matsu was raised in the presidential debates between Kennedy and Nixon in 1960. Kennedy argued that the line was "undefensible" and should be changed to a "clearly defined" line "drawn at the island of Formosa." Nixon's response echoed Eisenhower's belief that the Nationalists could not "force our Nationalist allies to get off of them [the offshore islands] and give them to the Communists," because so doing would trigger a "chain reaction" that would compromise the security of Taiwan itself (The Second Kennedy-Nixon Presidential Debate). Both Kennedy and Nixon appeared to agree that the type of commitment the United States should extend to Taiwan depended on whether the defense line could be moved and clarified. Kennedy suggested that the ambiguity in the existing policy followed from Eisenhower's inability to persuade the Nationalists to abandon the offshore islands. He argued that the line could be redrawn at Taiwan's shore, putting 100 miles of water between Chinese and Nationalist forces and making it possible to establish a less ambiguous conditional deterrent commitment. Nixon did not take issue with the possibility of changing the policy if the defense line could be moved and clarified. His contention was that the line could not be moved and clarified without incurring unacceptable costs and thus the probabilistic deterrent commitment formed by Eisenhower should remain in place.

In comparing the defense lines in Korea and the Taiwan Strait, the relatively short and wide demilitarized zone in Korea was easier to monitor and defend than the Nationalist-held offshore islands, which were close to China's mainland and far from each other and the main Nationalist command on Taiwan. Given these differences, it was more feasible to enforce the specific conditions contained in the United States–ROK Mutual Defense Treaty and ratification agreement than it would have been to enforce a similar conditional commitment to defend the offshore islands. Unless the United States could successfully move the defense line away from the offshore islands and clarify what constitutes a violation of the defense line, the optimal U.S. deterrence commitment for the offshore islands was a probabilistic commitment.

Summary

The evidence analyzed in this chapter supports a causal relationship between the observability of destabilizing moves and the third-party defender's choice of a deterrence commitment. Because the United States was worried about revisionism in Japan, South Korea, and Taiwan in the early 1950s, it chose between forming a conditional commitment and a probabilistic commitment in each case. Although there is some variation in the relative strength of the U.S. commitment in its treaties with Japan and South Korea, as well as in Truman's neutralization strategy in the Taiwan Strait, each of these commitments is a conditional commitment. Only the 1954 United States–ROC commitment is probabilistic. The reason for this difference stems from the difficulty of monitoring actions that might lead to war between the Nationalists and the Communists in and around the offshore islands. Because initiations of conflict were observable across the Taiwan Strait and the demilitarized zone, it was possible to form conditional deterrent commitments when the defense lines were established in those locations. In Japan, observability was not an issue because the U.S. occupation enabled the United States to gain significant control over Japan's military. On the other hand, the Nationalist and Communist disputants were physically too close to one another on the islands off the coast of China and too far from Taiwan for the United States to costlessly observe which side was responsible for initiating hostilities.

The U.S. mutual defense treaty with the ROC at the end of the 1954–55 Quemoy crisis provides strong evidence for the hypothesis summarized in Table 7.1. A canny strategist, Chiang recognized that he needed U.S. support to fulfill his objective of reconquering mainland China. He believed that maintaining control of the offshore islands was also key to this goal, as their proximity to China's coast sustained Nationalist hopes in the dream to return to the mainland. Furthermore, Chiang believed that the loss of the islands might give the United States grounds to pursue a two-China solution. Therefore, Chiang manufactured a link between the survival of the offshore islands and the defense of Taiwan by reinforcing the offshore islands with a disproportionate percentage of his military, refusing to evacuate the islands, and linking the psychological survival of Nationalist Taiwan to the defense of the offshore islands. Unlike the Taiwan Strait, the offshore islands' location did not provide a natural defense line because of the close proximity of the Nationalist forces to the Communist military on the mainland, the length of the line, the dynamic status quo, the distance from Taiwan, and the difficulty in determining what kind of an attack constituted a provocative action. Thus, Chiang's concentration on the offshore islands complicated a straightforward definition of a conditional deterrence strategy, which was precisely his goal. However, the U.S. administration recognized the danger of being drawn into a large-scale, and possibly nuclear, war in Asia if it extended a strong military commitment to Chiang. Unable to draw a line in the sand, Eisenhower formed a probabilistic deterrence commitment. In the mutual defense treaty with the ROC government in Taiwan, the United States was purposely vague about what vicinities the defense commitment included, and it secretly constrained Chiang's ability to unilaterally move against the Communists without U.S. consent. Thus, the United States used a probabilistic commitment mechanism to minimize the moral hazard problem, which was exacerbated by the difficulty of monitoring hostilities along the complicated defense line.

8

Constructing Security in Today's World

Since the 1990s, the security of the Taiwan Strait and that of the Korean peninsula have reemerged as international priorities. When the government of China conducted missile tests off the shore of Taiwan in 1995–1996, Taiwan's military went on heightened alert and the United States flexed its muscles by sending naval forces to the area. The crisis triggered questions and concerns about the suitability of the U.S. policy of strategic ambiguity to effectively manage tensions between China and Taiwan. China also faces growing questions about its security commitment to North Korea. In 1993, the government of North Korea announced its intention to withdraw from the nuclear nonproliferation treaty. The threat that North Korea might acquire a nuclear weapon rekindled tensions between North Korea and the United States–ROK alliance. The road to the present time has been rocky, with occasional bursts of violence, such as North Korea's shelling of the South Korean island of Yeonpyeong in 2010.

Although these crises did not escalate to war, they do raise questions about whether the policies of China and the United States, which were formed for these regions decades ago, are adequately designed to meet the current demands of the disputes. The U.S. policy of strategic ambiguity is a probabilistic commitment; it causes concern because of the intuitive belief that uncertainty tends not to enhance peace. China's policy toward North Korea is a conditional commitment, but North Korea's fearless pursuit of nuclear weapons and growing aggression toward South Korea raise the specter that China's commitment may not be an effective mechanism for restraining North Korea and may even unwittingly encourage its aggressiveness.

In this chapter, I provide an explanation for the original design of these two commitments, and then examine whether factors have changed that would also create incentives for China and the United States to change their policies. First, though, I will briefly summarize the main themes developed in this book.

Summarizing How Commitments Manage Deterrence and Moral Hazard

Deterrence and moral hazard both play a role in the formation of military alliances and extended deterrence commitments. How a commitment is designed depends on factors that influence how adversaries and allies are expected to react to promises of assistance in conflicts. These factors include: (1) the degree to which allies agree with each other about the value of fighting a war on each other's behalf, (2) the extent to which they agree about the ideal peaceful settlement of a disputed issue between an alliance member and its enemy, (3) disparities in allies' war-fighting capabilities against a prospective adversary, and (4) the observability of the actions leading to war between an alliance member and its enemy. With respect to the first factor, governments that do not share an ally's interest in fighting a war for their ally's security are motivated to devise commitments that curtail the risk of moral hazard that may result from an ally's expectation that a defender will come to its aid in war. The second factor relates to allies' preferences over policy outcomes. Firm commitments may motivate the recipients of the commitment to drive a hard bargain with its enemy to extract as much as possible in negotiations. If allies disagree about the ideal settlement, then the outcome of such a settlement may make the defender country worse off. In these circumstances, the defender may opt for a conditional or probabilistic commitment.

Allies' relative capabilities, the third factor that might affect the design of deterrence commitments, affect the incentives of weaker allies' behavior in crises. Commitments made by powerful defenders can dramatically improve weaker allies' ability to fight and win, which, in turn, emboldens them to push for more concessions from their enemies. The more powerful the third-party defender and the less powerful the ally, the greater the moral hazard distortion to the behavior of the ally. This leads to an added measure of caution on the part of the third party as it decides what type of commitment to adopt. Such disparities in allies' capabilities are likely to result in the formation of probabilistic commitments.

Finally, whether the disputants' actions in crises are observable to a third-party defender might also affect the tendency of the ally to behave aggressively. If the defender cannot determine in real time who is responsible for initiating and escalating a crisis to war, then there is an incentive on the part of the ally to take advantage both of the obscurity and the commitment to aggressively pursue its interests at the expense of its adversary. Because defenders cannot make and enforce conditional commitments in these circumstances, they will choose probabilistic commitments, unconditional commitments, or no commitments instead.

Strategic Ambiguity in Taiwan

The disagreement over the sovereignty of Taiwan is perhaps the most dangerous dispute in the world today, because of its potential for drawing the

United States into a conflict with China (Tucker 2009). On several occasions during the past two decades, Americans have been reminded of the hazards lurking in the Taiwan Strait. In 1995–1996, the government of the People's Republic of China (PRC) tested missiles along the Taiwan coast and carried out amphibious assault exercises. The Clinton administration responded by sending two aircraft carrier battle groups to the area. After the missile crisis, tensions remained high, with the PRC publicly condemning what it perceived to be a pro-independence movement at work in Taiwan's democratic process and the People's Liberation Army (PLA) investing more heavily in military training and materiel specifically targeting Taiwan. Meanwhile, Taiwan President Lee Teng-hui continued to edge toward greater autonomy for Taiwan with statements such as his infamous comment in 1999 that business between China and Taiwan should be characterized by a "special state-to-state" relationship.

When pro-independence candidate Chen Shui-bian, who sought to expand Taiwan's participation in international organizations and wanted to hold a referendum among Taiwanese voters to establish self-determination, was elected president of Taiwan in 2000, the PRC stepped up its efforts to deter Taiwan independence. The government aggressively built up missiles along the mainland coast opposite Taiwan and passed the 2005 Anti-Secession Law, which threatened to use force to deter Taiwan independence and to compel unification if peaceful unification failed.

Even with a heightened sense of danger of war over Taiwan during this time period, the U.S. commitment to defend Taiwan remained ambiguous. The first pillar of the U.S. policy, which is contained in three official communiqués between the United States and the PRC, acknowledged that there is only one China and Taiwan is part of China. The ambiguous aspect of the U.S. commitment to defend Taiwan was laid out in the 1979 Taiwan Relations Act (TRA) after the United States abrogated its 1954 mutual defense treaty with the Republic of China (ROC) government. The TRA states that the United States expects "the future of Taiwan will be determined by peaceful means (Taiwan Relations Act, Sec. 2b). Additionally, the act states that the United States reserves the right "to resist any resort to force or other forms of coercion that would jeopardize the security, or the social or economic system, of the people of Taiwan" (Taiwan Relations Act, Sec. 2b) but that such a decision must be a joint decision between the president and the Congress. In sum, the policy holds that, even though the United States acknowledges there is only one China and that Taiwan is part of China, it nevertheless may intervene to defend Taiwan from China if the president and Congress agree to do so.

The commitment meets the definition of a probabilistic commitment laid out in the typology in Chapter 2. In the policy of strategic ambiguity, there is no blanket commitment of guaranteed military assistance in the event of war, nor are there specific conditions that may arise in a conflict that automatically trigger a U.S. military response. Instead, U.S. intervention would be decided by the executive branch and a vote of agreement in Congress. There is widespread uncertainty about how the United States would respond if the PRC and Taiwan became engaged in a war, because U.S. intervention depends, in large part, on the mood of Congress at the time of a decision.

The purpose of the policy, which has been more or less supported by every U.S. presidential administration since the adoption of the TRA in 1979,[1] is to deter the PRC from attacking Taiwan while simultaneously restraining Taiwan from provoking China by moving toward independence.[2] There is some evidence that the policy has, in fact, served as an effective mechanism for restraining Taiwan. Public opinion polling in Taiwan has shown that Taiwanese voters would support independence if they believed it could be achieved without the risk of retaliation from China, and the degree to which they feel threatened by China depends on whether they believe that the United States will defend Taiwan if there is a war. Because voters' opinions about whether the United States will defend them are mixed, it is possible to infer from public opinion that the U.S. policy of ambiguity helps restrain Taiwan from behaving overly aggressively toward China (Benson and Niou 2005; Niou 2004).

However, many influential voices have called for a change in the U.S. policy, proposing that the United States clarify its intentions. Detractors often object to the probabilistic commitment because uncertainty is generally believed to be associated with war, not peace. From this perspective, the uncertainty created by the policy of ambiguity may enhance the chances for a dangerous mistake by one of the actors involved in the dispute. For instance, China might underestimate U.S. intentions and initiate hostilities with Taiwan, or Taiwan may be overconfident in its belief that it will receive U.S. support and push so aggressively for autonomy that its actions might trigger a violent backlash from Beijing. An additional cause of worry is the fact that the costs of making a mistake in the Taiwan Strait are too high to leave matters to chance; a misstep carries extraordinary risks by bringing the two most powerful countries in the world into conflict.

Since the scare of the 1995–96 missile crisis, there have been three main proposals for a policy change. The first, voiced by some influential academics and policy makers, called for the United States to adopt a conditional deterrent commitment. Former Assistant Secretary of Defense Joseph Nye recommended that the current U.S. policy be replaced with an unambiguous commitment to defend Taiwan if and only if China attacks it without provocation.[3] Though not as explicit, former Secretary of State Henry Kissinger's 1999 proposal was in a similar vein, suggesting that U.S. policy should insist that Taiwan foreswear moves toward independence.[4] The policy of conditional deterrence

---

[1] The administration of George W. Bush began by deviating from the policy but, as will be discussed later, ended up reverting to the probabilistic commitment.
[2] Numerous scholars have written about the deterrence-versus-restraint objective of the strategic ambiguity policy. See, for example, Tucker (2009); Christensen (2011); Rigger (2006); Kastner (2006); Crawford (2003); and Hickey (1997).
[3] See Joseph S. Nye, Jr., "A Taiwan Deal," *Washington Post* (March 8, 1998), sec. C.
[4] See Henry Kissinger, "The Way to Avoid Confrontation," *Yomiuri Shimbun*, October 25, 1999.

was fleshed out in greater detail by former Deputy Assistant Secretary of State Thomas Christensen (2002), who stated that the new policy would create the benefit of demonstrating that "the United States has strong interests in Taiwan maintaining that [democratic] status and will not fight for Taiwan if it chooses to defy U.S. interests by declaring independence" (19). Christensen claimed that "a clear but conditional commitment to Taiwan's security might best serve U.S. interests," because it would prevent war while preserving Taiwan's democratic form of government by reducing Beijing's fear that Taiwan will become independent under the protection of the United States (20).

A second option for shifting policy was championed for a short time by President George W. Bush when he took office in 2001. The Bush administration arrived in Washington with the intention of strengthening U.S. alliances, walking back Clinton's engagement of China, and bolstering Taiwan's democracy and security in light of China's buildup of missiles across the Taiwan Strait from Taiwan (Tucker 2009, 255–259). In April 2001, George Bush announced that the United States would "do whatever it took" to defend Taiwan, and Vice President Dick Cheney followed the comment a few days later by saying that perhaps strategic ambiguity was not an appropriate response to China's increasingly threatening posture toward Taiwan (Tucker 2009, 261). Although the United States appeared to be on course for a firmer and less ambiguous security relationship with Taiwan, Bush doubled back on its policy in response to increased adventurism by Taiwan President Chen Shui-bian, who began pressing for a referendum on independence and characterized the relationship between China and Taiwan as "one country on each side" of the Taiwan Strait (Christensen 2011, 249). In an effort to reestablish a distance between the United States and an increasingly aggressive Taiwan government, Bush stated in 2003, "We oppose any unilateral decision by either China or Taiwan to change the status quo" (Tucker 2009, 268). However, the Bush administration never specified what actions would be regarded as violations of the status quo; by the end of the Bush administration, U.S. policy toward the Taiwan issue had reverted back to the long-standing probabilistic commitment of strategic ambiguity.

A third proposal advocated abandoning the TRA and the U.S. relationship with Taiwan. The most prominent position claimed that the future of United States–China relations was too important to allow the Taiwan issue to cause a distraction (Gilley 2010; Glaser 2011). This viewpoint rests on a basic principle that the United States does not gain from an outcome that benefits Taiwan at China's expense. Rather, from this perspective, a settlement of the Taiwan issue that favors the PRC is also in the U.S. interest, because the Taiwan issue stands between a bright horizon of cooperation between the United States and China. Another argument contends that strategic ambiguity has become too confusing and dangerous. Thus, the United States should continue to sell arms to Taiwan but make it clear that there is no security commitment, even an ambiguous one, to defend Taiwan (Carpenter 2005).

By applying the argument I have laid out in this book, it may be possible to understand why the U.S. policy originated as a probabilistic commitment as opposed to other potential mechanisms – such as conditional and pure conditional commitments – also designed for balancing deterrence and restraint. Another goal is to explain why there have been pressures to change the policy – and why it has remained unchanged. Finally, the implications of the theory in this book also allow us to identify conditions under which the policy may change in the future. By pinning down the relative preferences and capabilities of China, Taiwan, and the United States as well as the observability of China and Taiwan's provocative actions, we may be able to justify analytically the 1979 version of the U.S. policy, and to explain what pressures led to calls for a policy change and why those proposals ultimately failed to gain traction.

What distinguishes the United States–Taiwan relationship in the era after the passage of the TRA – and, especially, since Taiwan's democratization – is that Taiwan's primary threat to the PRC now consists in becoming independent from China rather than staging a military expedition to reclaim the mainland. Of course, the PRC views Taiwan as a renegade province and, ideally, prefers to unite Taiwan with the mainland under the PRC leadership. The official position of the U.S. government, as set forth in the TRA, implies that the United States feels strongly about the peace and security of Taiwan but is indifferent about the disposition of a negotiated settlement of the disagreement. However, decision makers in the United States are not always perfectly indifferent as to how the matter should be settled. For example, the suggestion made by the third group of detractors described earlier, who propose that strategic ambiguity should be abandoned, is motivated by a preference for settlement of the Taiwan issue that favors the PRC, so United States–China relations can progress without distraction. On the other hand, others, such as Nancy Tucker, suggest that peaceful unification is not in the interests of the United States and Japan because China would control critical sea lanes, possess forward naval capability, and gain access to proprietary military technology by acquiring U.S. weaponry sold to Taiwan (Tucker 2002). Moreover, what outcome is favored often appears to differ across administrations. Contrast, for example, Jimmy Carter's low value placed on Taiwan's survival to George W. Bush's desire to elevate the status of Taiwan's democratic government.

In addition to there being variation in preferences for the settlement of the disagreement over Taiwan's sovereignty, shifts in the relative capabilities of all three actors may also influence the U.S. commitment toward Taiwan. Although the United States has consistently been the strongest of the three actors, both China and Taiwan have become more powerful relative to the United States in the past two decades. The relative capabilities of China, Taiwan, and the United States can be established using the capabilities index in the Correlates of War dataset (Singer, Bremer, and Stuckey, 1972; Singer 1988). Scholars have used the capabilities index to estimate the probability of a country winning a war against another country (see, for example, Bueno de Mesquita 1983). At

Constructing Security in Today's World

the time the TRA was being considered by Congress in 1978–1979, the ratio of capabilities between China and Taiwan significantly advantaged China. Estimating Taiwan's likelihood of winning a hypothetical war by calculating its capabilities as a percentage of the combined capabilities of both China and Taiwan, Taiwan stood only approximately a 5 to 6 percent chance of winning in a head-to-head matchup. Full U.S. assistance would increase those chances to approximately 55 percent, implying that the U.S. contribution amounted to an increase of almost 50 percent.

Of course, there are inherent difficulties related to the military objective of conquering Taiwan that strengthen the Taiwan–United States bond beyond a comparison of raw capabilities. Taiwan is an island approximately 100 miles away from China's coast. For the government of China to raise a PRC flag over Taipei, the PLA would need to launch a long-distance attack over open waters and then carry out a difficult amphibious assault on inhospitable terrain after arriving on the coast of Taiwan. The difficulty of establishing a beachhead and waging an offensive campaign on Taiwan gives the Taiwan military a defensive advantage. Perhaps even more problematic from China's perspective is the fact that the open-water attack would place it at a significant disadvantage to U.S. naval superiority. There were legitimate doubts that the PRC could undertake a successful amphibious lift sufficient to take over Taiwan (O'Hanlon 2000), although by that time the PRC had already begun a buildup of missile capability sufficient to significantly damage Taiwan's infrastructure and economy. Thus, the capabilities index alone yields an overly generous estimate of China's ability to prevail over Taiwan and the United States in a war for Taiwan's sovereignty. It is useful to use the capabilities ratio to establish a baseline for the analysis, for we may assume that it sets a minimum estimate of the probability that the United States and Taiwan might prevail over the PRC. Given that the United States and Taiwan would be further advantaged by only having to defend the island of Taiwan from an offensive attack, their probability of winning against the PRC likely exceeds the estimate based on the ratio of capabilities.

Figure 8.1 presents a depiction of the U.S. options in 1978, based on the theory presented in Chapter 5, given a range of potential preferences for the ideal settlement and the relative strength of the United States. The horizontal axis represents the amount that the United States could potentially contribute to a war between China and Taiwan, and the vertical axis represents the ideal settlement of the Taiwan issue from the standpoint of the United States. The various marked regions in the figure represent the types of security commitment the United States might select under various parameter values. The characterization of the commitments in the figure assumes that the United States places value on the security of Taiwan, as Congress in fact did in 1978–79, regardless of its preference for the disposition of the settlement of the dispute between the PRC and ROC. Note that, consistent with the theory I have presented in this book, the commitments predicted in Figure 8.1 are more likely to become

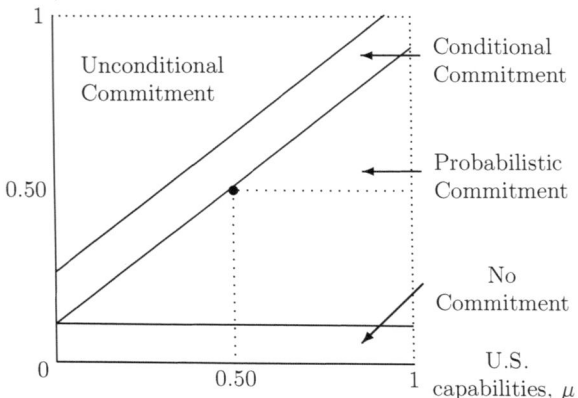

FIGURE 8.1. The effect of U.S. capabilities and preferences on its security commitment to Taiwan in 1979.

unconditional if the U.S. preference for the settlement converges on Taiwan's ideal outcome, and the likelihood of an ambiguous commitment increases if the U.S. capabilities grow large.

The point in the center of the figure represents the most extreme corner of the set of reasonable parameter values that fit the situation in 1978. The point represents the conservative estimate of the U.S. capabilities as estimated by the raw capabilities ratio in 1978 and an estimate of the U.S. preference of the ideal peaceful settlement of the dispute that was overly generous in Taiwan's direction. Because Taiwan enjoyed the tactical advantage of being able to defend the island from an amphibious assault, in reality the potential U.S. contribution was probably greater than 0.5, placing a more accurate estimate of U.S. capabilities somewhere to the right of the point in the figure. Carter administration officials took the position that there was no security threat to Taiwan, because the PRC lacked the capability to attack and take Taiwan (Tucker 2009, 119). From this perspective, even modest contributions of assistance from the United States would have an outsized impact on a hypothetical war. Thus, we assume that the U.S. capabilities in 1978 lay somewhere between 0.5 and 1.

Estimating the U.S. ideal settlement at 0.5 in 1978 is also a conservative approximation, as the Carter administration not only disagreed with Taiwan's position that the ROC should be the legitimate ruling government for all of China but also favored clarifying the issue by formally establishing the de facto reality that the PRC was the official government for all of China. Thus, a more accurate assessment of the U.S. preference at the time would lean more toward the PRC, which implies that the actual estimate should be less than 0.5 and somewhere below the point in the figure.

Constructing Security in Today's World 177

Combining these two estimates on both dimensions yields a set of feasible parameter values, demarcated by the square in the bottom right corner of the figure, that approximate the actual environment in 1978. In this region, there are only two possible commitments that the United States might have selected – they are a probabilistic commitment and no commitment, although a probabilistic commitment represents the largest area of the region. The logic here helps explain why the United States ended up devising a probabilistic commitment. The strong support in the United States for a secure Taiwan led the United States to form some sort of deterrent commitment, but the stark difference in capabilities and divergence of preferences over the policy settlement between the United States and Taiwan created strong incentives for the United States to blunt Taiwan's interest in taking advantage of the relationship to push its view of one China. The result was the ambiguity of the TRA.

The logic for the inception of the U.S. probabilistic commitment in the TRA is intuitive enough. One particularly compelling question, though, is why there was so much pressure to change the policy by the 1990s and early 2000s. It is especially interesting when we consider that some important factors did not change between 1978 and around 2001. The U.S. interest in Taiwan's security remained relatively solid, as did the U.S. concern that overcommitment to Taiwan might lead Taiwan to provoke China. In fact, one might argue that the emergence of Taiwan independence, rather than retaking the mainland, as the new pathway by which Taiwan might provoke China posed more realistic options for Taiwan that even increased the moral hazard risks of commitment to Taiwan. Nevertheless, many called for a clear conditional commitment to replace a probabilistic commitment. And, the Bush administration clearly made bolder moves toward an unconditional commitment.

The main reason that pressures for a policy change mounted was that during the time between 1978 and 2001, when Bush made his "whatever it takes" statement in support of Taiwan, the relative capabilities of the three actors underwent a shift. Taiwan's ability to defeat China in head-to-head war increased to 7 percent based on raw capabilities alone; in addition, because China also became more powerful during this time period, the value of how much the United States could improve Taiwan's relative strength in a hypothetical war between China and Taiwan dropped. According to the measure of raw capabilities, the U.S. impact amounted to approximately 0.47, compared with 0.50 in 1978. Moreover, this estimate, though still generous toward China for which a successful amphibious assault still likely remained out of reach, is nevertheless more accurate than the 1978 estimate of 0.50 because by the early 2000s China had developed a strong missile arsenal capable of doing severe damage to the island of Taiwan and potentially to U.S. forces in the Taiwan Strait and perhaps abroad.

The shift in relative capabilities likely caused some disaffection with the U.S. policy of ambiguity by the late 1990s, especially because the stakes of

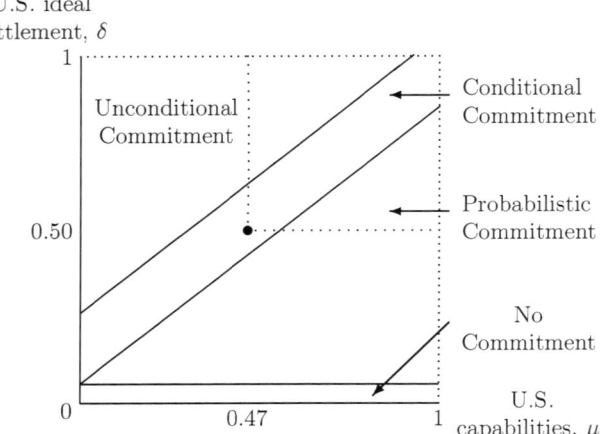

FIGURE 8.2. The effect of U.S. capabilities and preferences on its security commitment to Taiwan in 2001.

the dispute between China and Taiwan changed from the leadership of all of China to the sovereign status of the island of Taiwan. Figure 8.2 displays the commitment options with the updated capabilities for 2001. The shift in capabilities results in modifications to the commitment regions as well as the optimal choice of the U.S. commitment. Comparing Figures 8.1 and 8.2, it is clear that if the U.S. preferences on Taiwan's security and the ideal settlement remain unchanged across the two time periods, then the U.S. would push for a conditional type of commitment in 2001 just because Taiwan and China became relatively stronger. It is reasonable, then, why some may have called for a change in policy in 2001; even though the U.S. government faced a deterrence-versus-restraint dilemma in the Taiwan Strait (Ross 2002), the minor reduction in the relative capabilities of the United States may have decreased Taiwan's expectations about what it could gain in bargaining just enough that those who were less concerned about the disposition of the eventual settlement of the dispute than the security of the region might have no longer perceived a need for a probabilistic commitment. Under these circumstances – where policy experts in the United States believe restraining Taiwan was critical but feel unthreatened by the potential policy implications of bargaining between China and Taiwan – it is understandable why they might call for a conditional commitment.

There were, however, others – most notably, those in the Bush administration – who favored an outcome more closely aligned with Taiwan's ideal settlement. What may have given rise to the support of Taiwan was democratization in Taiwan and the Taiwan government's change in focus from aspiring to retake mainland China to pushing for greater autonomy from the PRC. The shift in what China and Taiwan were bargaining over – from the leadership of

China to the sovereignty of Taiwan – brought sympathizers of Taiwan's democracy much closer to Taiwan's ideal point. On the policy dimension of Figure 8.2, we might represent these pro-Taiwan tendencies as lying somewhere above the 0.50 mark on the y-axis. The square region in the top right-hand corner of Figure 8.2 represents the set of optimal commitments the United States might choose within the feasible range of parameter values for the U.S. capabilities and pro-Taiwan preferences at the time. For those who have sufficiently high values of policy preferences on the y-axis, it is natural that they might prefer an unconditional commitment to Taiwan.

Understanding the third proposal for a policy change, the abandonment of Taiwan, does not require so sophisticated an explanation, because the viewpoint is primarily motivated by a claim about what U.S. preferences on the status of the Taiwan issue should be. The main argument is that Taiwan's interests are no longer as important to the United States as more important issues related to United States–China relations (Glaser 2011), especially because Taiwan's interests may best be served by the United States withdrawing its influence completely so that Taiwan can interact directly with China without distraction (Gilley 2010). Figures 8.1 and 8.2 both show that for sufficiently low values of U.S. preferences on the y-axis, the United States should abandon Taiwan, even if its interests in Taiwan's security remain high. Abandoning Taiwan would give China a strong advantage in negotiations between China and Taiwan, resulting in a settlement that clearly favors China. If, in fact, the preferences of the U.S. government shift toward a solution to the Taiwan problem that strongly favors China, then the clear policy implication is that the United States should abandon Taiwan. However, it is doubtful that the preferences of the general public or the government of the United States have reached this point.[5]

The logic of my theory of designing security commitments has provided some insights about why alternatives to strategic ambiguity became increasingly popular as Taiwan and China became more powerful and as the shift in the disputed issue from reclaiming the mainland to Taiwan independence brought about changes in Americans' preferences about how the dispute should be settled. With many calls for a policy change, why did the United States revert to strategic ambiguity rather than revise the policy? One obvious possibility is that the capabilities of the United States are far greater than the approximately 0.5 level estimated in Figures 8.1 and 8.2. If U.S. assistance in a war would be of significantly greater benefit to Taiwan, then, as can be seen in Figure 8.2, an ambiguous commitment is the dominant choice for a wide range of U.S. preferences on the ideal settlement on the y-axis. In other words, the more Taiwan stands to benefit from U.S. assistance in a war against China, the more aggressively it will push for concessions from the PRC in crisis bargaining. Because Taiwan's aggressive bargaining can result in a settlement far from

---

[5] See Tucker and Glaser (2011) for an argument about why it is not in U.S. interests to abandon Taiwan.

what the United States would prefer, then the United States can do better by inducing less aggressive bargaining on Taiwan's part by adopting a probabilistic commitment.

A more plausible explanation for the survival of the U.S. policy of strategic ambiguity is related to the difficulty of drawing up a commitment that specifies all the conditions under which Taiwan may violate the commitment. The argument in this book has shown that unobservable actions inhibit a government's ability to form conditional commitments. In a similar vein, if it is too costly for the United States to specify and monitor all the ways its actions might nullify the U.S. obligation to defend Taiwan, then if China attacks Taiwan it would be difficult to determine whether it was provoked or not. Early in the United States–Taiwan relationship, the United States worried that overcommitting to Chiang Kaishek would embolden him to take military actions against the PRC in an effort to retake China's mainland. Today, the threat of Taiwan's independence presents a new kind of challenge for the United States, as Taiwan may now provoke China through political actions pertaining to independence rather than military actions related to retaking the mainland. Specifying and monitoring all the possible ways in which Taiwan's actions qualify as a move toward independence pose significant costs to a third-party defender. The task is made even more problematic by the fact that Taiwan, as a political entity with a foreign policy and military, already engages in many of the behaviors of autonomous states. Hence, just continuing some existing activities may be construed as moving toward independence. Alternatively, the United States would have to pay the costs of distinguishing which actions are new moves toward independence and which actions would get grandfathered in.

Indeed, drawing a line when it comes to a political issue such as independence for a quasi-autonomous entity such as Taiwan creates challenges for all three players. China has an interest in deterring Taiwan's independence and, accordingly, has threatened, in its anti-secession law, that it might use force to prevent Taiwan from moving toward independence. On the Taiwan side, President Ma Ying-jeou has pledged not to pursue independence in his "three noes" policy as a stepping-stone toward negotiations and better relations. The United States, too, has discouraged independence. When President George W. Bush began to back away from his early efforts to tighten relations with Taiwan, he announced that the United States opposed any unilateral move toward independence. Demonstrating the success of China's deterrent threat, Taiwan's promise not to pursue independence, and the U.S. efforts to restrain Taiwan require that actions leading to independence be identifiable. However, no actor has specified a list of behaviors that would constitute a breach of promise. Meanwhile, Taiwan buys arms from the United States, has joined the World Health Organization with the PRC's blessing, and has recently expressed interest in participating in more international organizations.[6]

---

[6] See Saunders and Kastner (2009) for some discussion about the problems associated with specifying an agreement between China and Taiwan prohibiting moves toward independence.

Constructing Security in Today's World

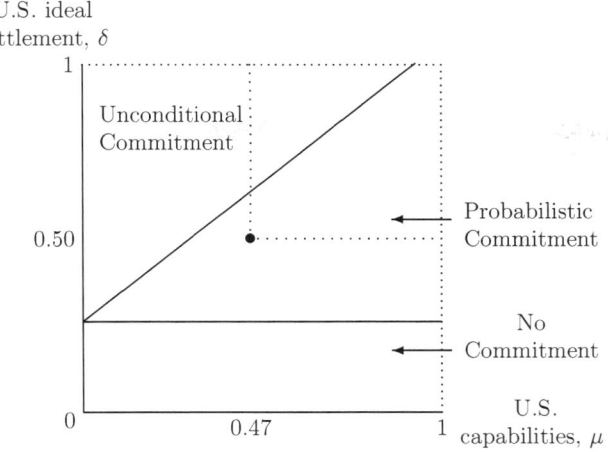

FIGURE 8.3. The effect of U.S. capabilities and preferences on its security commitment to Taiwan if Taiwan's moves toward independence are costly to observe and enforce.

The difficulty of specifying and monitoring actions leading to independence causes the third-party defender to form a commitment contingent on there being a war and not on any action that might provoke a war. If, in fact, specifying and monitoring moves toward independence are cost prohibitive, then the United States would be unable to enforce a pure conditional commitment that would obligate it to intervene if and only if China attacks and Taiwan did not first move toward independence. There would also be problems for a standard conditional commitment that promises assistance if China attacks Taiwan and says nothing about what the United States would do if Taiwan moved toward independence. Although a conditional commitment such as this is enforceable, because an attack on Taiwan would be observable, it may exacerbate moral hazard by inducing Taiwan to be especially aggressive in taking actions toward independence. The promise to defend if China attacked would provide cover behind the U.S. military for Taiwan to behave so aggressively that either China would make sizable concessions to avoid war or attack Taiwan.

The main implication of this monitoring problem for how the United States forms its security commitment with Taiwan is that the United States might be better off selecting an unconditional commitment, a probabilistic commitment, or no commitment. Figure 8.3 shows the type of commitment the United States might select to manage security in the Taiwan Strait given the problem of specifying and monitoring Taiwan's activities related to independence. The probabilistic commitment region encompassing the point, which represents an estimate of U.S preferences and capabilities in the status quo, overlaps with much of the conditional commitment area in Figure 8.2. The U.S. selection of a probabilistic commitment is fairly robust to differing characterizations of the status quo. If, for example, the U.S. capabilities are greater than the estimate point in the figure, which is likely to be the reality given the military advantage of defending Taiwan, then the selection of a probabilistic commitment remains the optimal option for all values of U.S. capabilities. Suppose, alternatively, that a future U.S. leader had pro-Taiwan sympathies. The logic of the argument suggests that the new leader would likely have to be more pro-Taiwan than George W. Bush was before it would overturn the policy of strategic ambiguity. If such a pro-Taiwan government gained power in the United States, the policy would likely shift toward an unconditional commitment, because the effect of moral hazard would actually benefit the pro-Taiwan leader, as it would induce aggressive bargaining by Taiwan and a more pro-Taiwan outcome.

On the other hand, for a pro-PRC U.S. leader, the difficulty specifying and monitoring independence-seeking actions imposes a lower threshold for switching from strategic ambiguity to abandonment. That is, compared with Figure 8.2, it is clear that there is a larger no-commitment region when the actions leading toward independence are too costly to specify and monitor. The reason Taiwan's ability to take hidden actions results in a higher likelihood that the United States will abandon Taiwan for a greater range of parameter values is that difficulty observing Taiwan's actions exacerbates the problem of moral hazard, resulting in a greater likelihood Taiwan will respond to any commitment, even a probabilistic one, by moving toward independence. Thus, a pro-PRC U.S. leader will be less likely to offer even a probabilistic commitment for some parameter values where the same leader would otherwise form a probabilistic commitment if undesirable actions by Taiwan could be costlessly monitored and prohibited.

The foregoing analysis describes a possibility of a policy shift only if the U.S. government changes to become significantly more sympathetic either toward Taiwan independence or unification. Otherwise, the current U.S. policy of strategic ambiguity makes sense given its goals of deterring China while simultaneously restraining Taiwan. The calls for changes in U.S. policy are understandable given that some relative power shifts since the passage of the TRA have altered actors' incentives somewhat. However, strategic ambiguity remains the optimal U.S. policy, primarily because the list of Taiwan's provocative actions are not easy to specify in a commitment; in addition, the United States is so powerful compared with Taiwan that any type of firm commitment – conditional or unconditional – would likely cause Taiwan to behave so aggressively that the impact on crisis bargaining may well result in an outcome that would make the United States worse off than what it can expect to receive by being ambiguous.

Looking forward, there are several implications for U.S. policy. The first is that a conditional commitment is not viable and may even intensify the crisis until it is possible to specify precisely what constitutes a move toward independence. Second, if the peace and security of Taiwan remain a priority for the United States but the United States becomes sufficiently pro-PRC, then abandoning Taiwan may actually benefit the United States because doing so would likely result in Taiwan making concessions to China without a significant increase in the probability of war. In recent years, policy experts have pressed the case that the United States should be more interested in a settlement of the Taiwan issue that favors the PRC. If pro-PRC sentiment in the United States grows dramatically and concern about Taiwan's security remains high, then the logical policy response would be for the United States to clearly remove any commitment to defend Taiwan. Third, as long as it remains problematic to condition a commitment on Taiwan's actions, a resurgence of pro-Taiwan sentiment among U.S. decision-makers might result in a shift to an unconditional commitment, even if the subsequent risk of moral hazard would cause those decision-makers to worry.

Other implications depend on shifts in capabilities. One surprising insight is that if China continues to get stronger relative to the United States and the capabilities difference between the United States and Taiwan remains the same, then the United States may gravitate toward a firmer commitment to enhance deterrence. The intuitive thought might be that the United States would instead be more likely to abandon Taiwan as China gets stronger. However, the increased relative strength of China would do a great deal to deter Taiwan from provoking China, and this reduces the pressure on the United States to restrain Taiwan. Under these circumstances and assuming that the U.S. interest in the security of Taiwan remains high, the United States would benefit from switching to a more transparent deterrent commitment. However, if the increased power of China also threatens to bring broader U.S. interests into harm's way, then perhaps the U.S. security interests in Taiwan would decrease. The short-term effect of such a transition in both power and preferences might be that the United States would remain ambiguous and may even become more firm and transparent until its own security interests clearly outweigh its interests in defending Taiwan, at which point it might weaken its commitment to Taiwan and perhaps even abandon it.

Finally, there are some implications for U.S. arms sales to Taiwan. The stronger the United States is relative to Taiwan, the greater the potential distortion to Taiwan's behavior as a result of moral hazard. Thus, if the United States or both the United States and China continue to grow stronger but Taiwan remains dependent on the United States for security, then, all else being equal, we might expect the policy of strategic ambiguity to continue indefinitely. Therefore, the best option for clarifying U.S. policy toward Taiwan, short of changing U.S. security interests or preferences for how the Taiwan issue should be settled, involves strengthening Taiwan's military capabilities. The combination of increased arms sales and, if possible, an effort to clarify what constitutes a move toward independence might make it possible to adopt a conditional deterrent commitment. However, the policy of strategic ambiguity will likely remain as long as U.S. interests remain consistent, the United States remains a dominant military force, and it is too costly to design a commitment conditional on the non-pursuit of independence-seeking activities.

China's Alliance with North Korea

The theory developed in this book has policy implications for security agreements beyond the Taiwan Strait. I now briefly examine one more military commitment in another one of the world's most perilous security environments. In 1961, China and North Korea signed the Sino-North Korean Mutual Aid and Cooperation Friendship Treaty. It was renewed in 2001, and is set for renewal again in 2021. In the treaty, China and North Korea agreed to use all necessary means to oppose any country or coalition of countries that attacks either alliance member. The commitment contained in the treaty meets the definition of a conditional commitment established in Chapter 2. As North Korea has turned its focus in recent decades to developing a nuclear weapons program, there is a risk to China that overcommitment might distort North Korea's behavior toward South Korea and the United States. Let us evaluate the circumstances involving China, North Korea, and the South Korea–United States alliance to determine what, if anything, might lead China to revise its commitment with North Korea.

Let us begin by analyzing the effect of shifts in China's and North Korea's capabilities on their security commitment. To get leverage on this effect, we need to pin down some estimated values for China's preferences regarding both North Korea's security and the ideal settlement of the policy disagreement between North and South Korea. First, consider how much the PRC government values North Korea's security. Throughout China's history, defending its northeastern border has been a top priority. Because the Korean peninsula connects northeastern China to Japan, controlling Korea – or, at the very least, ensuring that it remains in friendly hands – has always been an important key to securing China's northeastern border. North Korea remains just as critical to China's security today. It serves as a crucial buffer not just between China and Japan, but also between China and the U.S. military stationed in South Korea. Therefore, throughout the analysis, we will assume that China places high value on North Korea's security.[7]

With respect to China's preference for how the dispute between North and South Korea will be settled, China has changed its view from 1961, when it signed the treaty, to the present time. The main point of dispute between North and South Korea has historically been who should govern a united Korean peninsula. Even after the armistice ending the Korean War was signed in 1953, North Korea, or the Democratic People's Republic of Korea (DPRK), was determined to find a way to reunite Korea – forcibly, if necessary. This desire continued throughout the 1960s. Regardless of what the PRC government, led by Chairman Mao, privately preferred, it publicly supported North Korea's goal to unite Korea under the DPRK. The 1961 treaty clearly states

---

[7] For the strategic importance of the Korean peninsula see Han (2004, 163) and Bedeski (1995, 516–518).

that China recognizes North Korea as the only legitimate government for all of Korea.

In the 1990s, the PRC signaled its shift away from supporting North Korea's agenda to unite the Korean peninsula. In 1991, the PRC supported extending membership for both North and South Korea into the United Nations. Then, in 1992, the PRC government normalized diplomatic relations with South Korea. In a major departure from previous statements, the PRC also publicly announced that it believed the U.S. military presence in South Korea helped stabilize Korea. For the DPRK, the PRC's normalization of relations with South Korea marked a betrayal of the one-Korea policy laid out in the Sino-North Korean treaty.[8] For the PRC, however, normalizing relations served its interests. Retaining North Korea as a buffer while gaining a valuable trade relationship with South Korea advanced China's economic modernization objectives of the 1990s without compromising its security goals. Reunification by either North Korea or South Korea through crisis bargaining would likely have undermined these benefits. Additionally, instability on the peninsula could have triggered a mass migration of refugees from North Korea to China. From the PRC's perspective, then, peaceful maintenance of the status quo division of the Korean peninsula served its interests well in the early 1990s. Circumstances remain similar today.

Now, let us consider the effect of China's and North Korea's capabilities on China's optimal choice of security commitment to North Korea given the assumption that China values North Korea's security and prefers the status quo division of Korea. In Figure 8.4, the point represents an estimate of both China's and North Korea's capabilities. The estimates are based on the 2001 capabilities index and are evaluated relative to both the capabilities of the United States and South Korea. It makes sense to group the United States and South Korea together as the expected adversary of North Korea, because the United States has troops stationed in South Korea and the United States and South Korea are bound by a military alliance. The capabilities estimate for China is 0.40 and is 0.07 for North Korea. As the figure demonstrates, this estimate narrowly predicts a conditional commitment, which is what the existing Sino-North Korea treaty is. However, relatively small shifts in the capabilities of either North Korea or China could destabilize China's incentives for maintaining this type of commitment.

How might China's commitment to North Korea change? Given that North Korea is working to build its nuclear weapons arsenal and China's recent growth puts it on a trajectory to continue developing, it is unlikely that the capabilities of North Korea and China will decrease relative to the United States and South Korea. Hence, a future shift in capabilities would most likely

---

[8] See Han (2004, 162) and Wang (1998, 189–190). For more discussion about China's transition away from supporting unification and current support for the status quo, see Bedeski (1995) and Wang (1999).

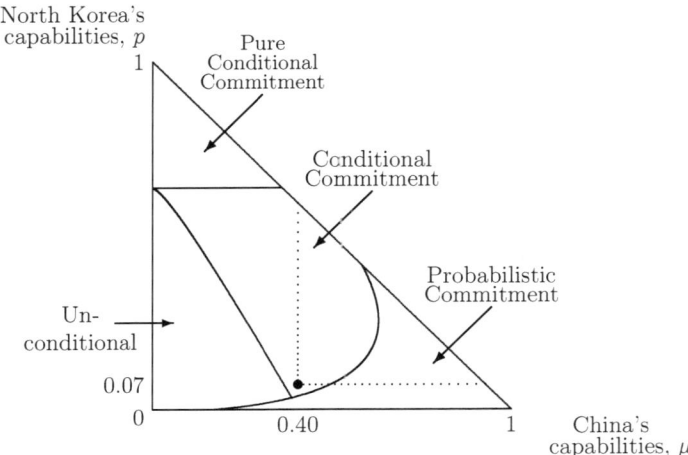

FIGURE 8.4. Effect of China's and North Korea's capabilities on China's security commitment to North Korea.

favor either North Korea or China or both. In Figure 8.4, the triangular region delineated by the dotted lines up and to the right of the point encompasses the set of commitments that correspond to positive shifts in capabilities for North Korea and China. The only other commitment in this region is a probabilistic commitment, which might emerge if the amount China could potentially contribute to a fight between North Korea and the United States–South Korea alliance increases. If China becomes more powerful, there is a greater potential for North Korea to exploit China's power for its own benefit against China's interests. A probabilistic commitment can diminish the amount North Korea expects to benefit from China's assistance and thereby moderate the level of North Korea's aggressiveness. Based on shifts in capabilities alone, then, the most likely scenario is that the policy remains a conditional commitment or, if anything, becomes a probabilistic commitment because of an increase in China's strength.

Shifts in capabilities are only one avenue by which China's commitment to North Korea may change. Changes in China's preferences toward North Korea may also affect the future security commitment. In fact, North Korea's transition in focus from uniting Korea to developing nuclear weapons may already have caused the goals of North Korea and China to diverge, and this divergence of preferences may be pressuring China to weaken its commitment to North Korea.

Figure 8.5 shows the effect of China's preferences on its choice of security commitment if the capabilities for China and North Korea are set equal to the status quo estimate shown in Figure 8.4. The point represents the optimal commitment if China has high value for North Korea's security and prefers

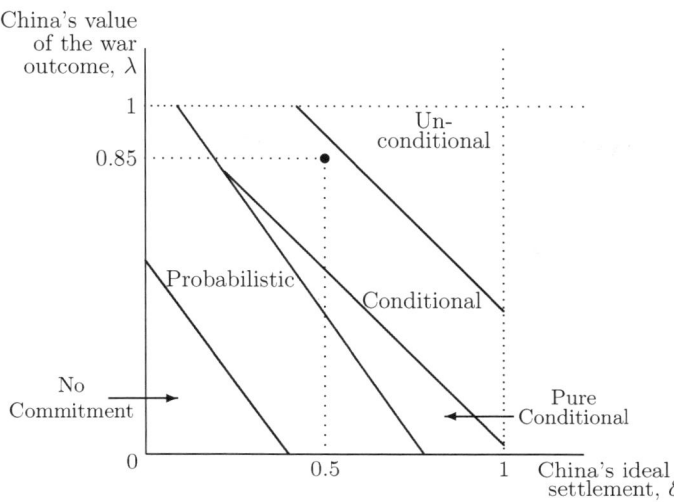

FIGURE 8.5. The effect of China's preferences on its security commitment to North Korea.

the status quo division of Korea. As discussed previously, there is little reason to believe that China's value for North Korea's security has diminished. Its preference for the ideal settlement, however, may have begun to diverge from North Korea's ideal, as now the potential for crisis is no longer just about who rules the Korean peninsula. The dispute now also entails a disagreement about North Korea's nuclear weapons program and its status in the international community.

What does North Korea want today? It is reasonable that, as before, it still ideally hopes to unite Korea under a DPRK government, even if it may believe that such a goal is infeasible. Beyond that, however, there is a solid argument that North Korea's primary goal is to be an established nuclear weapons state and to have special security guarantees (Cha 2009b). Victor Cha, former director of Asian affairs on the National Security Council from 2004 to 2007 and deputy head of the U.S. delegation to the Six-Party Talks during that time, has concluded from his experience negotiating with North Korea that the DPRK government wants to be accepted as a nuclear power on par with India and Pakistan, with the amount of weaponization subject to negotiation but, ultimately, the ability to retain a baseline level of nuclear energy and weapons granted indefinitely (122–124). Additionally, Cha claims that the DPRK ideally would also like positive security assurances that the United States and others will ensure the survival of the regime as it wades through economic reforms that could spell the government's demise (125–127).

The shift in stakes in the North Korea problem has implications for China's ideal settlement. If China's preferences have not changed, but North Korea's appetite has grown, then China's relative preferences for the settlement have shifted away from North Korea's ideal point toward the United States–South Korea alliance. Downward shifts in China's preferences for the settlement along the x-axis in Figure 8.5 predict a weakening in China's commitment toward North Korea.

Depending on how much China's preferences have actually changed, it may already prefer a probabilistic to a conditional commitment. Consistent with this possibility, many claim that the Sino-North Korean treaty can no longer be interpreted as a clear defense pact. China experts point to understated anniversary celebrations of the Sino-North Korea alliance as evidence that China is deliberately downplaying the treaty's significance (Wu 2005, 42). Additionally, much has been made of comments by prominent Chinese scholars, whose statements are likely screened by government censors; thus, that they have been made public may suggest that they are consistent with the government's current thinking regarding the status of the security commitment to North Korea. For example, Shen Jiru at the Institute of World Economy and Politics declared that the mutual defense article in the treaty should be removed. However, because the treaty includes a clause stipulating that the treaty obligations cannot be abrogated except by mutual agreement, the PRC cannot simply drop the provision of mutual defense.[9]

Another scholar, Shi Yinhong of Renmin University in Beijing, stated that "China will not support anyone's aggression on the Korean peninsula, whether it's from North Korea or a counterattack from the United States-South Korea alliance against North Korea's aggression." Although Shi did not say how China would respond if there was conflict on the Korean peninsula, he did affirm, in a comment reminiscent of the strategic ambiguity in the U.S. Taiwan Relations Act, that "North Korea's survival is so vital to China's interest."[10]

The analysis of China's commitment to North Korea suggests that China's security promise to defend North Korea if it is attacked may be weakening, and the risk of moral hazard is likely the reason. As China becomes stronger and its interests continue to diverge from North Korea's, the conditional commitment in the existing Sino-North Korean treaty will likely distort North Korea's behavior, encouraging it to behave more aggressively in its actions toward South Korea and the United States. North Korea's recent hostile behavior in the Yellow Sea lends support to this view. In March 2010, the South Korean destroyer *Cheonan* sank; an investigation led by South Korea's Ministry of National Defense and carried out jointly with other foreign experts concluded

---

[9] See Glaser and Liang (2008, 169) and Han (2004, 173).
[10] Both quotes are in Sunny Lee, "China, North Korea: Unlikely Friends," *Asia Times*, July 21, 2011, http://www.atimes.com/atimes/Korea/MG21Dg02.html. See also Han (2004, 173), which cites Shi's interview in the *South China Morning Post*, August 27, 2003. For more on the dissimilarity of interests between China and North Korea as well as their surprisingly weak relationship, see Ji (2001).

Constructing Security in Today's World

that North Korea was responsible for the sinking. Then, in November 2010, North Korea forces launched a shelling campaign targeting Yeonpyeong Island. Actions such as these, in which South Koreans were killed, marked a step up in the level of North Korea's bellicosity from its previous challenges, which in the past two decades have involved such behavior as testing nuclear weapons and missiles but seldom included attacking and killing South Koreans.

If these trends continue, it is possible that the PRC will move toward a probabilistic commitment. We have seen that there is some indication already that the defensive commitment in the Sino-North Korean treaty is no longer credible and that Beijing may already be using ambiguous language to reinterpret its defense commitment. Because unique characteristics of the relationship between China and North Korea may prevent China from abrogating the treaty and formally adopting a new probabilistic commitment, Beijing may instead work to weaken the credibility of the existing military commitment. Interestingly, it may be that this solution – forming an unambiguous commitment that lacks credibility – has a similar effect on deterrence and restraint as a probabilistic commitment.

Summary

In this chapter, I have explored the implications of the theory I have presented in this book for the U.S. policy of strategic ambiguity toward the Taiwan problem and China's commitment to defend North Korea in the Sino-North Korean treaty. Even though the specific facts of the actual problems may not exactly correspond to the details of the analysis, the overall implications are intuitive and provide insights about what to look for in these cases going forward. The theory's policy implications can help guide our thinking on many other security problems in the world today, such as the U.S. relationship with Israel, NATO enlargement, and tensions between Russia and former Soviet republics such as Georgia. The theory also provides the groundwork for thinking about related mechanisms for managing security relationships given the problems of deterrence and restraint.

Potential extensions to the theory include examinations of arms sales, direct military aid, joint military cooperation, and mediation. One possible avenue, which was raised in Chapter 1 and emerged again at the end of this chapter, is that world leaders may use other mechanisms for minimizing moral hazard. For example, states might form firm and transparent commitments and then manipulate the credibility of those commitments to manage risks of moral hazard and conflict as well as the policy outcomes that emerge from crisis negotiations. This avenue, which was suggested by Fearon (1997), might be consistent with China's current security strategy toward North Korea. Another potential avenue for managing international security in the face of dual concerns of deterrence and ally restraint is sending conflicting messages simultaneously (Snyder 1984). The approach I have taken in this book is to analyze theoretically and empirically commitments that are openly ambiguous. However, leaders may also occasionally attempt to use backchannels to signal private, conflicting messages to disputants. In spite of the empirical challenges involved with identifying such cases, it would nevertheless be interesting to investigate the incentives that such a strategy would create.

References

Accinelli, Robert. 1996. *Crisis and Commitment: United States Policy Toward Taiwan, 1950–1955*. Chapel Hill: University of North Carolina Press.
Acheson, Dean. September 7, 1958. "Text of Acheson's Statement on United States Policy Regarding China." *New York Times*, p. 3.
Ackerman, Bruce and Oona A. Hathaway. 2011. "Limited War and the Constitution: Iraq and the Crisis of Presidential Legality." *Michigan Law Review* 109:447–518.
Albertini, Luigi. 1957. *The Origins of the War of 1914*. 3 vols. Oxford, UK: Oxford University Press.
Arnott, Richard E. and Joseph E. Stiglitz. 1988. *The Basic Analytics of Moral Hazard*. Cambridge, MA: National Bureau of Economic Research.
Arrow, Kenneth J. 1963. "Uncertainty and the Welfare Economics of Medical Care." *American Economic Review* 53(5):941–973.
Baldwin, Leland. 1954. *Recent American History*. New York: American Book Company.
Banks, Jeffrey S. and Rangarajan K. Sundaram. 1993. "Adverse Selection and Moral Hazard in Repeated Elections." In *Political Economy: Institutions, Competition, and Representation*, ed. William A. Barnett and Melvin J. Hinich. New York: Cambridge University Press, pp. 295–311.
Beck, Nathaniel, Jonathan N. Katz, and Richard Tucker. 1998. "Taking Time Seriously: Time-Series-Cross-Section Analysis with a Binary Dependent Variable." *American Journal of Political Science* 42(4):1260–1288.
Bedeski, Robert E. 1995. "Sino-Korean Relations: Triangle of Tension, or Balancing a Divided Peninsula." *International Journal* 50:516–538.
Bennett, D. Scott and Allen Stam. 2008. *EUGene: Expected Utility Generation and Data Management Program*. University Park: Department of Political Science, Pennsylvania State University.
Benson, Brett V. 2006. *A Theory of Strategic Ambiguity: Credibility, Transparency, and Dual Deterrence* (Ph.D. dissertation). Duke University, Durham, NC.
Benson, Brett V. 2011. "Unpacking Alliances: Deterrent and Compellent Alliances and Their Relationship with Conflict, 1816–2000." *Journal of Politics* 73(4):1111–1127.

Benson, Brett V., Patrick R. Bentley, and James Lee Ray. Forthcoming. "Ally Provocateur: Why Allies Do Not Always Behave." *Journal of Peace Research.*

Benson, Brett V. and Emerson M. S. Niou. 2005. "Public Opinion, Foreign Policy, and the Security Balance in the Taiwan Strait." *Security Studies* 14(2):274–289.

Bolton, Patrick and Mathias Dewatripont. 2005. *Contract Theory.* Cambridge, MA: MIT Press.

Boulding, Kenneth Ewart. 1962. *Conflict and Defense: A General Theory.* Oxford, England: Harper.

Boyle, Peter G., ed. 1990. *The Churchill-Eisenhower Correspondence, 1953–1955.* Chapel Hill: University of North Carolina Press.

Bremer, Stuart A. 1992. "Dangerous Dyads: Conditions Affecting the Likelihood of Interstate War, 1816–1965." *Journal of Conflict Resolution* 36(2):309–341.

Bueno de Mesquita, Bruce. 1983. *The War Trap.* New Haven, CT: Yale University Press.

Bueno de Mesquita, Bruce and David Lalman. 1986. *War and Reason.* New Haven, CT: Yale University Press.

Carpenter, Ted Galen. 2005. *America's Coming War with China.* New York: Palgrave Macmillan.

Carter, David B. and Curtis S. Signorino. 2010. "Back to the Future: Modeling Time Dependence in Binary Data." *Political Analysis* 18(3):271–292.

Cha, Victor D. 2009a. "Powerplay: Origins of the U.S. Alliance System in Asia." *International Security* 34(3):158–196.

Cha, Victor D. 2009b. "What Do They Really Want?: Obama's North Korea Conundrum." *Washington Quarterly* 32(4):119–138.

Chang, Gordon H. 1988. "To the Nuclear Brink: Eisenhower, Dulles, and the Quemoy-Matsu Crisis." *International Security* 12, no. 4: 96–123.

Chang, Gordon H. 1990. *Friends and Enemies: The United States, China, and the Soviet Union, 1948–1972.* Stanford, CA: Stanford University Press.

Chang, Gordon H. and He Di. 1993. "The Absence of War in the US-China Confrontation over Quemoy and Matsu in 1954–55: Contingency, Luck, Deterrence?" *American Historical Review* 98(5):1500–1524.

Chang-il, Ohn. 1993. "South Korea, the United States, and the Korean Armistice Negotiations." In *Korea and the Cold War: Division, Destruction, and Disarmament*, ed. Kim Chull Baum and James I. Matray. Claremont, CA: Regina Books, pp. 209–230.

Cho, Soon Sung. 1967. *Korea in World Politics, 1940–1950: An Evaluation of American Responsibility.* Los Angeles: University of California Press.

Christensen, Thomas J. 1996. *Useful Adversaries: Grand Strategy, Domestic Mobilization, and Sino-American Conflict, 1947–1958.* Princeton, NJ: Princeton University Press.

Christensen, Thomas J. 2002. "The Contemporary Security Dilemma: Deterring a Taiwan Conflict." *Washington Quarterly* 25(4):7–21.

Christensen, Thomas J. 2011. *Worse Than a Monolith: Alliance Politics and Problems of Coercive Diplomacy in Asia.* Princeton, NJ: Princeton University Press.

Christensen, Thomas J. and Jack Snyder. 1990. "Chain Gangs and Passed Bucks: Predicting Alliance Patterns in Multipolarity." *International Organization* 44(2):137–168.

Clausewitz, Carl von. 1989. *On War.* Princeton, NJ: Princeton University Press.

Clubb, O. Edmund. 1959. "Formosa and the Offshore Islands in American Policy, 1950–1955." *Political Science Quarterly* 74(4):517–531.

Cohen, Warren I. 1980. "Acheson, His Advisers, and China, 1949–1950." In *Uncertain Years: Chinese-American Relations, 1947–1950*, ed. Dorothy Borg and Waldo Heinrichs. New York: Columbia University Press, pp. 13–52.

Colaresi, Michael P. and William R. Thompson. 2005. "Alliances, Arms Buildups, and Recurrent Conflict: Testing a Steps-to-War Model." *Journal of Politics* 67(2):345–364.

Crawford, Timothy Wallace. 2003. *Pivotal Deterrence: Third-Party Statecraft and the Pursuit of Peace*. Ithaca, NY: Cornell University Press.

Crawford, Timothy Wallace. 2005. "Moral Hazard, Intervention and Internal War: A Conceptual Analysis." *Ethnopolitics* 4(2):175–193.

Crozier, Brian. 1976. *The Man Who Lost China: The First Full Biography of Chiang Kai-shek*. New York: Scribner.

de Waal, Thomas. April 20, 2010. "Missiles over Tskhinvali: Review." *National Interest*. http://nationalinterest.org/bookreview/missiles-over-tskhinvali-3449.

Diehl, Paul F. "Contiguity and Military Escalation in Major Power Rivalries, 1816–1980. *Journal of Politics* 47(4):1203–1211.

Donovan, Robert J. 1982. *Tumultuous Years: The Presidency of Harry S. Truman, 1949–1953*. New York: W. W. Norton and Company.

Dulles, Foster Rhea. 1972. *American Policy Toward Communist China, 1949–1969*. New York: Thomas Y. Crowell Company.

Dyomkin, Denis. September 20, 2008. "Russia Says NATO Provoked Georgia Conflict." *Star Online*. http://thestar.com.my/news/story.asp?file=/2008/9/20/worldupdates/2008-09-20T032850Z_01_NOOTR_RTRMDNC_0_-355700-1&sec=Worldupdates.

Eisenhower, Dwight D. 1963. *Mandate for Change, 1953–1956*. Garden City, NY: Doubleday and Company, Inc.

Fearon, James D. 1994. "Domestic Political Audiences and the Escalation of International Disputes." *American Political Science Review* 88(3):577–592.

Fearon, James D. 1995. "Rationalist Explanations for War." *International Organization* 49(3):379–414.

Fearon, James D. 1997. "Signaling Foreign Policy Interests: Tying Hands versus Sinking Costs." *Journal of Conflict Resolution* 41(1):68–90.

Fearon, James D. and David D. Laitin. 2004. "Neotrusteeship and the Problem of Weak States." *International Security* 28(4):5.

Finkelstein, David M. 1993. *Washington's Taiwan Dilemma, 1949–1950: From Abandonment to Salvation*. Fairfax, VA: George Mason University Press.

Gaddis, John Lewis. 1987. *The Long Peace: Inquiries Into the History of the Cold War*. New York: Oxford University Press.

Gartner, Scott Sigmund and Randolph M. Siverson. 1996. "War Expansion and War Outcome." *Journal of Conflict Resolution* 40(1): 4–15.

Garver, John W. 1997. *The Sino-American Alliance: Nationalist China and American Cold War Strategy in Asia*. Armonk, NY: M. E. Sharpe, Inc.

George, Alexander L. and Richard Smoke. 1974. *Deterrence in American Foreign Policy: Theory and Practice*. New York: Columbia University Press.

Gibler, Douglas M. and Meredith Reid Sarkees. 2004. "Measuring Alliances: The Correlates of War Formal Interstate Alliance Dataset, 1816–2000." *Journal of Peace Research* 41(2):211–222.

Gibler, Douglas M. and John A. Vasquez. 1998. "Uncovering the Dangerous Alliances, 1495–1980." *International Studies Quarterly* 42(4):785–807.

Gibler, Douglas M. and Scott Wolford. 2006. "Alliances, Then Democracy: An Examination of the Relationship between Regime Type and Alliance Formation." *Journal of Conflict Resolution* 50(1):129–153.

Gilley, Bruce. 2010. "Not So Dire Straits." *Foreign Affairs* 89(1):44–60.

Glaser, Bonnie S. and Wang Liang. 2008. "North Korea: The Beginning of a China-U.S. Partnership?" *Washington Quarterly* 31(3):165–180.

Glaser, Charles. 2011. "Will China's Rise Lead to War? Why Realism Does Not Mean Pessimism." *Foreign Affairs* 90(2):80–91.

Gleditsch, Kristian S. and Michael D. Ward. 2001. "Measuring Space: A Minimum Distance Database." *Journal of Peace Research* 38(6):739–758.

Goff, Brian L. 1997. "Batter Up! Moral Hazard and the Effects of the Designated Hitter Rule on Hit Batsmen." *Economic Inquiry* 35:555–561.

Han, Sukhee. 2004. "Alliance Fatigue: Sino-North Korean Relations in Flux." *Korean Journal of Defense Analysis* 16(1):155–179.

Hickey, Dennis. 1997. *Taiwan's Security in the Changing International System*. Boulder, CO: Rienner.

Hölmstrom, Bengt. 1979. "Moral Hazard and Observability." *Bell Journal of Economics* 10(1):74–91.

Hsieh, Chiao Chiao. 1985. *Strategy for Survival: The Foreign Policy and External Relations of the Republic of China on Taiwan, 1949–79*. London: Sherwood Press.

Hunt, Michael H. 1980. "Mao Tse-tung and the Issue of Accommodation with the United States, 1948–1950." In *Uncertain Years: Chinese-American Relations, 1947–1950*, ed. Dororthy Borg and Waldo Heinrichs. New York: Columbia University Press, pp. 185–234.

Huth, Paul. 1988. *Extended Deterrence and the Prevention of War*. New Haven, CT: Yale University Press.

Huth, Paul and Bruce Russett. 1984. "What Makes Deterrence Work? Cases from 1900 to 1980." *World Politics* 36(4):496–526.

Huth, Paul K. 1999. "Deterrence and International Conflict: Empirical Findings and Theoretical Debates." *Annual Review of Political Science* 2(1):25–48.

Jervis, Robert. 1976. *Perception and Misperception in International Politics*. Princeton, NJ: Princeton University Press.

Jervis, Robert. 1994. "What Do We Want to Deter and How Do We Deter It?" In *Turning Point: The Gulf War and US Military Strategy*, ed. L. Benjamin Edington and Michael J. Mazarr. Boulder, CO: Westview, pp. 122–124.

Ji, You. 2010. "China and North Korea: A Fragile Relationship of Strategic Convenience." *Journal of Contemporary China* 10(8):387–398.

Jin, Park Chan. 1975. "The Influence of Small States Upon the Superpowers: United States-South Korean Relations as a Case Study, 1950–1953." *World Politics* 28(1):97–117.

Johnson, Jesse C. and Brett Ashley Leeds. 2011. "Defense Pacts: A Prescription for Peace?" *Foreign Policy Analysis* 7(1):45–65.

Kastner, Scott L. 2006. "Ambiguity, Economic Interdependence, and the U.S. Strategic Dilemma in the Taiwan Strait." *Journal of Contemporary China* 15(49):651–669.

Kim, Stephen Jin-Woo. 2001. *Master of Manipulation: Syngman Rhee and the Seoul-Washington Alliance, 1953–1960*. Seoul: Yonsei University Press.

Kuperman, Alan J. 2008. "The Moral Hazard of Humanitarian Intervention: Lessons from the Balkans." *International Studies Quarterly* 52(1):49–80.

Lai, Brian and Dan Reiter. 2000. "Democracy, Political Similarity, and International Alliances, 1816–1992." *Journal of Conflict Resolution* 44(2):203–227.

Lebow, Richard Ned. 1981. *Between Peace and War: The Nature of International Crisis*. Baltimore: Johns Hopkins University Press.

Lebow, Richard Ned and Janice Gross Stein. 1989. "Rational Deterrence Theory: I Think, Therefore I Deter." *World Politics* 41(2):208–224.

Leeds, Brett Ashley. 2003a. "Alliance Reliability in Times of War: Explaining State Decisions to Violate Treaties." *International Organization* 57(4):801–827.

Leeds, Brett Ashley. 2003b. "Do Alliances Deter Aggression? The Influence of Military Alliances on the Initiation of Militarized Interstate Disputes." *American Journal of Political Science* 47(3):427–439.

Leeds, Brett Ashley, Andrew G. Long, and Sara McLaughlin Mitchell. 2000. "Reevaluating Alliance Reliability: Specific Threats, Specific Promises." *Journal of Conflict Resolution* 44(5):686–699.

Leeds, Brett Ashley, Michaela Mattes, and Jeremy S. Vogel. 2009. "Interests, Institutions, and the Reliability of International Commitments." *American Journal of Political Science* 53(2): 461–476.

Leeds, Brett Ashley, Jeffrey M. Ritter, Sara McLauglin Mitchell, and Andrew G. Long. 2002. "Alliance Treaty Obligations and Provisions, 1815–1944." *International Interactions* 28:237–260.

Levy, Jack S. 1981. "Alliance Formation and War Behavior: An Analysis of the Great Powers, 1495–1975." *Journal of Conflict Resolution* 25(4):581–613.

Levy, Jack S. 1990. "Preferences, Constraints, and Choices in July 1914." *International Security* 15(3):151–186.

Lewis, John Wilson. 1962. "Quemoy and American China Policy." *Asian Survey* 2(1):12–19.

Li, Xiaobing. 1990. "Chinese Intentions and 1954–55 Offshore Islands Crisis." *Chinese Historians* 3(1):45–59.

Liska, George. 1962. *Nations in Alliance: The Limits of Interdependence*. Baltimore: Johns Hopkins University Press.

MacArthur, Douglas. 1964. *Reminiscences*. New York: McGraw-Hill.

Maoz, Zeev. 2005. Dyadic MID Dataset (version 2.0). http://psfaculty.ucdavis.edu/maoz/dyadmid.html

Maoz, Zeev and Bruce Russett. 1993. "Normative and Structural Causes of Democratic Peace, 1946–1986." *American Political Science Review* 87(3):624–638.

Marshall, Monty G., Keith Jaggers, and Ted Robert Gurr. 2002. *Polity IV Project Political Regime Characteristics and Transitions, 1800–2002*. College Park, MD: Center for International Development and Conflict Management, University of Maryland.

May, Ernest R. 1975. *The Truman Administration and China, 1945–1949*. Philadelphia: Lippincott.

Morgenthau, Hans. 1960. *Politics Among Nations*. 3rd ed. New York: Alfred A. Knopf.

Morrow, James D. 1991. "Alliances and Asymmetry: An Alternative to the Capability Aggregation Model of Alliances." *American Journal of Political Science*, 35: 904–933.

Morrow, James D. 1993. "Arms Versus Allies: Trade-Offs in the Search for Security." *International Organization* 47(2):207–233.

Morrow, James D. 1994. "Alliances, Credibility, and Peacetime Costs." *Journal of Conflict Resolution* 38(2):270–297.

Nalebuff, Barry. 1986. "Brinkmanship and Nuclear Deterrence: The Neutrality of Escalation." *Conflict Management and Peace Science* 9(2):19–30.

Nalebuff, Barry. 1991. "Rational Deterrence in an Imperfect World." *World Politics* 43(3): 313–335.

Niou, Emerson M. S. 2004. "Understanding Taiwan Independence and Its Policy Implications." *Asian Survey* 44(4):555–567.

Niou, Emerson M. S. and Peter C. Ordeshook. 1994. "Alliances in Anarchic International Systems." *International Studies Quarterly* 38(2):167–191.

O'Hanlon, Michael. 2000. "Why China Cannot Conquer Taiwan." *International Security* 25(2):51–86.

Park, Chang Jin. 1975. "The Influence of Small States upon the Superpowers: United States-South Korean Relations as a Case Study, 1950–53." *World Politics* 28(1):97–117.

Payne, Robert. 1969. *Chiang Kai-Shek*. New York: Weybright and Talley.

Powell, Robert. 1990. *Nuclear Deterrence Theory: The Search for Credibility*. Cambridge: Cambridge University Press.

Pressman, Jeremy. 2008. *Warring Friends: Alliance Restraint in International Politics*. Ithaca, NY: Cornell University Press.

Rao, Geping. 1989. "The Kuomintang Government's Policy toward the United States, 1945–1949." In *Sino-American Relations, 1945–1955: A Joint Reassessment of a Critical Decade*, ed. Harry Harding and Yuan Ming. Wilmington, DE: Scholarly Resources, Inc.

Rauchhaus, Robert. 2005. "Conflict Management and the Misapplication of Moral Hazard Theory." *Ethnopolitics* 4(2):215–224.

Rauchhaus, Robert. 2009. "Principal-Agent Problems in Humanitarian Intervention: Moral Hazards, Adverse Selection, and the Commitment Dilemma." *International Studies Quarterly* 53(4):871–884.

Rigger, Shelley. 2006. *Taiwan's Rising Rationalism*. Washington, DC: East-West Center.

Ross, Robert S. 2002. "Navigating the Taiwan Strait: Deterrence, Escalation Dominance, and U.S.-China Relations." *International Security* 27(2):48–85.

Rovere, Richard H. and Arthur M. Schlesinger Jr. 1951. *The General and the President, and the Future of American Foreign Policy*. New York: Farrar, Straus and Young.

Rushkoff, Bennett C. 1981. "Eisenhower, Dulles and the Quemoy-Matsu Crisis, 1954–1955." *Political Science Quarterly* 96(3):469–470.

Saunders, Phillip C. and Scott L. Kastner. 2009. "Bridge over Troubled Water? Envisoning a China-Taiwan Peace Agreement." *International Security* 33(4):87–114.

Schaller, Michael. 1979. *The U.S. Crusade in China, 1938–1945*. New York: Columbia University Press.

Schelling, Thomas C. 1960. *The Strategy of Conflict*. Rev. ed. Cambridge, MA: Harvard University Press.

Schelling, Thomas C. 1966. *Arms and Influence*. New Haven, CT: Yale University Press.

Schelling, Thomas C. 2006. *Choice and Consequence: Perspectives of an Errant Economist*. Cambridge, MA: Harvard University Press.

Schnabel, James F. and Robert J. Watson. 1979. *The History of the Joint Chiefs of Staff: The Joint Chiefs of Staff and National Policy*. Vol. 3, *The Korean War*, Part 1. Wilmington, DE: M. Glazier.

Schroeder, Paul. 1976. "Alliances, 1815–1945: Weapons of Power and Tools of Management." In *Historical Problems of National Security*, ed. Klaus Knorr. Lawrence, KS: University of Kansas Press, pp. 247–286.

Senese, Paul D. and John A. Vasquez. 2008. *The Steps to War: An Empirical Study*. Princeton, NJ: Princeton University Press.

Shavell, Steven. 1979. "On Moral Hazard and Insurance." *Quarterly Journal of Economics* 93(4):541–562.

Sigal, Leon V. 1970. "The 'Rational Policy' Model and the Formosa Straits Crises." *International Studies Quarterly* 14(2):121–156.

Signorino, Curtis S. and Jeffrey M. Ritter. 1999. "Tau-b or Not Tau-b: Measuring the Similarity of Foreign Policy Positions." *International Studies Quarterly* 43(1):115–144.

Simon, Michael W. and Erik Gartzke. 1996. "Political System Similarity and the Choice of Allies: Do Democracies Flock Together, or Do Opposites Attract?" *Journal of Conflict Resolution* 40(4): 617–635.

Singer, J. David. 1988. "Reconstructing the Correlates of War Capabilities Dataset on Material Capabilities of States, 1816–1985." *International Interactions* 14(2):115–132.

Singer, J. David, Stuart Bremer, and John Stuckey. 1972. "Capability Distribution, Uncertainty, and Major Power War, 1820–1965." In *Peace, War, and Numbers*, ed. Bruce Russett. Beverly Hills, CA: Sage Publications, pp. 19–48.

Siverson, Randolph M. and Michael R. Tennefoss. 1984. "Power, Alliance, and the Escalation of International Conflict, 1815–1965." *American Political Science Review* 78(4):1057–1069.

Slantchev, Branislav L. 2005. "Military Coercion in Interstate Crises." *American Political Science Review* 99(4):533–547.

Smith, Alastair. 1995. "Alliance Formation and War." *International Studies Quarterly* 39(4):405–425.

Smith, Alastair. 1996. "To Intervene or Not to Intervene: A Biased Decision." *Journal of Conflict Resolution* 40(1):16–40.

Snyder, Glenn H. 1984. "The Security Dilemma in Alliance Politics." *World Politics* 36(4):461–495.

Snyder, Glenn H. 1997. *Alliance Politics*. Ithaca, NY: Cornell University Press.

Snyder, Glenn H. and Paul Diesing. 1977. *Conflict among Nations: Bargaining, Decision Making and System Structure in International Crisis*. Princeton, NJ: Princeton University Press.

Spanier, John W. 1965. *The Truman-MacArthur Controversy and the Korean War*. New York: W. W. Norton and Company.

Starr, Harvey and Benjamin A. Most. 1976. "The Substance and Study of Borders in International Relations Research." *International Studies Quarterly* 20(4):581–620.

Sulzberger, C. L. March 19, 1955. "Negotiating With Red China and Our Allies." *New York Times*, p. 14.

Tao, Wenzhao. 1989. "Hurley's Mission to China and the Formation of U.S. Policy to Support Chiang Kai-shek against the Chinese Communist Party." In *Sino-American Relations, 1945–1955: A Joint Reassessment of a Critical Decade*, ed. Harry Harding and Yuan Ming. Wilmington, DE: Scholarly Resources Inc., pp. 78–95.

Taylor, A. J. P. 1961. *The Origins of the Second World War*. New York: Atheneum.

Trachtenberg, Marc. 1991. *History and Strategy*. Princeton, NJ: Princeton University Press.
Tsou, Tang. 1959. "The Quemoy Imbroglio: Chiang Kai-Shek and the United States." *Western Political Quarterly* 12(4):1075–1091.
Tuchman, Barbara W. 1971. *Stilwell and the American Experience in China, 1911–45*. New York: Grove Press.
Tucker, Nancy Bernkopf. 1980. "Nationalist China's Decline and Its Impact on Sino-American Relations, 1949–1950." In *Uncertain Years: Chinese-American Relations, 1947–1950*, ed. Dororthy Borg and Waldo Heinrichs. New York: Columbia University Press, pp. 131–171.
Tucker, Nancy Bernkopf. 1983. *Patterns in the Dust: Chinese-American Relations and the Recognition Controversy, 1949–1950*. New York: Columbia University Press.
Tucker, Nancy Bernkopf. 2002. "If Taiwan Chooses Unification, Should the United States Care?" *Washington Quarterly* 25(3):15–28.
Tucker, Nancy Bernkopf. 2009. *Strait Talk: United States-Taiwan Relations and the Crisis with China*. Cambridge, MA: Harvard University Press.
Tucker, Nancy Bernkopf and Bonnie Glaser. 2011. "Should the United States Abandon Taiwan?" *Washington Quarterly* 34(4):23–37.
Vasquez, John A. 1993. *The War Puzzle*. Cambridge: Cambridge University Press.
Wagner, Harrison. 2005. "The Hazards of Thinking about Moral Hazard." *Ethnopolitics* 4(2):237–246.
Waltz, Kenneth Neal. 1979. *Theory of International Politics*. Reading, MA: Addison-Wesley.
Wang, Fei-Ling. 1998. "China and Korean Unification: A Policy of Status Quo." *Korea and World Affairs* 22(2):177–198.
Wang, Fei-Ling. 1999. "Joining the Major Powers for the Status Quo: China's Views and Policy on Korean Unification." *Pacific Affairs* 72(2):167–185.
Ward, Michael D.. 1982. *Research Gaps in Alliance Dynamics*. Vol. 19 of *Monograph Series in World Affairs*. Denver, CO: Graduate School of International Studies, University of Denver.
Weitsman, Patricia A. 2004. *Dangerous Alliances*. Stanford, CA: Stanford University Press.
Wu, Anne. 2005. "What China Whispers to North Korea." *Washington Quarterly* 28(2):35–48.
Yuen, Amy. 2009. "Target Concessions in the Shadow of Intervention." *Journal of Conflict Resolution* 53(5):745–773.
Zagare, Frank C. and D. Marc Kilgour. 2000. *Perfect Deterrence*. Cambridge: Cambridge University Press.
Zagare, Frank C. and D. Marc Kilgour. 2003. "Alignment Patterns, Crisis Bargaining, and Extended Deterrence: A Game-Theoretic Analysis." *International Studies Quarterly* 47(4):587–615.
Zagare, Frank C. and D. Marc Kilgour. 2006. "The Deterrence-versus-Restraint Dilemma in Extended Deterrence: Explaining British Policy in 1914." *International Studies Review* 8:623–641.
Zhang, Shu Guang. 1992. *Deterrence and Strategic Culture: Chinese-American Confrontations, 1949–1958*. Ithaca, NY: Cornell University Press.

References

Government Documents

The American Presidency Project: Harry S. Truman: The President's News Conference, http://www.presidency.ucsb.edu/ws/index.php?pid=13678#ixzz1PIhdfCDG.

Clark, Mark W. Mark W. Clark to JCS, May 13, 1953, JCS Records, RG 218, CCS 383.21 Korea (3-19-45), sec. 128, NA.

Eisenhower, Dwight D. to U.S. Senate, January 11, 1954, Speeches Series, Ann Whitman Files, Eisenhower papers; *New York Times*, January 13, 1954.

Eisenhower, Dwight D. 1954. Mutual Defense Treaty between the United States of America and the Republic of China. December 2.

Eisenhower, Dwight D. Confidential to Albert Coady Wedemeyer, 28 February 1955. In *The Papers of Dwight David Eisenhower,* ed. L. Galambos and D. van Ee, doc. 1316. World Wide Web facsimile by The Dwight D. Eisenhower Memorial Commission of the print edition; Baltimore, MD: Johns Hopkins University Press, 1996, http://www.eisenhowermemorial.org/presidential-papers/first-term/documents/1316.cfm.

Exchange of Notes Between the Secretary of State and the Chinese Minister of Foreign Affairs. December 10, 1954. TIAS 3178; 6 UST 450.

Foreign Relations of the United States (FRUS), 1952–1954, XV, p. 1455.

Korean War Armistice Agreement, July 27, 1953; Treaties and Other International Agreements Series #2782; General Records of the United States Government; Record Group 11; National Archives.

Memorandum for Use in Presenting to the President the Problem of Military Assistance to the Chinese National Armies, June 27, 1947, Office of Chinese Affairs, Film C0012, Reel 11, frames 37–38, NA.

Memorandum of Conversation. Korean Situation. June 25, 1950. DGA/Box 65/May-June 1950.

Ambassador John Muccio to Butterworth, November 1, 1949: Truman Library, Muccio oral history interview no. 177, December 27, 1973; State Department 895.00 file, box 946.

Mutual Defense Treaty Between the United States of America and the Republic of China. December 2, 1954. 6 UST 433; TIAS 3178.

Mutual Defense Treaty Between the United States of America and the Republic of Korea. October 1, 1953. UST 2368; TIAS 3097; 238 UNTS 199.

Walter S. Robertson to John Foster Dulles, June 26, 1953, Top Secret File, 795.00/6-2653, declassified by the State Department under the Freedom of Information Act (FOIA), Case No. 391. Security Treaty Between the United States and Japan. September 8, 1951. 3 UST 3329; TIAS 2491.

The Second Kennedy-Nixon Presidential Debate, October 7, 1960 Debate Transcript. http://www.debates.org/index.php?page=october-7-1960-debate-transcript.

Statement By The President, June 27, 1950. GME/Box 71/Korea. June 27, 1950. Department of State, U.S. Relations with China (Washington: Government Printing Office, 1949), p. 192.

Taiwan Relations Act, January 1, 1979. Public Law 96-8, 96th Congress, H.R. 2479.

Truman, Harry S. January 5, 1950. Harry S. Truman: The President's News Conferences. Available in John T. Woolley and Gerhard Peters, The American Presidency Project [online]. Santa Barbara, CA. Available at http://www.presidency.ucsb.edu/ws/.

U.S. Congress. Senate. Committee on Foreign Relations. Mutual Defense Treaty with Korea; Report on Executive A. Washington, U.S. Govt. Print. Off., 1954 (83rd Cong. 2d sess. Executive Report No. 1) p. 5.

U.S. Department of State Bulletin XXIX (August 17, 1953):203-204.

U.S. Department of State. 1949. *U.S. Relations with China: With Special Reference to the Period 1944-1949.* Washington: Government Printing Office.

U.S.-Japan Security Treaty, 1951.

U.S.-Republic of China Mutual Trade Agreement, 1954.

Index

Acheson, Dean, 148, 154, 155, 156
Ackerman, Bruce, 53
Alliance Treaty Obligations and Provisions (ATOP) project, 26–27, 41, 77
Anti-Secession Law, 171, 180
Armenia, 67
ATOP (Alliance Treaty Obligations and Provisions) project, 26–27, 41, 77
Austria, 1, 27, 28, 30, 33, 37
Austria-Hungary. *See* Triple Alliance (1882)
Azerbaijan, 67

Balkans, 8, 30
Bedeski, Robert E., 184, 185
Belgium, 4, 28–29
Britain. *See* United Kingdom
Bush (George W.) administration, 54, 173, 174, 177, 180, 182

Carter administration, 174, 176
CCP (Chinese Communist Party). *See* Chinese Communists
Cha, Victor, 187
Chen Shui-bian, 171, 173
Cheney, Dick, 173
Cheonan, 102–103, 134, 188
Chiang Kaishek. *See* Chinese Nationalists, as revisionists; Chinese Nationalists, U.S. support of
China, People's Republic of, 143. *See also* Chinese Communists
  and Korea. *See* China–North Korea alliance
  and Taiwan, 169, 170–171. *See also* U.S. commitments to Taiwan
China–North Korea alliance
  in 1953 Korean War assessment, 159
  in 1961 mutual defense treaty, 169, 184–189
  in 2010 *Cheonan* incident, 103
Chinese Communists
  in Chiang entrapment strategies, 153, 155, 160, 168
  in Chinese civil war, 8, 58, 59, 70, 152–153
  and defense line, 158–161, 167
  and dynamic status quo, 157–159, 161, 165, 167, 168
  in Quemoy crisis, 2, 9, 11, 54–55, 161–163
  in U.S. deneutralization strategy, 159
  in U.S. neutralization policy, 148–149, 154, 155
  in U.S. withdrawal from Asia, 153, 154
  and U.S.–ROC treaty, 163–164. *See also* U.S.–ROC mutual defense treaty (1954)
  in war against Japan, 67–69, 152
Chinese Nationalists, as revisionists, 152–155
  deterrence of, 2, 145, 168. *See also* U.S.–ROC mutual defense treaty (1954)
  emboldenment of, 68–69, 158
  entrapment efforts by, 153, 160
  U.S. awareness of, 2, 69, 70, 152, 155, 156

Chinese Nationalists, U.S. support of
  domestic pressures in, 8, 153–154
  financial, 8, 58, 67–69
  military, 54–55, 58–59, 153
  psychological, 161, 162
  reduction of, 8, 70, 153–154, 156
  revival of, 148–149
  risks of. *See* Chinese Nationalists, as revisionists
Christensen, Thomas, 8, 49, 154, 172–173
Churchill, Winston, 161, 162
Clark, Mark, 156
Clausewitz, Carl von, 91
Clinton administration, 171, 173
Clubb, O. Edmund, 161
Collective Security Organization of the Commonwealth of States (1993), 96
commitment design, models of, 90, 104, 106–107
  baseline, 90, 104–108
    case 1, 108–113
    case 2, 108, 113–115
  conditional and unconditional commitment, 90, 105, 115–117
    case 1, 117–120
    case 2, 120–124
  hidden-actions, 90–91, 105, 106–107, 124–127
  testing implications of, 128–129, 134–136
    hypothesis 1 (preferences), 130–131, 135, 138
    hypothesis 2 (third-party capabilities), 131–132, 135, 138
    hypothesis 3 (protégé capabilities), 132–133, 135, 138–140
    hypothesis 4 (contiguity), 133–134, 135, 140–141
compellence, as objective of third-party security commitment, 32, 34–35, 36–37
Composite Index of National Capability, 174, 175, 185
conditional commitment, as non-optimal option, 11–12, 182, 183
  correspondence to alternative choice, 104. *See also* conditional commitment, formal analysis of: in model of hidden actions
  hidden actions and, 103, 104, 133, 140–141, 145, 170, 180
  in historical analysis, 142, 144–146. *See also* U.S.–ROC mutual defense treaty (1954)
  relative capabilities and, 132, 182
conditional commitment, as preferred option, 11, 94–95, 100, 127, 141
  observability and, 142, 144, 145. *See also* Japan: U.S. alliance with; U.S. commitments to Taiwan; U.S.–ROK mutual defense treaty (1953)
  preference incongruence and, 101, 104, 144
  relative capabilities and, 102, 104, 133, 138–139, 141, 178. *See also* Sino-North Korean Mutual Aid and Cooperation Friendship Treaty (1961)
  security concerns and, 101
  time consistency and, 98
conditional commitment, definitions of, 4, 32–34, 36, 37, 94–95
conditional commitment, effect on protégé behavior of, 72–73, 99–100, 129–130. *See also* conditional commitment, as non-optimal option; conditional commitment, as preferred option
  preference incongruence and, 130
  revisionism and, 72, 74, 88, 101, 181
  statistical analysis of, 79–86
conditional commitment, formal analysis of, 105, 116, 127
  in model of conditional and unconditional commitment, 105, 116, 123
    case 1, 118, 119, 120
    case 2, 122, 123
  in model of hidden actions, 105, 124, 125, 126
conditional compellent commitment, as type of alliance commitment, 18, 32, 33, 36–37, 40
conditional deterrent commitment, as type of alliance commitment, 18, 32, 33, 37, 40
Congress
  and Chinese Nationalists, 58, 153, 154, 163
  and Taiwan Relations Act, 171–172, 175
  as ultimate decision maker, 32, 96, 157, 163, 171–172
  and U.S.–ROK treaty, 146, 147
Correlates of War capabilities index, 174, 175, 185

Index

Correlates of War (COW) dataset, 79, 174
Crawford, Timothy, 8, 47, 92
Crimean War, 27, 30
Czechoslovakia, 1

Dachen islands, 158, 160, 161, 162, 166
Declaration by the United Nations (1942), 33, 36
defensive alliance, definition of, 26
deterrence, as objective of third-party security commitment, 32, 34–35, 37–41
Diesing, Paul, 3
DPRK (Democratic People's Republic of Korea). See Korea, North
Dulles, John Foster, 2, 9, 150, 163–164

Eisenhower policies in Korea, 156–157, 159, 165. See also U.S.–ROK mutual defense treaty (1953)
  defense line positioning in, 161, 166
  limits of war with, 54, 56
Eisenhower policies in Taiwan Strait, 2, 145, 159–168. See also U.S.–ROC mutual defense treaty (1954)
  criticism of, 7, 164–165, 167
  first-mover complications in, 2, 12, 103, 146, 157–158, 160–161, 165–167
  observability issues in, 150, 165, 166, 168
  realignment as nonfactor in, 8
  relative capabilities as factor in, 11–12, 160–161
  time-consistency problem in, 54–55
emboldenment, definition of, 47
England. See United Kingdom
entrapment, definition of, 47–48
Eritrea, 95
EUGene software, 75

Fearon, James, 3, 5, 6–7, 19, 20, 22, 51, 59, 60, 93, 189
Formosa. See Taiwan, sovereignty of; U.S. commitments to Taiwan
Formosa Resolution, 163
France, 1, 4, 27, 28, 30, 33, 36, 37

Gaddis, John Lewis, 165
game-theoretic models

conflict bargaining, 46
  baseline, 59–62, 90
  with third-party intervention, 59, 62–66
  standard alliance, 24–26, 105–106
  standard extended deterrence, 18–22, 105–106
  See also commitment design, models of; moral hazard effect, models of; typology of alliances
Gauss, Clarence, 69
George, Alexander, 22, 164
Georgia, 66–67, 92
Germany, 1, 4, 36, 38. See also Pact Of Steel (1939); Soviet Union: post-World War II anti-German agreements of; Triple Alliance (1882)
Glaser, Charles, 179
Grey, Edward, 1, 8
Guomindang (GMD). See Chinese Nationalists, U.S. support of

Han, Sukhee, 184
Hathaway, Oona A., 53
Hurley, Patrick, 69
Hussein, Saddam, 1, 53
Huth, Paul, 20

Indochina, 159
Iraq, 1, 53–54
Israeli–Palestinian conflict, 49, 103
Italy, 36, 37. See also Pact Of Steel (1939); Triple Alliance (1882)

Japan
  North Korea as buffer between China and, 184
  Russian alliance with, 38–39
  UK alliance with, 39
  UN declaration against, 36
  U.S. alliance with, 142, 146–147, 149–152, 167–168
  U.S.–Chinese alliances and, 58, 67–69, 148, 152
Jervis, Robert, 3
Ji, You, 188
Johnson, Jesse C., 74, 82
Johnson, Louis, 158

Kastner, Scott L., 180
Kennedy, John F., 167
Kilgour, Marc, 6, 8, 23
Kissinger, Henry, 172

Korea, North
  aggression toward South Korea and U.S., 169, 188–189. See also *Cheonan*; Korean War; Yeonpyeong
  and China. *See* China–North Korea alliance
  nuclear weapons program of, 169, 185, 186, 187
  security guarantees wanted by, 187
  Soviet Union in, 155
  unification goals of, 184–185, 186, 187
  Yeonpyeong attack by, 169
Korea, South
  demilitarized zone and, 95, 144, 146, 156
  PRC normalization of relations with, 185
  revisionism of, 144, 165, 167. *See also* Rhee, Syngman
  tensions with North Korea, 169, 188–189. See also *Cheonan*; Korean War; Yeonpyeong
  U.S. disengagement from, 155–156
  U.S. treaty with. *See* U.S.–ROK mutual defense treaty (1953)
Korean War, 148
  armistice agreement of, 148, 156, 166, 184
  defense line positioning in, 161, 166, 167
  as limited war for U.S., 54, 56, 162
  Taiwan Strait deneutralization in, 159
  Taiwan Strait neutralization in, 95, 148, 154–155
  as U.S. setback, 165
Kuperman, Alan J., 47
Kuwait, 1

Lee Teng-hui, 171
Leeds, Brett Ashley, 74, 82
Liska, George, 46

Ma Ying-jeou, 180
MacArthur, Douglas, 155
Mao Zedong, 2, 9, 54, 69, 161, 184
Maoz, Zeev, 75
Marshall, George C., 152–153, 154
Matsu islands, 160, 161–162, 166–167
Medvedev, Dmitry, 66
moral hazard, definitions of, 2, 43, 44
moral hazard effect, models of
  of alliance types to revisionist protégé on MID initiation, 74, 82–86
  of compellent or deterrent alliance on MID initiation, 74, 80–82
  of disaggregated alliance types on MID initiation, 74, 82, 85
  of major-power alliances to revisionist protégé on MID initiation, 75, 86–88
Morgenthau, Henry, 69
Morrow, James D., 20, 23
Muccio, John, 156

NATO (North Atlantic Treaty Organization), 67, 79, 189
Netanyahu, Benjamin, 49
Netherlands, 28–29
Niou, Emerson M. S., 23
Nixon, Richard, 167
North Atlantic Treaty Organization (NATO), 67, 79, 189
NSC 146/2, 159–160
nuclear warfare, 9, 56, 159, 165, 168. *See also* Korea, North: nuclear weapons program of
Nye, Joseph, 172

Obama administration, 49, 54
offensive alliance, definition of, 26
Ordeshook, Peter C., 23
Ottoman Empire, 37

Pact of Steel (1939), 27, 28, 33, 35, 36
People's Liberation Army (PLA), 158, 160, 171
perfect Bayesian equilibrium (PBE), 60–61, 62, 106–107, 108
Pescadores, 2, 12, 150
Poland, 1, 33, 35
PRC. *See* China, People's Republic of
probabilistic commitment, 10, 13, 141
  in agreement dataset, 135
  as balancing mechanism, 93, 95–97, 98
  in bargaining behavior, 72–74, 85, 88, 102
  in baseline commitment design model, 108
    case 1, 111, 112–113
    case 2, 114, 115–116
  in conditional and unconditional commitment model, 105, 116
    case 1, 118–119, 120
    case 2, 122, 123
  in contemporary U.S.–Taiwan policy, 169, 171–183
  credibility and costs of, 57–58, 95–96, 98
  in dyad-year deterrence dataset, 75, 77, 78

Index

in existing alliance models, 30, 32, 41
in extension of initiator analysis, 80, 82, 85
in hidden-actions model, 124, 125, 126
as likely option, 43–44, 101, 104, 127, 141
  preference incongruence and, 128, 129, 130–131, 136–138, 170
  relative capabilities and, 100, 102, 104, 128, 131–132, 138, 170
  unobservable actions and, 103–104, 127, 128, 133, 140, 141, 170. *See also* probabilistic commitment, historical analysis of
as type of alliance commitment, 18, 32, 38–39, 40, 41
probabilistic commitment, historical analysis of, 142, 144, 145, 167
and destabilizing moves in Taiwan Strait, 146, 157, 158, 165–166
ROC–ROK comparison in, 144, 166–167
U.S.–ROC treaty in, 151, 157, 163–164
U.S.–ROK alliance classification in, 143, 146, 147, 151
probabilistic deterrent commitment, as type of alliance commitment, 18, 32, 38–39, 40, 41
pure conditional commitment
  bargaining behavior distortion by, 100, 101
  in conditional and unconditional commitment model, 105, 116, 120, 122, 123
  credibility and costs of, 57, 58
  demilitarization policy as, 95
  in empirical analysis results, 136, 138–139, 140
  in hidden-actions model, 125
  as likely option, 101, 102, 127, 141
  neutralization policy as, 95, 149, 151
  nonprovocation agreement as, 39, 75, 95
  relative capabilities and, 100, 102, 141
  as type of alliance commitment, 32–34, 39–41, 95
  in U.S.-Taiwan scenario, 181
pure conditional deterrent commitment, as type of alliance commitment, 32–34, 39–41, 95

Quemoy islands, 2, 158, 160–162, 166–167. *See also* Eisenhower policies in Taiwan Strait

Rauchhaus, Robert, 47

Republic of China (ROC). *See* Taiwan, sovereignty of; U.S. commitments to Taiwan
Republic of Korea (ROK). *See* Korea, South
revisionism, definition of, 73
Rhee, Syngman, 146, 147, 156–157
Ridgway, Matthew, 54, 162
Robertson, Walter S., 156–157
ROC (Republic of China). *See* Taiwan, sovereignty of; U.S. commitments to Taiwan
ROK (Republic of Korea). *See* Korea, South
Romania, 4, 27, 29
Roosevelt, Franklin, 68
Russia
  in 1854 UK–France alliance, 37
  in 1855 UK–France–Sweden alliance, 37
  in 1856 Crimean War treaties, 30
  in 1914 July crisis, 1
  in 1916 Japan–Russia alliance, 38–39
  in 1953 U.S. dilemma, 54
  in 1990s Armenian actions, 67
  in 2008 Russian–Georgian war, 66, 92
  See also Soviet Union

Saakashvili, Mikheil, 67
Saunders, Phillip C., 180
Schelling, Thomas, 5, 7, 20, 34, 52, 79, 158–159, 161, 164–165
Schroeder, Paul, 46
Second United Front, 68, 69, 152
security commitment, definition of, 17, 91
Senese, Paul D., 79
Seventh Fleet, 148–149, 155, 159
Shen Jiru, 188
Shi Yinhong, 188
Sino-North Korean Mutual Aid and Cooperation Friendship Treaty (1961), 184–189
Smith, Alastair, 23
Smoke, Richard, 22, 164
Snyder, Glenn, 3, 6, 9, 23, 48, 49, 51, 92
South Ossetia, 67, 92
Soviet Union
  and aid to China, 68
  former republics of, 67
  post-World War II anti-German agreements of, 28, 30, 31, 33, 38
  in 1948 USSR–Romania alliance, 4, 27, 29–30
  as U.S. adversary, 143, 154, 155, 162, 165
  See also Russia

Stilwell, Joseph W., 69
Sulzberger, C. L., 160
Sweden, 33, 37

Taiwan. *See* Taiwan, sovereignty of; U.S. commitments to Taiwan
Taiwan Relations Act, 171–172, 173, 174–175, 177
Taiwan, sovereignty of, 161, 170–171. *See also* U.S. commitments to Taiwan
TRA. *See* Taiwan Relations Act
Treaty of Paris (1856), 30, 37
Triple Alliance (1882), 28, 31, 33
Truman administration
  and Chinese civil war, 8, 58, 152–154
  and Korean conflict, 154, 155–156
  and Taiwan Strait neutralization, 95, 142, 148–149, 151, 154–155, 158–159
Tucker, Nancy, 174, 179
Turkey, 30, 37
typology of alliances, 32–42. *See also specific types of alliance commitments*

unconditional commitment
  avoidance of, 15, 145
  bargaining behavior distortion by, 99, 101, 129
  in conditional and unconditional commitment model, 105, 116
    case 1, 118, 119
    case 2, 123
  credibility of, 95–96
  emboldening effects of, 72–73, 74, 85, 86–88, 103
    statistical analysis of, 78–79, 82–86. *See also* moral hazard effect, models of
  in existing alliance models, 4, 27–28
  in hidden-actions model, 125–127
  as likely option, 127, 141
    contiguity and, 140, 141
    deterrence and, 92, 104, 141
    moral hazard and, 92, 141, 182
    preference congruence and, 101, 130, 176, 178–179
    unobservable actions and, 104, 124, 133, 170
  and policy implications for U.S., 176, 177, 179, 181–182, 183
  relative capabilities and, 15, 99
  as type of alliance commitment, 18, 21, 27, 32, 33, 35, 36, 37–38, 40, 41

unconditional compellent commitment, as type of alliance commitment, 18, 32, 33, 36, 40
unconditional deterrent commitment, as type of alliance commitment, 18, 32, 33, 36, 37–38, 40
United Kingdom
  in 1832 UK–France alliance, 27–29, 33, 35, 36
  in 1854 UK–France alliance, 33, 36–37
  in 1855 UK–France–Sweden alliance, 33, 37
  in 1856 UK–Austria–France alliance, 28, 33, 37
  in 1905 UK–Japan alliance, 33, 39
  in 1912 Belgian protection treaty, 4
  in 1914 July crisis, 1, 8
  in 1939 UK–Poland alliance, 28, 30–31, 33, 35
  in 1950s U.S.–Taiwan policy, 154, 161
United Nations, 36, 53, 95, 156, 185
United States
  and China, 184, 185, 188. *See also* Chinese Nationalists, U.S. support of; Japan: U.S.–Chinese alliances and; U.S. commitments to Taiwan;
  and Georgia, 67
  and Iraq, 1, 53–54
  and Japan, 142, 146–147, 149–152, 167–168. *See also* Japan: U.S. alliance with; Japan: U.S.–Chinese alliances and
  and Korea, 143, 169, 185, 187, 188. *See also* Korean War; U.S.–ROK mutual defense treaty (1953)
    in *Cheonan* incident, 103
  relative capabilities of, 185–186
  and Taiwan. *See* Chinese Nationalists, U.S. support of; U.S. commitments to Taiwan
U.S. commitments to Taiwan
  in 1949 abandonment of Nationalists, 154
  in 1950 neutralization strategy, 148–149, 151, 154–155, 157–159, 167
  in 1953–1954 Eisenhower policies. *See* Eisenhower policies in Taiwan Strait
  in 1960 Kennedy-Nixon debates, 167
  in 1978–1979 Carter policies, 171–172, 174–177
  since 1990s, 171–184
  in 1995–1996 missile crisis, 169, 171

current, 5–6, 8, 11, 179–183
proposed changes to, 172–174, 177–179
U.S.-ROC mutual defense treaty (1954), 143
  abrogation of, 171
  ambiguity of, 2, 4, 11–12
  as ATOP defensive alliance, 30, 32
  as probabilistic commitment, 32, 38, 145, 150–151, 164–168
  secret notes for, 9, 10, 150, 164
U.S.-ROK mutual defense treaty (1953), 142, 156–157
  in comparisons to other treaties, 146, 149–150, 166, 167–168
  conditional nature of, 143, 151, 156–157, 167
    supplementary materials and, 143, 146, 147–148, 151
  probabilistic language of, 143, 146, 147, 151

Vasquez, John A., 79
Vietnam War, 56

Wagner, Harrison, 47
Wang, Fei-Ling, 185
Ward, Michael D., 23
Wedemeyer, Albert, 59
Weitsman, Patricia A., 46
World Health Organization, 180

Yeh, George K. C., 150
Yeonpyeong, 169, 189
Yuen, Amy, 50, 51

Zagare, Frank, 6, 8, 23

Made in the USA
Middletown, DE
29 July 2015